The Author: Born in Yokohama in 1892, Eiji Yoshikawa was forced by family circumstances to leave school and find work at the age of eleven. His teens were spent in a series of more or less menial jobs, his scant spare time being devoted to reading and early attempts at writing haiku and stories. In 1910 he went to Tokyo intending to work his way through school. Growing contacts with the literary world and a first prize in a literary competition won him increasing attention, till in 1922 he joined the staff of a Tokyo newspaper, which began serializing a novel of his. In 1923, after the Great Earthquake, he decided to become a professional writer, and a series of large-scale publications in the following decades gradually established him as his country's leading historical novelist, writing works combining both popular and literary appeal. They include *Shinran* (1934), *Miyamoto Musashi* (1935; tr. as *Musashi*, 1981), *Shinsho taikoki* (1937; tr. as *Taiko*, 1992), and *Shin Heike monogatari* (1950; tr. as *The Heike Story*, 1956). In 1960 he was given the prestigious Order of Culture, and in 1962 the Mainichi Art Award. He died of cancer in 1962.

Yoshikawa in his late sixties

Fragments of A Past

A Memoir

Eiji Yoshikawa

Translated by Edwin McClellan

KODANSHA INTERNATIONAL
Tokyo • New York • London

Distributed in the United States by Kodansha America, Inc., 114 Fifth Avenue, New York, N.Y. 10011, and in the United Kingdom and continental Europe by Kodansha Europe Ltd., 95 Aldwych, London WC2B 4JF. Published by Kodansha International Ltd., 17-14 Otowa 1-chome, Bunkyo-ku, Tokyo 112, and Kodansha America, Inc. Copyright © 1992 by Kodansha International Ltd. All rights reserved. Printed in Japan.

First edition, 1992
First paperback edition, 1996
96 97 98 99 10 9 8 7 6 5 4 3 2 1
ISBN 4-7700-2064-3

Contents

Preface

Yoshikawa Eiji (here and in the main text Japanese surnames will precede given names) began publishing this memoir in serial form in the monthly magazine *Bungei Shunju* in 1955. He ended it after twenty-one installments, with the description of his mother's death in 1921. It was then brought out as a book in 1957 under the title of *Wasure-nokori no ki*.

Yoshikawa tells us that he was at first reluctant to write it. He had a very reticent side to him—he says that his own children knew nothing about his childhood or youth—and it must have taken some determination on his part to describe with such candor and fullness of feeling his early experiences of extreme poverty, of growing up with a drunken, tyrannical father, and of having to watch his mother, whom he loved deeply, live a life of endless torment and humiliation.

He was sixty-three at the time, a famous and hugely successful historical novelist. A gifted storyteller, he could describe duels or street scenes in seventeenth-century Osaka or Kyoto with unmatched flair and persuasiveness. He was erudite, and had a fine historical sense; but he was not a highbrow writer, he wrote novels principally to entertain. He was not one of those self-absorbed autobiographical novelists whose careers had been built on harrowing confessional writing and who inevitably enjoyed a more prestigious position in the Japanese literary establishment; nor was he a man with intellectual pretensions (he had only had an elementary school education) from whom the reader might expect soul-searching revelations about the self or the human condition. For such a writer as himself to embark on a highly personal account of his early life and times seemed to him something of an anomaly.

But in finally succumbing to the repeated urging of the editor of *Bungei Shunju* to write his memoir, he was simply acknowledging his need to leave a record of his memories for his children, to whom he had not been able to talk about his past, and, perhaps more importantly, to make real the world which he and his generation had grown up in and which seemed to him to be fading fast from his countrymen's memory. Time had passed quickly in Japan, and his childhood and youth seemed to belong to another age entirely. He looks back to the Meiji era (1868–1912) in sad and fond remembrance, and tries to evoke for us a time when children like himself were brought up by parents who had been shaped by the feudal past, when peddlers, apprentice boys, and dockworkers (he had been one of all these) knew only how to endure, when poverty was seen as a mark of moral failing by the more fortunate, and when high-spirited progress went hand-in-hand with a special forlornness, associated forever in his mind with flickering gaslight, naive, romantic songs, and lost dreams. The Yokohama that he had known as a child had been nearly obliterated twice, once in the great earthquake and fire of 1923, and once in the bombing during World War II. And the war itself, which ended ten years before he began writing his memoir, was an event which split apart the different generations. Sixty-three was not very old, but historically Yoshikawa felt himself to be a man from a time long gone.

However reluctant he might have been initially to write his memoir, we soon find him writing it with a sureness and freedom uniquely his. He has an impeccable sense of timing and drama, a sharp eye for personal idiosyncrasies whether sad or funny, a generosity of spirit, and no fear of seeming frivolous or improper. Yoshikawa puts on no airs, neither is he self-serving in the way of many memoirists or professional autobiographical novelists. He describes himself often in miserable situations, but he never loses sight of others, and there is remarkably little self-pity in such anecdotes. When he tells us at the end of the book that he is glad to have lived when he did, we believe him.

As for his meager formal education, I think that it was less of a disadvantage to him than he might have thought. He was brought up by literate parents, and he read voraciously from the time he was a little boy. Some of the Edo-period (1600–1868) writers and dramatists he was reading as a teenager would only be half understood at best by most Japanese university graduates today. While his lack of formal education may have had some negative effects on his writing—his style, for instance, can be maddeningly eclectic and unpredictable, at least for the translator—I think that all in all it was an advantage to him as an autobiographer, for it seems to have freed him from those incapacitating needs to understate, to be sophisticated, and generally to live up to one's academic credentials.

Yokohama, where Yoshikawa was born and raised, was still a very young city at the turn of the century, younger than Tokyo (known as Edo before the Restoration of 1868), or Kyoto and Osaka, far to the west. A fishing village before the signing of the Harris Treaty between Japan and the United States in 1858, it rapidly became a thriving port city after it was opened to foreign trade. By 1892, when Yoshikawa was born, it had become one of Japan's major cities with a style all its own. Flamboyant and cosmopolitan, it was a city which prided itself on its entrepreneurial know-how and expertise in foreign manners and tastes. There, Japanese businessmen mingled with foreigners at the Negishi Racecourse, and smoked cigars and drank whisky with them in clubs and expensive restaurants. The Chinese tailors in Yokohama could make you a European suit vastly better cut than those baggy affairs made by Tokyo tailors for their dour civil-servant customers. Presents that you exchanged with your friends and neighbors were apt to be fancy foreign goods. Japanese women of means in Yokohama dressed more daringly than their counterparts elsewhere, sprinkled themselves with exotic scents, and used cosmetics liberally. (Yoshikawa's mother did not, however, for she was not from Yokohama and by upbringing had more restrained tastes.) It was a city where money was quickly made and just as quickly spent. It was more than a little crass, but it was smart all the same; it had what was then known as "the Hama style."

It was to this city, then, that Yoshikawa's father came to make his fortune. He was of samurai birth, though of low rank. Willful and arrogant to the point of self-destructiveness, he was in many ways a typical example of the dispossessed samurai turned new-age entrepreneur. He was an able man, nevertheless, and for the first few years of Yoshikawa's boyhood was one of the lesser nouveaux riches of Yokohama. But after a sudden turn in his fortunes when Yoshikawa was eleven, the family was thrown into deep poverty from which it did not recover for a decade. Yoshikawa's story of how the family survived is more than personal history; it is social history of the rarest kind, told by an unusually observant, humane, and intelligent man.

The book ends with Yoshikawa's mother's death in 1921, by which time the author had begun to make his mark as a writer of popular fiction and the family had come to know some comfort. It is therefore not about his career as a writer, his intention from the beginning being to tell us about his childhood and youth, his relationship with his parents, and about life in Yokohama (and in Tokyo toward the end) during a very special period in Japan's history.

There is much cruelty and pain in the story, but there is much kindness and love in it too. Yoshikawa was a rich man when he wrote it, but he seems not to have become a snob or a prude, and the people he loves most are those who live in the mean streets and those who are erratic. This is evident in his best novels also, where some of the most memorable scenes are those peopled by the humble and the poor. I think he identified with them, without condescension or sentimentality, and that may be one reason why he has been so widely read. When in his historical novels he romanticized those who were above the ordinary by birth or achievement, he did so with an unerring sense of the aspirations and dreams of the less distinguished.

In 1925, four years after his mother's death, Yoshikawa adopted the personal pen name of Eiji, retaining his original surname. His true given name was Hidetsugu, which is why in the book he is called by the diminutive Hide-chan (and occasionally Hide-san, which is more respectful, though friendly). His father, of course, calls him plain Hide. Yoshikawa's adoption of his new pen name marked the launching of his career as a full-time writer, and from then on his success was assured. It is a pity, one feels, that his mother—or, for that matter, his father, whose death preceded hers by three years—did not live to see him become so successful.

I am glad, however, that Yoshikawa ended his autobiography where he did, for with the death of his mother one part of his life came to an end. And I very much doubt that had he gone on to write about the rest of his life, he could have done so with so much passion, no matter how rich his later experiences might have been.

There is a certain amount of repetition and the occasional inconsistency in his story. This is partly because he wrote it in installments, and partly because sometimes his memory was faulty. He did add some new material when it was being republished as a book, but otherwise he seems not to have been inclined to do much rewriting.

Edwin McClellan
New Haven, 1992

A Tiny Stipend

I am constantly getting letters from people I don't know. I suppose this is a common experience with people like myself—writers and others who have won public recognition of a kind. Only recently, for instance, I found an envelope in the mail addressed to me by one Nakano Keijiro of the Board of Education of Odawara City. Probably from one of my readers, I thought as I opened it; but I was wrong. The letter ran, in effect, as follows:

> You may not remember, but once before the war this city, on the initiative of the then mayor, Mr. Masuda Nobuyo, hosted a public lecture which you gave in the Civic Hall. As head of the Odawara Public Library and a member of the local historical society, I was one of those who officially welcomed you. It was my privilege on that occasion to give an introductory address entitled "Mr. Yoshikawa's Ancestors." That was a very long time ago, and I am afraid our paths have not crossed since. But I wonder if we might presume on you again? On November 3—Culture Day—we shall be holding our customary celebration in the very same Civic Hall. We have received gracious cooperation in the past from various locally born people who have distinguished themselves in the cultural sphere. I wonder then if you would consider visiting us once again and addressing us on the day of our celebration. We can discuss details later, should you be willing to come.

When I began this manuscript I rummaged through my box of correspondence to find the original letter, but it wasn't there. To tell the truth, I'm not one to keep old letters; nor is it my habit to keep a diary. When I travel, I don't normally think to take a camera or a notebook with me; and on the odd occasion when some fancy moves me to take them, I never use them.

I am not, in short, a conscientious keeper of records; which is why, I suppose, I find so admirable those who are. There have been times when—the New Year being the best time to begin a diary—I went to a stationer's as the year approached its end and bought myself a diary, and after the New Year began keeping it. But the exercise would soon be discontinued, not because of indolence or forgetfulness, but because of disgust at my own inability to be candid. Anything I thought too awkward to set down I replaced with dots and dashes. I was deceiving myself, and the awareness would leave an unpleasant aftertaste. So in the end I would lay the diary aside. This too was cheating, but at least it was more comfortable. And here I am, living out my days still in a haze of compromise.

Thus when a publisher suggested that I write some kind of autobiographical account covering roughly the first half of my life, I was quite appalled by the idea. Not that I don't enjoy reading other people's accounts of their lives. But usually they have a much greater capacity for self-analysis than I do, or unlike me have experienced true suffering. If I were to write about my life, I felt, it would be of little interest to others; even now, in fact, I feel that I ought to resist the temptation. So far, not even my family has heard me talk much about my own past. There are some things that my younger siblings, perhaps, would remember dimly. But the only father that my teenage sons know is, I am sure, the one they see before their very eyes.

It so happened, though, that when the publishers Kadokawa Shoten decided to include my *Shinran*[1] in their *Collection of Showa*

1. One of Yoshikawa's early historical romances (1922), based on the life of the priest Shinran (1173–1262).

Literature, I was called upon to provide a chronological summary of my life and career to go with it. For the first time, then, I prepared such a summary, describing the main events of my sixty-year life. It was hardly a standard example of its kind, for I had had hardly any formal education, nor had I been raised in any conventional way. When it came out, it caused some amusement among my less charitable friends. "I didn't read the novel," one of them said, "but I did read the chronology. Now *that* was interesting." I noted his reaction as possibly true but had little inclination to inquire further.

Already, before this, I'd been urged several times to write an account of the first half of my life. And of course I'd consistently refused. But in the process of refusing time and time again I came to develop, as so often happens in such situations, a vague sense of obligation to do what I was being asked to do; and in spite of my conscious determination, I found myself sketching the rough outlines of an autobiography in my mind.

I tried to explain to the man I was dealing with, a Mr. S of *Bungei Shunju*. How could someone with such a capacity for evasion that he couldn't even keep a diary bare himself before others? Besides, to talk about my past would be to talk about my parents and their household, that tiny, obscure pocket of feudalism lingering on miserably into the Meiji and Taisho eras. And why should I—their child, another leftover from that obscure feudal existence—presume I had anything worth telling to those who came after? That I was a writer made no difference; I was more aware than anyone, in fact, of my own limitations as an author, of the dubious nature of any public recognition I might have received. . . .

But I soon realized that if you are the sort to go away quietly every time an author makes excuses, you have no business being chief editor of *Bungei Shunju*. "There's no reason why you should force yourself to say things you don't want to," he said. "Just because you're a writer doesn't mean you're under some special obligation. Just say what you feel you can. If you can't do the first half of your life, we'll be happy with the first quarter. So let's hear from you."

And so, in the end, he had his way.

I began this chapter with the letter from Mr. Nakano Keijiro. I did so because my father happened to be from Odawara, and the letter provided what I thought might be a convenient opening to my narrative. The letter, moreover, was correct: I did once go to Odawara to give a lecture. The Civic Hall on the day was packed. I had given such lectures before, but as it turned out, this one caused me some embarrassment.

It began with Mayor Masuda saying something like this: "I have a bone to pick with Mr. Yoshikawa. Despite the fact that his forebears came from Odawara, he has rarely, if ever, been here or mentioned it in his writings. And its citizens of course are quite ignorant of his connection with it—which is why I have bullied him into coming here and being introduced to you all."

During the ensuing storm of applause I saw quite a few people in the audience looking at me in some puzzlement. For it was not true that I had ignored or avoided Odawara. Far from it. In those days, indeed, whenever I had to closet myself in an inn to finish a manuscript, I would almost invariably go to Tonosawa or somewhere else in the vicinity of the city. And though it was true that I had never had the pleasure of meeting the mayor, there were people in the area whom I saw frequently.

Worse was to come, when Mr. Nakano Keijiro got up on the podium and spoke on behalf of the local historical society. He began by listing the various modern men of letters who had their roots in Odawara. When he came to me he said: "In preparation for this event, we of the historical society did some research on Mr. Yoshikawa's ancestors, but I am afraid we learned very little. We did find references to his great-grandfather and grandfather in the registers of the Odawara domain, noting their places of abode, their posts, and their stipend; but that was about all. It appears that Mr. Yoshikawa's grandfather, Yoshikawa Ginzaemon, was a foot samurai of the domain with a house in Shimogahara, and once served as a guard at the Nebugawa barrier station. Now, as to his stipend at the

4

time . . ." and here, if I remember rightly, Mr. Nakano paused and smiled a little, then in a slightly different tone continued: "Well, according to the entry, it was five *koku*[2] of rice with a supplement of ten men's rations." At the mention of this pitifully small stipend, the audience burst into laughter, drowning out Mr. Nakano. All of them, including the mayor and the other important persons sitting in their special seats, looked at me, and when they saw me blushing, with a sheepish grin on my face, they shook with still louder laughter, till the very walls of the lecture hall began to shake with them.

It was the first I'd heard of the five *koku* and ten men's rations. When I was a child, Father had mentioned "the Odawara domain" whenever he had the chance. "As a samurai child, you . . ." was a favorite opener of his when addressing me. I assumed, from childhood well into adulthood, that our family had been of fairly substantial samurai standing, with an income of, say, a hundred or two hundred *koku*. I was not prepared to be told that they were quite as humble as that; neither, I should imagine, was the audience. Even in a small domain like Odawara, a stipend of five *koku* and ten men's rations would have put you at the bottom of the samurai hierarchy; one step further down and you would be a common foot soldier.

This in itself was nothing to be embarrassed about. The trouble was that far too much fuss had been made about my coming for the lecture: posters and banners declaring "Odawara Welcomes Yoshikawa Eiji Home!" and the like. No wonder that when the audience actually saw me—the object of all this publicity, sitting there as Mr. Nakano spoke—and pictured one of my ancestors as a guard holding a six-foot stick and standing like a scarecrow by the gate of

2. A samurai's yearly stipend was normally expressed in terms of *koku* of rice, one *koku* being equal to 180 liters, the amount held necessary to sustain one person for a year. The cash value of five *koku* would barely have kept the Yoshikawa family in a state of genteel poverty.

the Nebugawa barrier station, they were overwhelmed by the comedy of it all. And when I went on the podium to speak, I was greeted with yet another round of laughter. Yet once the laughter had subsided, I found myself feeling very much at ease and talking as though to people I knew well; so that in the end the occasion remains in my memory as an extremely pleasant one.

I have no memory of my grandfather Ginzaemon, who died when I was a baby. According to Mother he was a quiet man, kind to his daughter-in-law. He had a white goatee; and though he was small, something about him suggested that he must have been a handsome young man. I have never forgotten the stories Father told me about him. In these, he emerged as a rather severe and frightening figure. It seems that, his paltry stipend notwithstanding, he was the archetypal head of a samurai household.

Although my name is Yoshikawa, most people in Yokohama, where I grew up, read the first character of the name as *kitsu* and called me "Kikkawa." Once, when I was a child, I asked Father about it. Yes, he said, our ancestors had indeed called themselves Kikkawa. And he took the opportunity to tell me something about them.

The name Kikkawa came originally from a place called Kikko which lay at the foot of Mt. Fuji. Our direct ancestors fought on the losing side in the battle of Sekigahara and, becoming lordless samurai, attached themselves, along with many other defeated warriors, to one of the victorious generals, Lord Okubo of the Odawara clan. These "outsiders," as they were called, were destined never to rise above the lower echelons of the domainal hierarchy. The Kikkawas at first became Buddhist priests, then doctors, and ended up as low-ranking samurai.

No doubt we were, as samurai, the lowest of the low, but Father never said so to me. It's possible too that in telling me about his own father, he chose to omit certain awkward facts. Maybe some of the things he told me were not absolutely true: I simply can't say. I was still innocent of the world, and had no reason to disbelieve anything he told me. But whatever the authenticity or otherwise of his anecdotes, they may well have helped form the person I was to become later, and as such are worth recording.

Father had an elder brother surnamed Akiyama; for some reason he had been adopted into a family of that name. In the civil war that preceded the Restoration he served as a soldier in the Odawara contingent stationed in Kyoto under the command of the young lord of the domain. At the end of hostilities he returned to Odawara suffering from a severe case of syphilis—a common fate, apparently, among young samurai of domains that sent contingents to Kyoto. He had reached the stage where, as the professional raconteurs like to put it, "his nostrils merged and his legs were next to useless." Despite his condition, however, he maintained a cheerful outlook on life and a stylish appearance. His hair was always beautifully groomed; his kimono and sash were chosen with exquisite care; and he would pass his time on the verandah on the south side of the house, holding a short-handled broom as though it were a samisen, quietly singing a Kyoto song to himself and interrupting it with plucking sounds he made in imitation of the samisen accompaniment. He had a dried horse's penis hanging under the eaves, with small shavings from which he would brew the principal medicine he took for his ailment. (Could people in those days still have believed in the efficacy of such a brew?)

I was told that whenever my grandfather Ginzaemon, on one of his frequent visits to the house, caught him contentedly sitting on the verandah singing a Kyoto song to himself, seemingly oblivious of his condition, he would fly into a rage. "You're a disgrace!" he would shout. "I've never met anyone so shameless!" On more than one such occasion, he even drew his sword: "If you're too feeble to do the proper thing yourself, your father will do it for you!"

All my uncle Akiyama could do when threatened thus was look up at his father imploringly—owing to his incapacity he would remain seated—and clasp his hands together in a plea for mercy. At times like these it probably took the combined efforts of the entire family to calm Ginzaemon down. I think it most likely too that gossip about Akiyama would sometimes reach Ginzaemon's ears, so that, finding it unbearable, he would rush to his son's house resolved to cut him down, only to be driven away by all the pleading.

After the Meiji Restoration the domainal system was abolished, and Akiyama, like all other members of the samurai class, had been paid a lump sum by the government in compensation. I gather that all he did with this money was to frequent the pleasure quarter in Odawara, declaring each time that "it cost almost nothing." So, little by little, he squandered the money without spending a penny on anything else.

I remember him in his last years, a pitifully bent figure who would appear at our house and try to cadge from his younger brother, my father. I still have vague childhood memories of him and Father in heated argument—he came begging so often that Father lost all patience with him—and of him leaving the house empty-handed and forlorn. I remember too that he would come when Father was not at home, and hang around, causing Mother, who was too kind to ignore him, no end of trouble.

Father told me another story about Ginzaemon, this one involving Father himself when he was still a young boy.

Father's given name was Naohiro, but until he reached his majority he was known as Jonosuke. One winter there was an epidemic of flu. His mother and their manservant both caught it, and had to stay in bed, so his elder sister, a young girl, was preparing dinner in the kitchen.

Jonosuke, barely ten at the time, was busy playing outside. Called repeatedly by his sister, he finally appeared at the kitchen door in a sulk. "Be a good boy, Jo," his sister said, "and go into town and buy some tofu." "No, I won't!" he answered. "Oh, come on, don't behave like that," his sister pleaded, almost in tears. But when she started reasoning with him, he said angrily, "How can you expect a samurai boy to go and buy tofu? If you don't stop insisting, I'll cut my belly open!" And he fingered the small sword he was wearing as if to carry out his threat. Thoroughly frightened, his sister could only give in meekly.

After dinner that night Jonosuke was called into his father's room. In front of his father, who was seated formally, was a small ceremonial stand; on it lay a dagger, partly drawn from its unlacquered sheath so that some of the blade was showing. The sight, my father told me, made him suddenly go cold. Glaring at him his father said: "Jonosuke, I hear that you frightened your sister by telling her you were going to cut your belly open. Now, I have always told you that samurai children must never lie. So now I'm waiting to see you keep your word. Remember—*you're* the one who refused to go and buy tofu because you're a samurai's son. Well then, behave like one! What—a bit scared, are you? Go on, cut your belly open!" Jonosuke began to blubber and say he was sorry, but his father was unmoved. "Go on, do it," was all he would say.

In great agitation Jonosuke's sister and the bedridden mother and manservant all went to Ginzaemon to plead for the boy's life. But no amount of crying and apologizing would placate him. The night wore on, and finally in desperation the girl and the servant rushed out into the dark to seek help from some relations. One after the other the relatives arrived and interceded on Jonosuke's behalf, but Ginzaemon wouldn't listen. By now it was almost morning. Then at last, around sunrise, he relented. "I cannot forgive him entirely," he said. "What I shall do is send him to live elsewhere." This was his final decision.

Jonosuke was immediately taken away to the home of some other member of the family. It was, of course, a common form of punishment at the time. Soon afterward, he was sent to a mountain temple some miles inland from Odawara to serve as an acolyte. The idea was that the hardship and discipline he would undergo there would do him good; in addition, the relation to whom he had been entrusted was probably too poor to keep him. He stayed there in the

9

mountains until he was fourteen. For being made to study, he was later grateful; but the conditions of his service, he said, were unbearably harsh.

I would do well, I feel, to remind myself occasionally that I am descended from such men: that I didn't just pop up out of nowhere, to be fashioned by myself as the fancy took me.

A Young Meiji Woman

I dislike the strange official habit of requiring, on questionnaires, application forms and the like, various kinds of personal information: your real name (if you have a *nom de plume*), your date of birth, and so on. Of what conceivable use is one's date of birth to others?

This, though, seems to be one of those rare occasions when I need to be specific. In the family register, then, I am entered as having been born on August 13 in the twenty-fifth year of Meiji [1892].

In actual fact, I've been told, I was born on the eleventh, but for some reason my birth was registered two days late. I know it hardly matters, but I can't help wishing that I had asked Mother about it while she was still alive. After all, my birth was more important to me personally than the earth itself, and I would feel better if I could be a little less vague about when precisely it occurred.

There's no denying however that, apart from a dim sense of having been born, our minds are a complete blank until we reach the age of awareness; for a while, we are nothing more than a few pounds of pulsating flesh. Our "memories" from that period are implanted in us later, by our parents and others around us. To attempt to relive the moment when one's self emerged in full consciousness can only bring frustration, and we might just as well acknowledge the futility of such an attempt. Even so, to have to resign ourselves to ignorance is irritating. Society generally agrees that ignorance is shameful; yet we happily refer to "we" and "I" without the slightest notion of when "we" and "I" came about.

Imagine a passenger on a train. The train started at Tokyo Station, but he doesn't know that. Nor does he remember going through Yokohama Station. As the train comes out of Tanna Tunnel he begins slowly to open his eyes, till finally, somewhere around Shizuoka, he suddenly realizes that he is in fact on a train. During the five-minute stop at Nagoya, he stares unbelievingly at the world outside the window, then in great agitation exclaims, "Hey! Where's this train going?" The other passengers watching him are of course much amused. They pity him, too, for his ignorance. The one difference between this imaginary train and the "train of life" is that the passengers on the latter are all like this man. Man's being born—my being born—simply has to be some kind of joke. . . .

Ironically enough, our human "rights" are ignored from the start by being bestowed on us arbitrarily, before we are in any condition to accept or reject them. I am reminded of an autobiographical piece that the novelist Naoki Sanjugo wrote many years ago for some magazine. It began: "Wondering what kind of a household I was going to find myself in when I came out bawling into this world, I nervously took a peek out through my mother's belly button. The house stood in one of those squalid side streets in Osaka. Pa's trade, it appeared, was selling secondhand clothes. There he sat, surrounded by piles of old clothes, counting coins. He was badly in need of a shave. Ma was in the kitchen, shouting at a bunch of whining kids. Hell, I said to myself, a slum family! But by then there wasn't much I could do about it."

Naoki's gentle mockery of himself and life has a point: to say that one has no control over the circumstances of one's birth doesn't mean that one wouldn't have liked, before coming out, to make sure that what could be observed through the belly button seemed acceptable. Either way, my own situation was different from Naoki's in that there were no whining kids present when I was born. My parents had had a daughter named Kuniko before me, but she had died shortly after birth. I was the child of young parents—Father was twenty-eight and Mother twenty-five—and I gather that, having lost their first child, they felt particularly protective toward me.

Mother was relatively prolific, and gave birth to six more children after me. With so many little chicks appearing one after the other, I can't have been the object of special care for very long. In later years, as Mother grew old and fell to repetitive reminiscing, her favorite topic was the hard time she'd had in rearing us. "You were all over me, from morning to night," she would say. "On my back, at my breast, in my lap—really, I never had a moment to myself. For years I don't think I ever sat down to a proper meal in peace." To reminisce like this, with us sitting around her listening attentively, was, I think, the greatest comfort of her old age.

At the time I was born my parents were living in Negishi. By now, it is part of Yokohama; in those days it was in the country outside the city. From the front of our house you could see the turf of the Negishi Racecourse.

The course, apparently, was built entirely at the initiative of foreigners following the establishment of the foreign concession in Yokohama and the signing of the Commercial Treaty, so it must have been there since before the Meiji Restoration of 1868. And I would guess that it was the building of this racecourse, and of many residences for foreigners on the bluff overlooking the sea, that so rapidly transformed the outcast settlements of Negishi and Aizawa into suburbs with a markedly international flavor.

My parents lived in a house rented from a certain Mr. Kameda, a local landowner. It was Mr. Kameda, it seems, who persuaded them to start—with rather shaky qualifications—a modest school for small children in their house. At first, of course, they only intended to take on a handful of pupils—children, moreover, of the outcast poor of Aizawa. But in time the children of foreigners living near my parents began coming too, and the experiment turned out to be an unexpected success.

The ill-treated outcast community of Aizawa huddled in isolation at the bottom of a hill, overlooked by a burial ground used not only by Japanese but by Chinese and other nationalities. Mr. Kameda, who had a deep sympathy for the children of this community, knew that at an ordinary primary school they would have been ostracized and bullied by the other children, and it was presumably this that made him persuade my parents to start a school for them.

Not surprisingly, the children became very attached to my mother and father—and their parents even more so. Not a day passed when someone didn't come to the back of the house and leave in the kitchen vegetables he had grown or fish he had caught. It was thanks to these gifts, rather than the fees, that my parents were able to live comfortably. And it was their gratitude—Mother often told us—that made the hard work worthwhile throughout the years that they ran the school.

What is interesting is that the foreigners, unlike the Japanese, were quite oblivious of the age-old discrimination practiced against these outcast people; blue-eyed Franks and Georges mingled quite happily with their Japanese schoolmates, reading the same Japanese primers, singing the same songs, and playing games with them—though such little scenes, of course, were also typical of turn-of-the-century Yokohama as a whole.

I was never told much about my father's activities from the time he left his hometown, Odawara, to the time he began teaching at this small international school on the edge of Yokohama; but it seems that the period was quite eventful.

Mother was not his first wife. He had previously been married to a woman he met while still in Odawara. He had a son by her, named Masahiro, which meant I had an elder half-brother. I understand that she was from the demimonde of Odawara, where she was known for her beauty. Father married her in spite of opposition from his family and unfriendly local gossip, the general disapproval being all the more severe because at the time he was a civil servant working in the saké tax office of the prefectural government.

As a saké tax inspector he was required to visit breweries throughout the prefecture, and no doubt it was in the course of these travels that he gradually acquired his taste for alcohol—later to develop into a serious addiction—and loose living in general.

His father Ginzaemon, it would seem, had so deeply implanted in him a sense of his identity as a samurai's son that his ideals, his whole view of himself, and his basic personality were all shaped by it. He was stubborn and uncompromising, with the burning desire to make a mark in the world that characterized the Meiji spirit. And despite his reputation as a womanizer, he apparently had no trace of the sophisticated young man-about-town.

There is a story about him that he used to tell us when we were children. He was rather proud of it, and I don't know how many times we were made to listen to it. It happened on one of his trips as a saké tax inspector, in the middle of winter. He was on one side of the Tenryu River. The brewery he wanted to visit was on the other side. The ferry was some way downstream, and the hour was late. So he decided to swim and, taking off his clothes, jumped in. Even so, he said, the current was so strong and the water so cold that by the time he was about halfway across he thought he would never make it.

As a young man, then, he seems to have viewed this simple, impulsive trait in himself with something close to pride. How his fellow bureaucrats would have viewed it is another matter. Later, when he took up with a woman from the demimonde, they almost certainly condemned him outright. Soon afterward, he was transferred to Nagano Prefecture; and he was living by himself in a boarding house in Nagano City when his wife, whom he had left behind in Odawara, was killed by a lover. The incident was reported in the newspapers. Humiliated, my father left the civil service for good and for a couple of years led a vagrant's life without going back to Odawara.

He liked doing paintings in the Nanga style, dashing off simple

15

landscapes or pictures of lotuses and chrysanthemums and signing them with sobriquets like Gyuseki [Ox Stone] or Itsumin [Hermit] or Sekisei [Voice of the Rock]. He was rather proud of his Chinese poetry, too. Yet another of his "accomplishments" was writing a postcard or a brief letter without the aid of a brush: he would chew on the end of a matchstick or a toothpick and use it to produce a smooth, flowing script that suggested the use of a bamboo pen.

He often said that it was his years at a mountain temple during his boyhood that had developed his artistic talent. Either way, for over a year after his resignation from the Nagano Prefectural Office he supported himself as an itinerant painter. His audacity in parading himself as a trained artist on the basis of a mere hobby picked up as a boy still astonishes me. I remember, as a child, seeing many of his pictures of plum blossoms, lotuses and the like. They were not very good, but to him they were a source of great pride; nothing gave him greater pleasure than to be asked by someone—it didn't matter who—to paint a picture for them. A carpenter who used to come and do work for us once said to my mother, "The best thing to do when the master is in a bad mood is ask him for a picture."

On returning to Odawara after two years of wandering, Father started a cattle farm in the foothills of Hakone. The newly opened port of Yokohama was not far from Odawara, and no doubt he felt that to survive in the new age one had to engage in some business or other that catered to foreigners. This was a very bold thing to do for a man born a samurai. Not surprisingly, he was criticized mercilessly by his relatives and the local inhabitants, who saw cattle-raising as a tainted occupation, totally unfit for a man of respectable birth; and once more he found himself leaving Odawara, this time to start another farm just outside Yokohama.

Even at that late date, the general attitude toward the slaughtering of cattle was such that anyone who did it would first put up dwarf bamboo all around the slaughterhouse, hang up a sacred straw festoon, and have a Shinto priest come and say prayers of purification. Either way, Father's second attempt at ranching didn't last long either. A severe epidemic of what was then popularly called "the cattle pest" killed almost his entire herd. "Every day," he used to tell us, "I did nothing but dig holes and bury dead cattle. It was the toughest time in my life." I have sometimes wondered if he didn't lose a little of his innate obstinacy and pride around that time and start doing some serious thinking.

It was around then that he married again. The woman who came as his second wife was my mother, Yamagami Ikuko. The go-between was a man by the name of Yoshimasu, who practiced Chinese medicine somewhere in Yokohama. This suggests that they were married at a time of bitter disappointment for my father, whose attempt to make a quick fortune as a farmer had ended in disaster. By then, Yokohama was full of businessmen, known as "treaty-port nouveaux riches," who had all prospered to a greater or lesser extent, but my father wasn't one of them.

Whenever my parents quarreled in the years that followed, Mother would tearfully blurt out, "I married you believing all those lies Yoshimasu told me about you." And Father would answer haughtily, "What lies, may I ask? Go and fetch Yoshimasu." I can hear them clearly, even now.

In the mid-Edo period there had been a famous doctor of Chinese medicine named Yoshimasu Todo; so no matter how much the family might have declined since then, the name Yoshimasu carried some weight in the history of the profession. We were told that our Dr. Yoshimasu was of that family, but whether he actually was descended from Yoshimasu Todo or not, I don't know. In appearance, manner, and speech he was certainly very much as one imagined a doctor of Chinese medicine in the old days. Whenever we children came home and saw his high clogs, with their padded, tatami-like uppers and white straps, standing in the vestibule, we would immediately guess that our parents had been quarreling again, and go back outside.

But though she often quarreled with her husband, Mother—who had after all been brought up in a Meiji household with all its

17

old-fashioned precepts—was in fact a perfectly ordinary Japanese woman of the traditional type. As a young woman, she must have known nothing of the world; and I am inclined to believe that at least to some extent she was misled by the intermediary in marrying such an impecunious person. Perhaps she exaggerated a little under the stress of the moment during those arguments with Father, but it is true that every time the old quack was called in to mediate, he would be conciliatory, not to say abjectly apologetic, toward Mother.

I don't want to be unfair to the worthy doctor, but surely only some distortion of the facts could have induced an innocent young Meiji woman to move with all her worldly possessions from Tokyo to the harsh environment of a treaty port, and there marry a young man with no fixed occupation, a man whose one notable characteristic, one might say, was his excessive obstinacy. I suspect that all her life she regretted her gullibility.

Even as children we sensed, albeit vaguely, the regret she felt, and sympathized with her. When she cried, we would cry with her, without knowing exactly why. And yet, however much she may have regretted her misplaced trust, the marriage was consummated; we were the issue of the union, and right up to the moment when, her will to live gone, she finally left us, she never—not once—spoke to us without love.

Mother was born in Sakura in Chiba Prefecture. The town had formerly been the seat of the lords Hotta, whom her family had served for generations as domainal samurai. "Grandpa"—her father, whose image impressed itself deeply on our young minds— was named Yamagami Benzaburo.

Once, during the Pacific War, I spent a day in Mother's birthplace. On my arrival, a local bigwig took me to the site of Mother's old house, where I lingered awhile before going to give a lecture at the local elementary school; finally, a relative took me to the family temple, where generations of Mother's forebears were buried.

From the look of the tombstones and the age of some of them I got a pretty good idea of the family's standing; quite simply, it was a class apart from Father's family, struggling along on a paltry stipend. Mother, I felt, had been justified in seeing her marriage as a comedown.

After the abolition of the domains, Benzaburo was made headman of the Usui district of Sakura. He seems to have been straightforward and generous in his dealings with people, a man much loved and respected. At the dinner given for me before I left, I was regaled with fond memories of him. He was remembered as a kindly, bighearted old gentleman, utterly comfortable with himself, fond of his saké and the people of the area in equal measure. He had many children, my mother being his fourth daughter.

On graduating from a local girls' school she was sent to Shiba Shinsenza in Tokyo to stay for a time at the house-cum-academy of Kondo Makoto, a scholar of National Learning and a pioneer oceanographer. Her elder sister Toyoko was married to Saito Tsunetaro, a fellow Toba clansman of Kondo's and professor of foreign languages at Kondo's academy. Toyoko, apparently, was extremely fond of her little sister and, wanting her near her, had prevailed on the Kondo family to take the young girl in as a kind of domestic trainee.

The academy, known as the Kogyokusha, specialized in nautical training. In effect, it was a successor to the Naval Institute founded by Katsu Kaishu and others under the Shogunate, and forerunner of the modern Naval Academy. Before moving to Shiba Shinsenza, it had been situated within the grounds of the main Edo mansion of the Toba clan. Mother seems to have thoroughly enjoyed being there, and would often speak of those days with nostalgia.

She was not a pretty woman, but had a small, neat figure and was extraordinarily fair-skinned. The students at the academy, all studying to become naval officers, would good-naturedly tease her about this, calling her "Oyuki-san" [*yuki* being the Japanese word for snow] instead of "Oiku-san," the familiar variant of her name. She would still be shy about telling us this, even though by then she was married with a large family.

Exactly what happened after that, what the circumstances were that eventually led her to go to Yokohama as Father's bride, I have no idea. I can imagine Father saying—had he been asked—that it was not because the intermediary had misrepresented things, but because, at the matchmaking interview, his own good looks and manly bearing had decided her then and there to take him as her future husband.

Physically I seem to have taken after Mother, for I am unusually slight and small. Father, on the other hand, was a tall, well-built man. In his prime he had the habit of lowering his head a little as he entered a room to avoid bumping into the doorframe above. The only physical feature I inherited from him is a mole just below the left-hand corner of my mouth, and even then his was much bigger.

Anyway, I was born the second child of these two people. Their sole means of livelihood around that time was the bizarre educational enterprise they had started in the house near the Negishi Racecourse, which meant that until I was almost four I grew up amongst a mixed bag of Japanese and foreign kids.

Though it was their landlord Kameda's idea that my parents should start a school, I can't help wondering if he could have persuaded them so easily if Mother had not once lived in the household of Kondo Makoto, an experience that must have impressed her with the pleasures of academic life, and even given her the confidence to assist her husband in such a joint venture.

However, it was not to teach little children that Father had come to Yokohama. By the time I was four, we had moved to a house in Ishikawa-cho, commonly known as Monki ["monkey"?] Hill, and Father had found new employment as secretary of the fish market in Minato-cho.

Changes in Children's Play

I n the beginning," they say, "was the word," but the individual's own personal history can only begin with his first memory. Everything preceding that is prehistory, an infantile age of the gods. Like a tadpole turning into a frog, the god takes on human shape, is given a passport to life, and suddenly a first memory touches off a process whereby one profane—in divine eyes—impression follows another till a dim awareness of the existence of himself and his surroundings takes root in his brain cells.

One of the harmlessly inane things you get asked in panel discussions on TV and the like is, "What's your earliest memory, and how old were you at the time?" The answers always differ widely. It seems you just can't generalize about the timing and nature of people's first recollections. Tolstoy's and all the other autobiographies describing the authors' early years seem to bear this out, and if some magazine cared to conduct a survey on the matter, I'm sure it would yield further confirmation.

Thinkers and literary people who set themselves up to be out of the ordinary dislike beginning accounts of their early childhood in such a vague way; I suppose they can't bear to admit ignorance as to the void that existed before memory, when they were no different from tadpoles or mosquito larvae. So, inevitably, they strive to find some memory of the self that preceded memory.

St. John's "the word," Buddhism's "time before one's forebears,"

21

and similar references in Shinto and Confucianism all seem to take as their basic premise a memory preceding human memory. From that premise, you might say, religion itself evolved: for without it as a point of reference in our consciousness, how would religion teach of sin and love? Every human being, after all, wants reassurance that he is a link in the chain of life and time, and not just an insignificant grub. The urge to confirm it for himself is built into him; indeed, without such confirmation, his doubts about the meaning of his birth—and the whole point of life itself—might well be more than he could bear.

History is an accumulation deriving from this instinct in our predecessors; and the same element is seen in the work of the historians and writers who have inherited it, which is why we often encounter startling passages where the writer tries to portray himself as he was before the advent of memory. In *Confessions of a Mask*, for example, Mishima describes the wooden basin in which he was given his first bath: how from inside the basin he saw a ray of light striking one spot on its brim, and the water lapping up as though to touch that golden spot. In *Portrait of My Inner Self*, Hasegawa Nyozekan describes in even greater detail his sensations while still in his mother's womb: how he was pulled out by the midwife and swung about above the basin, and how, angered and frightened out of his wits by the cruelty of this treatment, he let out his first scream.

These of course are not memories but literary imaginings. But the desire that inspired them is common to us all. In *Of Human Bondage* Maugham writes: "Life has no meaning. It emerged simply as a result of a physical process in the environment. Life is meaningless, death is meaningless. In the final analysis life is a fabric which we may weave according to any design of our choosing. Our actions and our feelings are simply patterns which we design as we like."[3] Yet before reaching this categorical statement, even Maugham cannot resist indulging in speculation and nostalgia concerning the

3. This is a paraphrase of a much longer passage.

void. And it is remarkable, in terms of the history of ideas, that the philosophical musings he offers from his ultimate sanctuary of nihilism should be so similar to the Zen priest's cry of enlightenment and the mysterious mutterings of the Taoist hermit.

I don't usually think of myself as abnormally susceptible to feminine charms, but perhaps at heart I am; for the earliest memory *I* have is of a woman, a pretty woman.

I can't say how old I was at the time. But I do remember that I was being carried on the back of a serving woman. And that I hadn't yet been weaned.

Vividly imprinted somewhere deep in my brain are these images: beside us, stone steps; a stone wall; and above it a window framed in green, the color of the paint by far the most striking color in the picture. A woman comes toward us, a pretty woman. She rubs her cheek against mine and says to somebody, "How nice the smell of milk is on a child!"

My earliest memory is just that. The strange thing about it, it struck me later, was that I should still have been unweaned at the time. Once, when Mother was still alive, I asked her if what I thought I remembered wasn't some kind of illusion. "That must have been when we were living on Monki Hill," she said. "Our front door was at the top of a flight of stone steps. It was a standard Japanese house, but a foreign missionary had lived there before us, and the windows and other places were painted in bright foreign colors."

Presumably, then, the memory was not an illusion. Besides, at the age of two I was, apparently, still being breast-fed; and since I was a tiny, delicate child, I was still being carried about on someone's back.

Even so, how is it that I remember the woman as being pretty, or that I can recall with such clarity her one isolated remark? And is it possible that the remark should have made such an impression on my auditory memory—as sounds or words—without any understanding of its meaning? I know these questions are unanswerable, yet I still have a compulsion somewhere inside me to believe that it all did take place: my own personal and most ancient myth.

In the second of my memories I am already walking. I was, perhaps, about three at the time.

Living near us was a carpenter who used to come and do work for us. (Later, I remember, one of his sons worked in Father's firm.) His wife had called in, and she and my mother were talking while I sat on Mother's lap, listening.

The carpenter and his wife had many children. One of them had drawn a picture, which she now showed proudly to my mother. I brought my face close and peered at it.

It was a picture of a ship, done in pencil. Smoke was coming out of the funnel. The masts were there, and the gangplank. It was just like the steamships we Yokohama children were accustomed to seeing in the harbor, except that the artist had carefully added guns on the bow and stern, with flames coming out of their mouths. The flames were bright red, as was the Rising Sun of the Japanese flag flying on one of the masts. Nothing else in the picture was colored.

Holding the picture in her hands, my mother gazed at it, then said: "It would be so nice if my one could learn to draw like this before too long."

A very simple scene, but I remember it with surprising clarity.

The Sino-Japanese War was over by then, but the repercussions, no doubt, were still making themselves felt even on children. In time, I too began to indulge in such "free drawing," and if I drew a ship, I too would feel compelled to show it with guns and the Rising Sun. In the same way, if I scribbled anything on a wall or on the ground, it would somehow reflect events that had occurred in the adult world. We children used to insult each other by shouting "Chink," and our songs still included wartime favorites that in retrospect seem comical in their crudeness and naiveté, songs such as the one that went, "So Japan and China broke off talks. . . ." Our repertoire also included genuine children's songs like "Snow is falling thick and fast" and "Big freeze, little freeze, blowing from

24

the mountains." We sang them all with equal gusto.

The most direct influence on our minds, I think, came from the images depicted on kites and picture cards. There were no children's magazines then, nor had the moving pictures reached us, though it is said that one was publicly shown for the first time in Japan in August 1920 at the Hama-za theater in Osaka. In my case, I was quite a bit older before, to my utter amazement, I saw slides even, much less moving pictures.

Essentially, I feel, changes in children's play represent changes taking place in society at large. Sometimes, indeed, the way children play betrays what is happening in the adult world even before it becomes common knowledge. On the other hand, the childish mind has naturally inherited, deep-rooted traditions of its own; and we too, in our time, were inhabitants of a world distinct from that of adults, untouched by their concerns and their commotions. In this sense, then, one could also speak of children's play as unchanging.

If "traditional" be the right word here, then I suppose all the games we played, and our playthings, were of the traditional variety: card-flipping,[4] nail-hurling,[5] swings, rope-jumping, marbles, tops, kites, hopscotch, stone-slinging, stilts, hoop-rolling, blowguns, guessing games, hide-and-seek, cards, fox-and-geese. . . . The list could go on much longer, I'm sure. They all owed their selection and popularity to the collective wisdom of us footloose children and the shopkeepers who sold us cheap toys and candy; the ideas about "culture" and the like current in grown-up society at the time cast not the faintest shadow on our world of play.

As for our physical surroundings, even the big streets were still unpaved, and we had no electricity in our houses; "change" meant

4. *Menko* in Japanese, a game in which you tried to flip over your opponent's card by throwing your own card down at it. The cards were made of pasteboard or lead, with colorful pictures on them. If successful, you kept your opponent's card; this was the element that made parents disapprove of the game.
5. *Nekki* in Japanese, a game in which you tried to knock down a nail or stick stuck in the ground by your opponent by hurling your own at it.

little more than the gas lamps that emitted their blue light along the Bund and those few streets where the horse-drawn buses ran.

The pastimes that most absorbed us were card-flipping, nail-hurling, and stone-slinging. It was through the picture cards that we first became acquainted with the likes of Minamoto Yoshitsune,[6] Colonel Fukushima,[7] and actors such as Danjuro and Kikugoro whom we had yet to see on the stage. In the grounds of the Hokke-ji temple near our house, there stood a shrine dedicated to Lord Seisho,[8] and the porch of this shrine became our favorite place for flipping cards. We found that rubbing the pasteboard cards on both sides with candle wax made them feel heavier and gave them a lovely sheen, so we would collect candle ends from the altar of the shrine and rub our cards with them on the wooden floor of the porch.

I've forgotten his name, but one of the boys I used to play card-flipping with was the son of a doctor who lived in the neighborhood. At sunset, this doctor would appear outside the gate of his house and, like some itinerant priest, blow a large conch horn. My playmate would turn pale with fright at the sound, and run off home. Once as I watched him I saw his father, the conch horn hanging from his neck on a red cord, grab him by the collar and beat him several times on the bottom. I remember being overcome with guilt, almost as though I myself were being spanked.

In every family, games like card-flipping and nail-hurling were thoroughly disapproved of, for they were seen as a form of gambling; so we played them in secret. Society at large neither provided guidance nor showed any interest in such matters, and the responsibility lay entirely with the family. It follows that home was a very restrictive place for us children.

One moonlit night, we were in a neighborhood that stood on a

6. 1159–89, legendary military hero.
7. Fukushima Yasumasa (1852–1919), who crossed Siberia alone on horseback in 1892; later general in the Russo-Japanese War.
8. Kato Kiyomasa (1562–1611), a famous soldier and powerful daimyo.

small hill. The houses all around us had hedges over which we could see their low roofs. Here and there lamps cast a dim, yellowish light. The houses were inhabited by artisans who painted pictures on whitewashed paper for sale to foreigners; during the day, you could see them working at their desks near bay windows that let in a lot of light. The results of their labor presumably went to the exporters on Benten-dori or to the foreign settlements. We would often stand on tiptoe outside the bay windows and watch in fascination as with practiced skill they painted flowers and birds, Mt. Fuji, and shrine gates on crepe paper, as well as folding fans, parasols, and egg-shaped Gifu lanterns.

The children who played in this neighborhood were the offspring of these artisans, or of Christian ministers, doctors, company employees, civil servants and the like. How it was that that evening we were out so late, I don't know, but there we were—looking, like a pack of stray dogs, for ways to amuse ourselves.

The event I am about to describe was, I think, the finale of the evening. We were gathered in a semicircle around a boy who went by the nickname of Octopus. He was older than the rest of us.

We stood there like conspirators, silently expectant. Octopus sat down, his back against a cedar hedge, and parting his clothes below the waist proudly pointed at his erect penis, no bigger than the spout of a teapot.

For some reason nobody even thought of laughing; we just kept staring at the thing. Then Octopus changed his sitting position slightly so that the pale, sharp moonlight was aimed directly at his crotch and the weird thing could be seen with startling clarity. That set us all snickering. "Suck it!" said Octopus to one of the boys standing close. "I'll hit you if you don't!" The boy went down on all fours like a puppy and put Octopus's thing in his mouth. The next boy was commanded to do the same. And so it went on, the back of one boy withdrawing on his hands and knees being immediately succeeded by another crawling up to Octopus.

I'm not certain, but I must have been about four at the time. Yet the scene has stayed in my memory with extraordinary vividness. I don't remember that I myself went down on all fours in front of Octopus; more likely, I ran away before I had to. What is absolutely certain is that it was the very first time the existence of the genitals was impressed upon me with such force.

Unsupervised, we thus occasionally discovered new, fanciful ways of amusing ourselves apart from the standard games. Academically speaking, I suppose, all kinds of things could be said about Octopus's psychology, his environment and so on, but there were other factors involved that only someone of my generation can understand. By now, we are incapable of recalling the darkness of those days when there was no electricity; and I'm sure that the darkness of the world around us was a major factor. We adapted ourselves to it, we romped about in it with no fear of stumbling. We were, in short, creatures of the wild.

My family moved frequently. From the house with the green windows we moved to a place that was larger and much further up the hill.

The house next door, with its front gate standing in line with ours, belonged to Mr. Konuma of the Japan Mail Steamer Company. It was through watching him leave for his office that I first came to think of people who worked for companies as rather grand. Every morning a rickshaw would arrive at his gate to fetch him. He had an elegant moustache, wore gold-rimmed spectacles, and the aroma of the cigars he smoked hung about him. A maid would follow him to the gate to see him off, and as the rickshaw pulled away would bow very low, her hands resting formally on the front of her thighs.

After a while, his fair-skinned, round-cheeked wife, who taught at a girls' high school somewhere, would appear, and seeing me would greet me with a nice, friendly smile. Her hair was done in the then fashionable style known as an "English bun." When she wore Japanese dress, she would wear a hakama and shoes; and when she wore Western dress she would swathe her face in a veil. Perhaps because they had no children of their own, they were extremely fond of me. Every Sunday without fail they invited me to come and play at their house, where they plied me with food and showed me models of steamships or books richly bound in leather. For some unknown reason, they always addressed me as "General."

Children are more sensitive than adults imagine to differences of life-style and appearance between their own and other families. I can still recall the design of the Konumas' living-room carpet and the mole on Mrs. Konuma's white cheek. And for years I kept remembering how once, when I was left to play by myself, I saw them kissing in front of a piano—or was it a harmonium? Even now, when a similar scene occurs in a movie, I feel as though I am seeing the Konumas again.

I don't think we lived next to them for very long. This time we moved a fair distance away, to a house by the rear entrance of the nursery garden on the Bluff. We were separated only by a single fence from a huge area devoted to the cultivation of trees and flowers, so it was like living in a large park.

Each time we moved, it was to a bigger house. I was too young to know much about what Father did for a living, but it was around then that he quit his job as secretary of the fish market and became, I believe, some kind of dealer in silk, selling raw silk locally or exporting fancy woven stuff. Dreaming perhaps of joining the ranks of the "treaty-port nouveaux riches," he spent his days visiting the customs house and trading firms in the foreign settlement. In the course of his activities he became acquainted with a Mr. Takase Risaburo, a prominent figure in Yokohama business circles; and together with him and two or three other businessmen he embarked on a scheme to set up a new firm called the Yokohama Pier Company. This undertook all kinds of things, from unloading cargo off foreign ships to supplying coal and provisions and acting as agents for trading companies.

The new venture must have been a success, for our style of life became more glamorous than that of the Konumas. My mother took to wearing pretty clothes, and we had more servants than before. But to the question whether this change in our fortunes brought us greater happiness or not, I paid no more attention than to changes in the season: I was too busy leading a life of pure mischief.

I remember one evening, on the main street of Aizawa, hanging on to the back of a horse-drawn night-soil cart returning from the city. It was a pleasant sensation, being carried along on the swaying cart, and children everywhere did it. The night-soil men no doubt kept an eye open for them, but this one was especially unaccommodating. Urging his horse to quicken its pace for a while, he then brought it to a sudden halt. Jolted by the abrupt motion, the night soil spilled out of the open barrels, covering me from head to toe. I don't remember how I got home, but I do remember being taken to the well by my mother and a maid and having bucketfuls of water poured over me. However much the material circumstances of our family might have improved, I myself remained a little savage.

Going to School

At the age of six I began attending a school in Chitose-cho with the long name of "the Yamanouchi Private Normal and Higher Elementary School of Yokohama City."

Postwar Yokohama has entirely lost its former aspect. For one thing, when I was a child, you had to negotiate really hilly terrain for over a mile to get to the school from the back gate of the nursery garden. First, you went through the nursery to the front gate along a zigzagging, up-and-down path, which brought you out onto that part of Yamate-dori popularly known as "Cherry Avenue"; then you went down Yugyozaka and crossed Kuruma-bashi, till at last you saw the painted gate of the school next to the Mariners' Shrine.

In all the publications concerning Yokohama City that I have looked at, I've not come across a single reference to the Yokohama Nursery Company. But to the foreign residents of the day, it must have meant a lot. It was so large, so full of trees and flowers gathered from all over Japan, that it could have been a public botanical garden. Beside the iron front gate that gave access to the main office building were a number of red-brick storehouses, and I remember seeing men bringing out lily bulbs and piling them up high on horse-drawn carts. Japanese lily bulbs were being exported in great quantities at the time, and this may explain how so large a nursery garden had come into existence. Either way, it is a fact that nowhere else in Japan have I seen a nursery so grand, with flowering plants and trees growing in such splendid, fragrant profusion.

Having been born in Yokohama, I never paid much attention to foreigners. But I do remember sensing something vaguely patrician in the leisurely way the beautiful, fair-haired women and their gentlemen companions walked about the garden, having nurserymen cut peonies or carry large pots of flowering wisteria for them, and pausing to look at the azaleas and irises on their way out. At such times, even the insects flying about seemed to carry the fragrance of flowers on their wings and emit a shining light from their bodies.

The path through the nursery garden from the back gate to the front was of course not a public thoroughfare, but I used it every day as a shortcut to my school downtown. Every morning when I left home Mother would stand outside the gate and smilingly watch me rush off down the steep path between the banks of flowering shrubs. "Just like a little bullet," she'd say to me afterward. It would seem that I was already a very undersized boy for my age.

I suspect that, unconsciously, all those flowers I passed by on my way to and from school throughout the four seasons had a long-lasting effect on me. I never in fact developed any particular fancy for flowers or gardening; but when, say, I am sitting at some official dinner and suddenly smell the cut flowers placed at the center of the table, I find my thoughts wandering back by some associational process to those days, days that become dearer and dearer to me as I get older and experience more of the hardships of life.

Once, in the early days of the Pacific War, Kikuchi Kan, the novelist, and I were coming back in a taxi from the Negishi Racecourse when I remarked casually that the nursery garden I'd known as a child was somewhere nearby. "Well then, let's go and take a look," he said. So we drove around a little uncertainly in what was to me more or less familiar territory. But there was no longer any trace of the nursery, and the search ended with us stuck in a shabby little alley and Kikuchi complaining steadily.

Then later, after the war had ended, I came upon a flower shop in Omagari in Koishikawa with a dust-covered window and a sign saying "Yokohama Nursery Company." For a while I stood rooted in front of it, wondering whether this could indeed be all that was left of the nursery garden I remembered with such fondness. But then I realized what an old fool I was being. For what was there to be wondered at? What I was looking at was simply another representation, on a small scale, of the confusion all around us, of Japan's tumultuous history in the half-century from Meiji through Taisho to Showa.

My real "home," then, has always been linked with those days when I lived beside the back gate of the nursery garden. It's no affectation to say that that was when I first fell in love with life. My friends at the time were Ichi-chan, son of a nurseryman, and Toku-chan, son of an umbrella mender. We didn't play much in the nursery garden, since not far from where we lived was the main street of Aizawa, and right behind it was a notorious slum known as the "I Ro Ha ['ABC'] Tenements." It was in a narrow alley, and what you saw first when you arrived was a variety theater with a dirty sign saying "I Ro Ha Playhouse." Then came an unbroken line of squalid single-story dwellings with a board-covered gutter running alongside it. The place presented a picture of dire poverty in all its manifestations. Those inhabitants who worked at all were engaged in marginal occupations: hammering rust off ships docked in the harbor, serving as part-time waitresses in questionable establishments, grave-tending in the Chinese cemetery, performing on the streets, selling lottery tickets, helping in the slaughterhouse, or cooking noodles on street stalls at night. Compared to these people, the day laborers you used to see hanging about in cities like Yokohama after the war were wholesomeness itself. By now, the squalor and poverty of the I Ro Ha Tenements seem to belong to an entirely different world.

Yet in this jungle of destitution we children sniffed out forbidden fruit that could never have been found in the nursery garden. In the cheap candy shop, we learned to play little games of chance that seemed much more like gambling and were therefore more thrilling than card-flipping; and in the same shop we acquired a taste for simple pancakes done quickly in front of you on a griddle, and for pieces of very dubious meat—dog, perhaps, or pig's innards—broiled on skewers. Pre-Meiji perforated coins, which by then were beginning to lose their currency and were carelessly left lying about in our homes, were welcome there, and would each buy us a bull's-eye.

Without exception the inhabitants of the I Ro Ha Tenements lived out their lives in a ceaseless, noisy struggle to survive. In summer men and women alike hung about almost totally naked, and would behave with casual indecency in full view of others. Always, somewhere, there would be a couple engaged in a loud quarrel. Yet they never tried to harm us—were, indeed, unfailingly kind to us. It was a world that seemed in our eyes to be open and free, a world where nothing was hidden behind curtains, where we were protected, as if in some sanctuary left over from primitive times, against customary censure.

Our parents of course thoroughly disapproved of our visiting the tenements, and whenever they found out that we were there would immediately haul us back home. But we were so drawn to the place that we would sneak back repeatedly, having first helped ourselves, with the adroitness of a magician, to some of the small change left lying about in the living room.

What was it, I wonder now, that made the place so irresistible? Not, surely, any unique attraction in its own right, but the simple fact that homes such as ours were far too neat and restrictive for us children. Like monkeys we swung from tree to tree in search of rare, tasty fruit, fruit that was forbidden at home.

Immediately opposite this row of tenements was a busy street that led from the foreign settlement on the Bluff to the Negishi Racecourse and the Chinese cemetery. The section I was most familiar with was known as the Aizawa neighborhood, and mention of the place brings back afresh memories of scenes of the kind depicted in popular genre pictures and songs of the time. Particularly vivid among these memories are the funeral processions of resident Chinese and Emperor Meiji's visits to the racecourse.

I doubt that such colorful, old-style funerals are to be seen anywhere in present-day China, even in the remoter areas. The coffin, laid on a litter decorated with gold leaf and bright distemper colors, would be borne on the shoulders of numerous men. Surrounding them were Taoist and other officiating priests dressed in heavy embroidered robes. Dragon-headed mourning banners and others of all kinds and colors preceded and followed them. There were men bearing offerings of whole pigs cooked in oil. Then came a long, meandering line of rickshaws, carrying what looked like members of the immediate family and other relations of the deceased, plus a professional woman mourner who with her hair in wild disarray wailed loudly and ceaselessly under the midday sun. The eerie wailing was accompanied by cymbals and gongs, the whole filling the street with the most exotic and haunting cacophony. If the funeral was that of some person of consequence in the Chinese community—a big merchant, say—there would be several hired mourners, with a seemingly endless procession of banners fluttering in the wind and people scattering colorful paper lotus petals or throwing rice cakes to the spectators on either side of the street. We children would be boisterous and elated at the marvelous spectacle we were witnessing, and when finally the tail end of the procession went past we would trot excitedly after it.

We behaved very differently, however, on those several occasions when the Emperor passed through this same poor, narrow street on the way to the racecourse. Then we would be on our best behavior and line up quiet and erect by the side of the road.

Emperor Meiji's fondness for horse racing was well known both in Japan and abroad. He must have attended the spring and autumn races at Negishi more than ten times in all. The visits invariably took place on a Sunday or a national holiday, which meant that we weren't turning out as part of some official school outing under the supervision of a teacher. Yet we all carried small paper Rising Sun flags, and, standing among the men and women of the I Ro Ha Tenements and the Aizawa district, would cheer and wave our flags as the Emperor, seated in his four-horse open carriage emblazoned with the gold chrysanthemum crest, passed by.

With so many spectators jostling each other on either side of the narrow street, there was hardly any space between them and the procession; sometimes those in front would be pushed forward against the horses of the mounted guards, alarming them, so that the Emperor's carriage would momentarily come to a halt. This was a great treat for us children, and we would cheer and wave our flags with added enthusiasm, so close to the Emperor that we might easily have touched him with our flags. From his open carriage the Emperor would smile at the people on either side from time to time, and raise his white-gloved hand. In the sky above the grandstand of the racecourse, fireworks would be going off in rapid succession.

To those of us who had grown up in those days, the pomp and excessive guardedness of later imperial processions in Taisho and prewar Showa were incomprehensible. How distant and cold they became, as though the people who thronged the streets were all potential enemies! My own memories, I felt, belonged to another world entirely.

The present Emperor is commonly held to have become democratic since the end of the war; but however true this may be, I don't believe one would ever see now a spectacle to match that of Emperor Meiji's procession wending its way through the shabby, crowded street in Aizawa. And although "Emperor's cups" and "Emperor's prizes" are presented at various sporting events, the Emperor himself is never there; nor does he seem to have time to share with his subjects the pleasure of spending a day at the races, as Emperor Meiji did.

The *Annals of the Meiji Period* quotes the following description, taken from *The People's Newspaper*, of Emperor Meiji's visit to the Negishi Racecourse in May 1899:

> Upon arriving at a little after ten o'clock His Majesty retired briefly to rest, then appeared on the grandstand. At the entrance to the paddock were displayed His Majesty's prize, a silver vase, and another prize, a cloisonné vase, give by Mrs. Aoki, wife of the foreign minister. The main topic of conversation among those present was who would be the lucky owners of these trophies.
>
> In addition to His Majesty's prize, to be given to the winner of the sixth and main race of the day, which was to be run at three o'clock, was the Peking Cup. A further money prize of 250 yen was to go to the winner, and fifty yen to the runner-up. The horses entered for the race were as follows:
>
> > Tortoise, owned by Mr. Allfield.
> > Terrapin, owned by same.
> > Ikubuchi, owned by Mr. Hugo.
> > Genghis, owned by Mr. Rusher.
> > Azuma, owned by Mr. Nishimura.
> > Mars, owned by Mr. Starlight.
>
> The six horses ran the mile and a half as if each wanted this to be his day. The large grassy area around the course was packed with several tens of thousands of Japanese and foreigners. Azuma was the first to pass the post, to be greeted by thunderous applause and stirring martial music from the brass band of the British warship *HMS Balfour*.

My father did not own a horse, but it seems that since much of the business of the Yokohama Pier Company which he managed involved negotiating with foreigners, he frequently went to the Negishi Club and was familiar with the racecourse. He sometimes took me to see the races, and I remember that the sport was much talked about at home. Possibly because racing in Yokohama was still in its early phase, no one thought of it as being in any way a tainted sport. And when the Emperor came to Negishi, it was as though the whole city of Yokohama was *en fête*. People seemed to talk about nothing but the races. It was like a Spanish town on the day of a bullfight.

Incidentally, there was a famous jockey of the day, a Mr. Kanzaki, who was known even to us children. Indeed, he was one of our heroes, and we idolized him. Years later, when I wrote *Song of the Rust Hammerers*, I made one of the characters a jockey and gave him the name of Kanzaki, thinking it would be all right since the story was set so long before. Some time after the book came out, I received a highly indignant letter from a descendant of his living in Kobe. "Kanzaki was not at all the womanizing playboy that you make him out to be," he wrote. "He was a decent family man and a jockey who never betrayed the trust of his admirers, whether Japanese or foreign." I immediately wrote back a polite letter of apology. This happened before the war, and I imagine even his family has forgotten about it by now.

I have never forgotten one particular day in my first year at elementary school. It was a terribly hot and bright summer afternoon, and the nursery garden as I passed through it on my way home from school was filled with the cry of cicadas. Water had been sprinkled to lay the dust around the front door and in the garden, and I sensed that we had a visitor. The house inside seemed very cool and still. As always, Mother came out to the entrance and wiped my face and feet with a damp cloth before I stepped up into the house. In the morning room she poured a cup of tea and told the maid to take it to the drawing room which was at the back of the house, then said to me, "You go and say hello." Going quietly to the end of the corridor, I peeped into the drawing room. The bamboo shades hanging from the eaves had been pulled down halfway, and layers of sunlight filtered into the room diagonally through the slats. A

38

single guest sat in the middle of the large room, his back straight, a rather forlorn figure.

He was young, perhaps ten years older than me, and dressed in a white summer kimono with black splash patterns and a hakama of striped Kokura duck cloth. He sat sideways to me, his head slightly bowed. Even to a child, he seemed a quiet, well-mannered young man. I went back to the morning room and whispered to Mother, "Who is it?" She drew me to her and whispered back, "Don't you know? He's your elder brother. He lives in Odawara, remember?" I was incredulous: that I should have an elder brother seemed absolutely unreal. I tensed up, feeling that something oddly dishonest and shameful was happening, and though Mother repeatedly urged me to go and present myself to the guest, I shook my head and refused to move.

Just then, we heard the bell of a rickshaw outside the front gate, and Father, a tall figure in a white summer suit and sun helmet, appeared in the front hall. He spoke briefly with Mother, who had gone out to meet him, then immediately went to the drawing room. For a while, silence fell over the house. Then the sound of sobbing reached my ears. I stole back to the end of the corridor and again peeped into the drawing room. The two sat facing each other. With one hand Father held my brother's hand tightly in his lap; the other hand was on his shoulder. Both he and my brother seemed to be crying.

The scene must have made a deep impression on me, for it has stayed with me ever since. But where Mother was at the time— whether with me or in the morning room still—I simply don't remember. Much later, when she thought that I was old enough to understand, she began little by little to tell me various things about my brother that I wanted to know.

His surname was not Yoshikawa but Ayabe, and his personal name was Masahiro. We had different mothers. He was born in Odawara, and was brought up by a family called Fujimoto who owned a restaurant bearing their name in the city, where he also went to middle school. When he came to Yokohama for the first time to see the real father he hadn't known since infancy, he was already seventeen.

At that meeting, apparently, he told my father that it was his ambition to become a doctor, and that he wanted to go to medical school in Tokyo, since appropriate training was not available in Odawara.

The family he had been given to for adoption was called Ayabe, and had been doctors for generations in the village of Isaida in the Odawara domain. It was presumably in order to follow in their footsteps that he wanted medical training. He was still entered in the Ayabe family register even though, because the head of the family had died after his adoption, he had been taken in and brought up by the Fujimotos, their relatives.

He had come to Yokohama, then, to seek Father's help in realizing his ambition. But it would seem that for some reason Father was against the idea, and this studious young man went back to Odawara the next day in defeat.

My half-brother as I remember him was a youth of almost feminine gentleness, in appearance a perfect example of the type commonly described as "slender and of medium height," and in keeping with this he had a large mole in his left eyebrow. Nothing about him resembled my unyielding father with his harsh samurai background—or, for that matter, me.

Masahiro grew up in the pleasure quarter of Odawara, and he cannot but have been influenced in many ways by the environment. I have been told that he could sing and play certain musical instruments as no mere amateur could; and that when, at a party, my parents heard him perform for the first time they could hardly believe their ears. At ordinary times, though, there was not the slightest suggestion of frivolity in his behavior or speech. He was a nice, restrained young man, and was well liked. He never did go to medical school, but there was an air of the medical student about him, as though if one were to get close to him one would catch a whiff of some medicine or other.

To Mother he was only a stepson, but she cared for him like a real mother, with a love and loyalty that couldn't have been more constant. She always tried to shield him from Father's quick temper; sometimes I'd feel, unjustifiably, that she was more attached to him than to me, and get jealous. Of course, I was only a child at the time, and it seems likely that she sought in Masahiro the kind of moral support that I certainly couldn't have given her.

I wondered sometimes who was Masahiro's real mother, but on this score Mother said absolutely nothing.

In his twenties Father, as I described earlier, had created a scandal by making a woman of the pleasure quarter his common-law wife, and had had to leave Odawara and work as a prefectural official in Nagano. During his absence, this beautiful woman had been murdered by a jealous lover. Now, this is mere conjecture on my part, but I can't shake off the conviction that this same woman, left behind in Odawara by Father, was Masahiro's mother.

Father, of course, would have been unwilling to speak about her to anybody, and Mother would never have dreamed of mentioning her to me. But as I got older and gained in understanding and intuition, the silence concerning the identity of Masahiro's mother began to bother me. And from what I saw and heard during visits to Odawara with Mother, and especially from the way Father and Masahiro tangled with each other, and the things Father would say to Masahiro in his more uncontrolled moments, I began to form an idea of my own as to who she might have been. If my guess is right, I pity him. In my later boyhood and youth, I myself was to experience what you might call hardships, but they pale into insignificance compared to the misfortune he faced from the time he was born.

We moved again. Our house this time stood on Yamate-dori, the road that ran past the front gate of the nursery, just where it went downhill to the top of Yugyozaka, which descended sharply toward town. From the drawing room we could see over the garden to where the whole of downtown Yokohama spread out below us.

My daily walk to the school in Chitose-cho was thereby reduced by about one third.

I never found being at school unpleasant. The school was a two-storied wooden building, and my classroom was downstairs. Every sound made upstairs—the shuffling of feet, the harmonium being played—reached us totally unmuffled. The place was a veritable beehive.

The principal of this private school was Yamanouchi Mosaburo, who died only last year at the age of ninety. Not surprisingly, he was more or less bedridden in his later years, but the year before last, when I was given the Kikuchi Kan Prize and my friends held a reception for me at the Tokyo Kaikan, he was good enough to come all the way from Yokohama to attend. Accompanying him was Otei-chan, the beautiful Eurasian who had once been my half-brother Masahiro's sweetheart. When Yamanouchi Sensei's turn came to stand and say a few words of congratulation, I saw tears running down his red cheeks.

He had a red face when I started going to his school. I don't know that he was a heavy drinker, but his nose was particularly red. His name is indispensable to any history of children's education in Yokohama, and during his lifetime he was on several occasions publicly commended for his work. He is, then, a well-remembered man; but it is the smiling face and eyes, so expressive of his fondness for children, that I, for one, shall never forget.

His first wife died when they were both young, but she was still living when I was at the school, and she also taught me. Married women of the middle class were never addressed in those days as "Okusan," but, more elaborately, as "Goshinzo-sama." So we all used to call her "Goshinzo Sensei." There were plenty of other teachers at the school, but the school was run as a joint husband-and-wife venture, so she taught too.

In point of fact, we boys looked forward eagerly to her classes.

Even to our innocent eyes, she was beautiful. I would gaze at her from afar as she stood in front of us, wondering who had the fairer complexion, she or my mother, and fancying that I could smell from where I sat the fragrance of the powder on her neck and cheeks. She always wore her hair in the swept-up "evening party" style, and her customary dress was a long-sleeved cotton kimono with a purple cotton hakama over it. Not even the smell of the cotton went unnoticed by us.

One thing that distressed Goshinzo Sensei was that when she was teaching us we boys invariably got unruly. We knew perfectly well what we were doing and why. When she could no longer ignore our misbehavior, she would step down from the platform and approach one of us. "Now—you come with me!" she would say, and lead the chosen culprit by the hand to the side of the platform, where he had to stand as punishment. This was precisely what each of us secretly wanted. In my own case, my heart would start pounding as she walked gracefully down the aisle, her pretty white hand about to reach out to one of us. And if it took someone else's hand, I was bitterly disappointed.

Our school stood on a busy street, with no grounds to speak of. If you looked through a crack in the old wooden wall on one side of the playground, you saw the Mariners' Shrine and its grounds immediately in front of your eyes. And on a festival day you were assailed by the cries of the vendors who put up their stalls early in the afternoon, and the smells of the food they sold.

In those days, the word coeducation didn't exist, but our school took in both boys and girls as a matter of course. Already I was at the stage where I liked certain girls and disliked others; and I would often envy a boy who shared a desk with a girl I liked.

Calligraphy being a required subject, an ink stick and an ink stone were essential items of our school equipment. On the same single sheet of paper we would write out characters again and again, on top of our previous attempts, until the paper shone black with layers of dried ink. On rainy days, we played a game called "taking ink sticks." The game involved putting the stub of an ink stick on a desk, then taking turns at trying to flip it over with another piece. The teachers got very cross when they caught us doing this. There was another game we often played when it rained. Whose bright idea it was I can't possibly remember, but one of us would think up a story in rough outline, then draw pictures in his exercise book, frame by frame as in a film, all the while giving an impromptu running commentary.

The storyteller, for example, would first draw something that looked like a willow tree, then something that looked like a stream, then something that might be a boy urinating: "Kimura, you see, is sent out on an errand. On the way, he suddenly wants to pee, so he stands by the bridge and begins peeing into the stream. It makes a lot of noise." At this point the storyteller would compose the next frame. He would draw a bridge, then what must be a girl because it had long braided hair hanging down at the back. "This is Miyazaki Chiyoko-san coming toward Kimura. See, she's looking at him." The next frame follows: "Kimura goes all red, stops peeing halfway, and runs away." The scene changes to Kimura's house. He is being spanked on the bottom by someone, presumably his mother. "When he gets home his mother is awfully angry with him for wetting his pants."

In a sense, they were impromptu versions of the picture-card shows that you can still see in the streets these days.

Both pictures and words, of course, were hopelessly crude, but to us children they were quite acceptable. The themes always concerned the personal experiences of children, who were modeled on members of our group and identified as such. When we used pencil and paper, we drew the pictures in a series of frames; and when we used slate and slate pencil, we drew one scene then rubbed it out and drew the next—drawing and erasing, drawing and erasing, and continuing our extempore storytelling all the while, so that the whole exercise became a pretty frenzied affair.

We played this game in the classroom, on rainy days. We had no name for it, and it's possible that someone in our group invented it and that we were the only ones who played it. I for one enjoyed it thoroughly; indeed, I was a more enthusiastic storyteller than anyone else. Whenever the others urged me to take over, I would agree with alacrity and start talking and scrawling like a boy possessed. Once, I modeled the principal figure of my fantasy on Takagi, a boy with a pockmarked face who was always bullying a girl I liked. Carried away by wishful thinking, I had him suffer various misfortunes: first he failed his school exams; next, his family lost their house in a fire; then as a result of these setbacks he had to go and work as a servant boy in a shop—and so on. Takagi didn't find this very funny, and as I prattled on he came up from behind and poured the ink left in his ink stone over my head. I turned my face toward him just as he did so and rubbed my head with my hand, ending up with ink not only in my hair but all over my face and hand too. For some time after that, whenever I had a bath and washed my hair, the water went black.

I feel in retrospect that such games, however frivolous-seeming, cannot be entirely without value for those who have actually played them. For me, indulging in those simple fantasies to amuse others may well have been my first, very elementary and quite unwitting practice in what was to become my vocation, the writing of fiction.

Cow's Milk and English

Not long ago, a new golfers' association called Asahi Quarterly Golf held its first tournament in Sagami. The prize-giving ceremony was to take place later in the day at a restaurant in Chinatown in Yokohama. Our group was the first to tee off, and we were finished by about two o'clock. The others still had half the course left to play. Knowing beforehand that I would be free for much of the afternoon, I had planned to spend it in nearby Yokohama.

This was before Yamanouchi Sensei, whom I mentioned briefly in the last chapter, died. I had heard that he was in ill health and confined to his bed, and I wanted to go and see him. His home now was a small room in the Yokohama Women's Academy in Yamate-cho. His wife, it seemed, divided her time between nursing him and doing some teaching at the academy. Perhaps, when one reaches the age of ninety, one becomes a child again, for as I sat in that small room talking to him I felt as though I were the school principal and he a little schoolboy. Moreover, he had acquired the habit in recent years of starting to cry the moment he saw me, and he was no different this time. Awkward and at a loss once again, I left him sooner than I'd intended.

It was still too early to go to the restaurant in Chinatown. Thinking that I might never have the chance again, I spent the next two hours driving around Yokohama in a taxi. I found to my surprise

46

that even in places where I'd expected to find no trace of the past, there still lingered recognizable fragments of long-remembered scenes. In the space of only three to four decades Yokohama had, after all, suffered a great earthquake, heavy wartime bombing, and a severe mauling at the hands of the American occupation forces, so that my experience that afternoon was rather like suddenly meeting in the most unlikely places old acquaintances whom one had imagined dead. And I found myself marveling at the tenacity with which the earth defends itself against the changes wrought by time.

The last place I went to see was the area above Yugyozaka, where I had lived from around the age of seven to nine. I got out of the taxi and walked about for a while, my memories of those days keeping me company. All the cherry trees on Cherry Avenue were gone, but a few traces of the old nursery business remained. A sign had been put up proclaiming the grounds to be the property of the company. It looked rather forlorn.

Just about where our house had been, a little way down the hill on the left-hand side, there now stood an elementary school.

Yugyozaka was still pretty steep, but the road itself had been much worse when I was eight or so. On rainy days I used to slip and fall constantly. Often the strap on one of my clogs would snap, and I'd continue my way up or down the hill in utter misery, trying to hold on to the umbrella while carrying the useless clog in the same hand. One side of the road was bordered by a tall bank, and the houses were all on the other side. They'd been built on a series of stepped, clearly demarcated lots—rather as in a modern housing development—which ended at the foot of the hill, where the Yugyo-ji temple stood.

Almost all the houses in this neighborhood belonged to foreigners, and we used to refer to them as a matter of habit and without any old-fashioned sense of exoticism as *ijinkan* [strangers' houses]. About the only Japanese besides us who lived there were a family who had a small general store at the corner of Cherry Avenue where it met Yugyozaka, and the jockey Kanzaki and his family, whose house was on the west side of the road.

Quite naturally, then, our playmates included genuine fair-haired foreign children with names like George and Frank. No consciousness of national difference bothered us, and we hardly ever got nasty with one another. Even so, I seem to remember that just occasionally we would get a bit parochial and petty, and that if it led to a real quarrel we found ourselves automatically forming two clearly divided sides: "us" and "them."

Whenever one of the foreign kids started crying, his father or mother would come charging out of their *ijinkan* and shout at us. They shouted in English, of course, which made it all the more terrifying, and we would flee the scene instantly. On the other hand, if any of us Japanese kids went home crying our mothers got angry with *us* and instead of rushing out, eyes popping with rage and shouting at the other kids, left us skulking in some corner of the house.

In our neighborhood, any woman at all noticeable for her good looks was apt to be a foreigner's mistress (*rashamen* was what we called them) or a housekeeper/nanny—*ama-san*—in the employ of a foreign family. The small general store I mentioned was just up from our house, and quite often I was sent out to buy something there. It was run by a dignified old couple with a pretty daughter who occasionally came to mind it for them. Now, this young woman was a *rashamen*; somehow, we children knew this without being specifically told, together with the fact that it was thanks to her that the old couple were able to live so comfortably.

I seem to remember that we children used the word *rashamen* frequently in conversation. As used by the community at large in the Yokohama of those days it was not a disparaging or discriminatory term. True, when Japanese used the word among themselves they would associate it in their minds with an unfamiliar way of life— with the powerful, un-Japanese fragrance, say, of foreign perfumes made from roses and violets—but that was all. The term "Nanking *rashamen*" [mistress of a Chinese], however, conveyed a different sort of meaning, being clearly understood to refer to a low way of life. There were all kinds even among the white men's *rashamen*, of course, but whether they merely visited their patrons or had their own establishments they seemed as a rule to enjoy a fair degree of security. And the foreigners themselves [i.e. *gaijin*, a term applied only to white foreigners], probably because they were all to some degree educated people, seem to have had some sense of responsibility toward their women. It was not at all unusual for them to continue sending money for years after they had gone back to their own countries, or to ensure that there was enough money for the children they had left in Japan to be properly educated. For such reasons, then, we didn't think of Eurasian children, of whom there were many in Yokohama in those days, as being all that different, though we did sometimes call them "*rashamen* kids."

The Japanese in the neighborhood tended to keep the extravagantly stylish *rashamen* at a respectful distance. With the *ama-san* they were more friendly, and would ask them, with the furtive, inquisitive look of someone delving into another person's secrets, to describe the living habits of their employers at the *ijinkan*.

Ama-san customarily wore white aprons even when they came out carrying shopping baskets or pushing baby carriages. Inspired by this novel style of dress, Mother made several small white aprons for me and my younger sisters to wear. The idea, I suppose, was simply to keep our clothes clean, but we called these garments, not aprons, but "*ama-san*," in recognition of their origin.

I myself stopped wearing them when I started going to elementary school, but by then they had become standard wear for children first in Yokohama then throughout Japan. Many years later Anzai Kazuyasu, a lawyer who ran the Yokohama Short Poetry Society at the time, said to me, "Did you know that the first person in Yokohama to put her children in '*ama-san*' was your mother?" According to Mr. Anzai, Mother once had occasion to go and see him at the district court, and she took me, still a young child, with her. He was intrigued by my apron, and complimented Mother on her idea. I don't remember the incident at all, but I've wondered since hearing his story whether I wasn't in fact the original "*ama-san*" wearer.

It was during those same days on Yugyozaka that I dreamed of becoming a jockey when I grew up. Mr. Kanzaki, whose house was very near ours, was then at the height of his fame as a champion jockey. Through the iron railing of his front gate, from either side of which ran a low fence covered with climbing roses, you could see a large front garden colorful with flowering plants. On either side of the garden was a long row of stables, and beyond it, in the middle, stood a grand Western-style house. Often at the gate stood carriages and rickshaws that had brought glamorous visitors—a leading kabuki actor, a famous geisha, a cabinet minister. And when the brightest star of them all, Kanzaki himself, looking handsome and austere, came riding out of the gate on one of his horses, it was like seeing a knight from some Western fairy tale.

By coincidence, this was when I began avidly reading Iwaya Sazanami's *Fairy Tales of the World*. It was, I suppose, my first true experience of books. *Boys' World*, published by Hakubunkan, still seemed rather difficult. But the *Fairy Tales*, perhaps because they were in medium octavo with No. 4 type, were easier to read; and though several dozen volumes had already been published by the time I started, I managed to get through virtually all of them.

I'm pretty certain they cost seven sen a copy. My parents were hardly likely to buy me a seven-sen book every time I wanted one, but there was a woman who ran a lending library at the little house with a sliding lattice door at the top of Ushijimazaka. There she would sit in the three-mat front room, surrounded by bookcases filled with children's books such as *Fairy Tales of the World*, the Kinkodo *Collected Fairy Tales*, *Lives of Great Japanese*, and *Aesop's Fables*.

Each volume of *Fairy Tales of the World* cost one sen to borrow.

With experience, I became rather clever: I would go with one sen in my pocket, borrow a volume, start reading it immediately as I walked away from the lattice door, then when I'd finished it rush back and say to the woman, "Auntie, I read this one before—can you change it for another one, please?" and go home with a different volume.

Finally, one day when I tried to play the same trick for the umpteenth time, the woman, sitting there in front of her sewing box, said to me, "Look, Hide-chan, from now on I'll let you have two books for one sen, so please don't make me get up twice every time you come." I still remember blushing with shame.

I had reached the age when one begins to be devious. Once at home—and I don't know what prompted me to do this—I picked up a silver twenty-sen piece when my mother wasn't looking and, unable to think of a better place to hide it, squeezed it in between the stitches of the tuck at the waist of my kimono. It wasn't such a good idea as I'd thought, for very soon the coin found its way down behind the lining of the kimono to the bottom, so that when I walked I could feel it bouncing up and down on my foot.

I wanted of course to spend it, but had no idea how. Sleeping and waking, the kimono haunted me; and whenever the coin touched my foot, my secret agony seemed to increase. Many times I thought of going to Mother and making a clean breast of it, but the longer I waited the harder it became, and in the end I bore in silence the awareness of my crime and the ever-present coin.

Then one day I furtively related my predicament to an older friend, a lanky fellow from the neighborhood whom we called "Abu-boy." Though still a child he already had a growth of beard around his mouth, and his face was distinguished by a certain lack of space between the eyes and eyebrows. He resembled the Arab seamen you often saw walking about the harbor barefoot and clad only in a loincloth. He was presumably of mixed parentage, but what kind of family he came from or what they did, I don't remember.

Anyway, what is certain is that I confessed my secret to this Abu-boy. As soon as I finished telling him, he picked up the hem of my kimono and bit off the stitching around the coin, then like a conjurer pulled out the milled silver twenty-sen piece. He kept it in his hand, and I couldn't bring myself to demand its return. "Let's go to Isezaki-cho!" he cried out suddenly. "I'll take you to Isezaki-cho!"

I followed him without demur.

I can't call to mind precisely everything we did that day, but I can still feel in my stomach what a strain it was for two youngsters at that time to consume almost twenty sen's worth of the kind of shop-prepared food we craved.

First, we went into a shop that served sweet bean soup with dumplings. One serving cost, I think, either one or one and a half sen. Then we went into the Nigiwai-za and watched the show standing up, stuffing ourselves with the bean-jam buns, peanuts and the like that we'd armed ourselves with. After we came out, we wandered about again like hungry puppies, stopping to eat whatever took our fancy. But it seems that even we were unable to spend all the twenty sen, for when the spree was over, I found I still had a two-sen copper piece left.

I don't remember where Abu-boy and I parted company, but I do recall walking home across Kuruma-bashi, weighed down by a grossly bloated stomach and wondering what I was going to do with the copper coin, which was considerably larger than the silver coin I started with. I was certainly not going to take it home with me.

I stopped and with what I hoped was a casual air gazed at the river; then, making sure that no one was approaching the bridge at either end, I flung the coin far out into the river. And I ran all the rest of the way home. What happened after that I don't remember. But something of that feeling of sheer relief as I hurled the coin away from me with the skill of a practiced stone-thrower has stayed with me to this day.

There was another incident involving Abu-boy at about the same time, one that left a strangely unpleasant aftertaste. After these two incidents I stopped playing with him; he too became distant, and whenever we met by chance on the street we would both look away.

From the end of our garden you could see over the roofs of a row of three or four houses. The couple in the house at the far end of the row owned a harmonium, and every Sunday morning at a given time you would hear the pleasant sound of hymns being played on it. The children of the neighborhood, myself among them, would gather there and sing the hymns, listen to interesting stories, and receive pretty picture cards to take home. It was there that I had first became friendly with Abu-boy.

It was a humble rented house, and the sliding doors between the two rooms, one larger and one smaller, had to be taken out in order to accommodate all the children together. The setting was so humble in fact that if it hadn't been for the harmonium, "Sunday school" would have been too grand a term to describe our gatherings. The couple must have been Christians, but I don't think they were missionaries. I suppose they just liked having children around and doing good work; there were many such families in Yokohama in those days. The couple had a pretty daughter. She was older than me, but I was much taken with her; I remember the indescribable pleasure of watching her lips as we sang hymns together.

Since we lived near each other, I could go and see her even when it wasn't a Sunday. One afternoon, I went into their back garden and approaching the verandah called to her to come out and play. There was no answer. The sliding doors were open and I could see into the house. Deciding that no one was in, I started to walk away when the sound of muffled giggling reached me from inside the room beyond the verandah. I turned and looked inside again, and this time saw Abu-boy and the girl lying on the floor, half-hidden by the harmonium, their bodies closely entwined. Her back was turned toward me, her face buried in Abu-boy's chest; and over the back of her head with its plaited hair I could see his eyes watching me.

Thrown into confusion by an emotion that was new and strange to me I left without a word. It was not sharp enough to be called jealousy; besides, I am sure what I'd seen was only a children's game. Nevertheless, the feeling that overcame me as I walked out of the garden alone was hard to bear. From then on, I never spoke to Abu-boy again, nor did I ever go back to that house to sing hymns.

Mother was always saying that she would like me to become a doctor. "Don't talk nonsense," Father would say. "Commerce is the thing of the future. He's going to be a businessman." Mother's ideas were no doubt influenced by her stay at an impressionable age in the Kondo academy; as for Father, he had every reason to want me to follow in his footsteps in Yokohama, for the export and import business he was engaged in, and the business of the Pier Company, were thriving as never before.

From around the time I was seven and in my second year at the elementary school, I started taking private lessons in English. This meant that for two hours every day I had to remain at school after regular classes for tutoring.

The arrangement was approved by Yamanouchi Sensei at the special request of my father, who saw English as the future language of commerce and also, as a matter of general principle, wanted his son to be exposed to a foreign language at an early age.

Another consideration, perhaps, also played a part in Father's decision: that he had detected undesirable traits in my character and behavior, which he hoped to correct by introducing radical changes in my training.

From then on, I was not allowed to play; suddenly the father I saw at home became an even sterner figure than before. In effect, he was subjecting me to the sort of discipline he himself had experienced as a boy in a samurai household.

School ended every afternoon at two or three o'clock. After the other children had left, my English tutor and I would sit facing each other in the empty classroom, and with the first book of the *National Reader* in front of me I would read aloud, over and over again, "It is a dog," "It is a hat. . . ." I would watch in desperation the daylight fading outside the window; and the longing to go home, to go out and play, would be almost unbearable. Sometimes tears would well up uncontrollably and fall on the open pages of the *Reader*.

About six months later, in January of the following year, I had to begin attending yet another daily tutorial, this time in the Chinese classics. It would be evening when I got home from the English tutorial; I would have my dinner immediately, then rush off to the house of my new tutor, who happened to live across the street from the girl I wrote about earlier.

This tutor lived with an elderly woman who seemed to be his mother, and his younger brother, who was a student; as far as I could tell, he wasn't married. I remember that he was from the Mito domain and that his name was Oka Koto. Thirtyish and small, he was a gentle person. He was always dressed formally in a hakama and a black cotton haori with the family crest on it, and would receive me, child though I was, with the utmost courtesy. We sat facing each other across a desk made of mulberry or some other wood.

The first textbook Mr. Oka had me read was a miscellany of excerpts from the unofficial histories and the eighteen official histories. Following this initiation, we moved on to the *Analects* and writings in evidential scholarship that I neither understood nor was expected to understand. Whenever we came to words and phrases I found difficult to read, Mr. Oka would tear off little pieces of red Chinese paper and licking them lightly affix them there in my Japanese exercise book. In my childish way I thought them quite elegant, rather like plum blossoms fallen onto the pages.

But though the tutor's house was near, it would be eight or nine o'clock by the time I returned home from the tutorial. Father would be back from the office by then, and sometimes he made me sit in front of him and go over my lessons in English and Chinese. I don't suppose these review sessions lasted long, but for me they were the worst ordeal of all and seemed interminable at the time. On winter nights the room would get rather warm, and no matter how hard I tried to stay awake I would start nodding off. At such times Father, of course, would wake me with an angry shout. This much I was used to, but on one occasion I became aware that he was opening the inner sliding doors by the verandah, and the next moment I found myself being pushed off it into the garden. I remember clearly that it was snowing that night. And when Mother appeared on the verandah I heard Father shout from behind the inner doors: "Don't be a fool! Who said I'd forgiven him! Close the rain shutters and leave him out there!" I stood outside for perhaps half an hour, wailing, and calling out my apologies to him. I was too frantic at the time to remember what else occurred, except that I eventually went around the garden to the kitchen, where Mother wiped my ice-cold bare feet with a towel. Then, still sobbing, I was led back to Father to continue our session.

Father of course must have believed that it was out of love for his son that he was making me work so hard. Indeed, I have no doubt that he saw his own severity as a truer expression of a father's love than any leniency. Fathers and educators today would probably find such an attitude difficult to understand; for me, it is utterly beyond comprehension.

And yet I am, for all that, a product of that family and that father; and my own children may well be bothered by things in me that are carried over from their grandfather. I like to think that in my own way I've responded thoughtfully to the passage of time and the changes that occur with it, but it is inevitable perhaps that somewhere inside me I should still retain some traces of my heritage. Thus I have my doubts about the current permissiveness among parents, and there are times, even, when I feel a kind of retrospective attachment to Father's severity.

One very stormy Sunday morning Father, for some reason or other, went to his office. In those days there were people called "lunch carriers" whose job was to go to their customers' houses with covered carts, pick up box lunches prepared at home for the menfolk, and deliver them to their offices before noon. But they didn't

56

work on Sundays, so before leaving the house Father apparently told Mother to have me and my little sister Kino—she was two years younger than me—take his lunch to him. Under one oil-paper umbrella held at an angle against the wind and with our feet bare, the two of us walked in the torrential rain all the way to his office on the Bund to deliver his lunch. He was in a very good mood when he saw us. He said what good children we were, sat us down in the janitor's room, and ordered a simple Western meal for each of us. At times like this he seemed a very warm and bighearted man.

There is nothing I have disliked more ever since I was a child than cow's milk. I gather that this is because I was forced to drink it once at the age of three or four, when I was very seriously ill. The dislike is as intense now as it ever was. If someone in the family has drunk milk out of a particular glass, I can always tell even after it's been thoroughly and repeatedly washed. "This has had milk in it," I'll say as I bring it to my mouth. Butter and cheese don't bother me at all, but my stomach rebels at the very mention of milk.

It has been more or less the same for me with English. Despite all Father did to have it drummed into me—so convinced was he that it was an absolutely necessary subject—my mind could no more absorb it than my stomach could absorb milk. Those afternoons I had to spend in the empty classroom watching the sun slowly go down and my own teardrops spreading on the pages of the *National Reader* were to my boy's mind like being shut up in prison, and in the end caused me to reject English just as my stomach had learned to reject milk. With the passing of the years I became acutely aware of my ignorance of the language; for a time, I actually forced myself to give up my avid reading of literary works and tried learning it, but to no avail. Not only was my mind seemingly incapable of taking in a foreign language, but my whole body seemed to rebel against prolonged exposure to it. And to this day, cow's milk and English continue to produce the same physiological response in me.

Toy Train

Our Yugyozaka days can't have lasted more than two or two and a half years, for I remember that it wasn't long before we moved from there to Minami-Ota, in the western outskirts of Yokohama. This meant of course that I had to change schools, taking leave of Yamanouchi Sensei, Goshinzo Sensei, and the rest. First, though, a few more memories of our Yugyozaka days remain to be related.

I saw Tokyo twice in my early childhood, and traveled in trains on two different occasions. The first time was either just before I started school or in my first year there, when Mother took me with her on a trip to her birthplace, Sakura, in Chiba Prefecture. It must have been an intensely poignant occasion for her, for it could only have been the first or second time she'd been there since her marriage.

Nowadays, one thinks nothing of going from Yokohama to Sakura and back the same day. But in those days, it would seem, the journey was regarded as a considerable undertaking. Certainly the circumstances and mood of train travel then were quite different from what they are now. Once the train had left Yokohama, it was green countryside all the way to Shinbashi Station in Tokyo, just like the scenery described in the "Railway Song"; and the passengers, watching the green fields passing by outside, looked as though they were being lulled into a gentle somnolence.

On that trip, we stopped in Tokyo and spent the night at my uncle-in-law's house, which stood within the grounds of Prince Kitashirakawa's palace.

The next morning I was taken around the palace and grounds by my uncle and one of the prince's staff. In what I was told was the prince's son's room I saw a nickel-plated miniature railway laid out in a large circle on the floor. On it stood an exquisite toy train with an engine that ran on alcohol.

After the war, imported toy trains were all the rage, and even adults went about buying freight cars, engines, stations, and sections of rail one at a time to add to their sets. But this train was the kind of thing that in those days only a princely family could have owned. Someone in the young prince's room started the engine for me, and with utter amazement I watched the train run.

My uncle-in-law, Saito Tsunetaro, was a widower when I met him, his wife—Mother's elder sister—having died two or three years before. He was apparently one of the eminent linguists of his day, and besides being a professor at the Peers' School was educational supervisor of the various young princes of the blood. It was thanks to the latter appointment that he lived in the grounds of Prince Kitashirakawa's palace.

The elder sister of Mother's who married him was named Toyoko. She left behind three children when she died. She was very loving toward Mother, and Mother treasured her memory all her life.

I never saw her, yet I seem to be able to recall the shape of her face and her features even now with uncanny clarity. I suppose this is because even when Mother was in the very depths of poverty, and until the last years of her life, she would from time to time bring out a photograph of her sister—which she kept with great care, as though it were some kind of sacred charm—and tell us about her sweet and generous nature. Moreover, Mother truly admired her brother-in-law and kept in touch with him after her sister's death.

She seemed to feel that he was the only relative left she could depend upon.

Unfortunately, there was an immediate, instinctive antagonism between him and Father: "cat and dog" would be an understatement. We children would often see or overhear Mother crying after some altercation between the two. I couldn't understand what made the two men so hostile toward each other. But as I got older and came to understand something of the complicated workings of the human mind and the inflexible attitudes drummed into us by family tradition, I became a little less puzzled. In short, Father hated to be outdone by anybody. He was confrontational even toward his relatives, and in times of adversity, when he felt himself at a disadvantage, he became all the more assertive and inflexible. He and Saito were so different in every respect—in personality and attitude, in their respective circumstances—that they were utterly irreconcilable right from the start.

But for me Saito was a close relative, one of whom Mother had always spoken with affection and admiration; so later, when I went up to Tokyo hoping to find a way to further my education, he was the first person I went to for advice. Before beginning this memoir I wanted for various reasons to find out more about him, but by then there was no one I could readily go to for such information.

Just recently, however, I received a most surprising letter from a reader of *Bungei Shunju*, giving information about Kondo Makoto's Kogyokusha, Mother's relationship with Saito, and other matters concerning her and her connections that was more definite and detailed than the scanty and fragmentary information I had at the time I wrote about her days at the Kogyokusha. Part of it runs as follows:

> . . . I have been reading the installments of your memoir in *Bungei Shunju* with much pleasure and a sense of personal association. The fact is that my mother was born the second daughter of Kondo Makoto; and when recently I happened to read to her your account of your mother and the Kogyokusha

she was very surprised to learn whose son you were, for it turns out that she and your mother were cousins.

Kondo Makoto had many grandchildren, but my mother is the only one left of her generation of the Kondo family—the only one, in other words, who remembers the old days. She is now seventy-nine. If there is anything you wish to find out from her, let me know before too long and I will ask her for you.

In the meantime, allow me to tell you a little about your mother's connection with mine and about the Kondo family.

Kondo Makoto's wife Maki (her original given name was Yukiko) was your maternal grandmother's sister. She came from a family called Yoshimasu, of the Sakura domain. . . . My mother tells me that when she was a girl living with her parents at the Kogyokusha in Shiba Shinsenza she and your mother were good friends and often played together. Your mother at the time was living with her elder sister and her husband, Saito Tsunetaro, instructor in English at the Kogyokusha.

I should perhaps add that my mother later married a man by the name of Suzuki Kin'ichi, who was a chief engineer with the Japan Mail Steamer Company. Her eldest brother was Vice Admiral Baron Kondo Motoki, who died in 1929. Her elder sister Shizuko, who died in 1942, was the wife of Vice Admiral Baron Yamanouchi Masuji. Her second eldest brother, Sukemune, who was an employee of a foreign business firm, died in 1928.

My husband is at present head of the Tokyo branch of the Hokkaido Bank. If you have any questions you think we may be able to answer, please get in touch with him at his office address. . . .

[Signed] Kawachi Kiyoko

The letter made me realize how close Mother's ties with the

Kondo family were, and how much more there was to her connection with Saito Tsunetaro than I had thought. And of course it gave me a clearer picture of the circumstances that led her to leave home and go to live in Tokyo when still so young. It also contained information that obliges me to acknowledge my earlier ignorance about the man who acted as go-between in my parents' marriage.

I wrote earlier that he was a doctor by the name of Yoshimasu, a resident of Yokohama and a practitioner of the Yoshimasu Todo school of Chinese medicine. What I did not know was that he too was from the Sakura domain, and that he came from the same family as Mother's mother. He would thus have known the Kondo family well; and it isn't at all strange that he should have been listened to when he urged Mother to go to Yokohama and marry Father. Unfortunately I know nothing more about this man who played such a crucial role in her life.

To get back to my subject: my very first sight of the great city of Tokyo as it was around the end of the century was when Mother and I spent a night in Aoyama on our way to Sakura.

I've never forgotten the morning that we left Saito's house. We rode all the way from Aoyama to Ryogoku Station in Honjo in a gently swaying rickshaw. We stopped several times on the way, and each time we stopped Mother had to wake me up. It was late spring, as I remember it. We got off in Ningyo-cho, and bought gifts and went into a restaurant to have sweet bean soup.

We grandchildren had all been brought up to think fondly of our grandfather in Sakura. When I met him, he was still in excellent health. I think he was living in retirement by then, after being the headman of his local district. He lived in a house surrounded by an old-fashioned high hedge, with a sweeping view of Lake Inbanuma from his garden. He always had saké served even with his breakfast, and every morning would have a friendly chat with the fish seller who came walking all the way in the dark from the sea with his selection of freshly caught fish. He was particularly fond of bonito sashimi, which he ate with the skin left on and served with grated garlic in soy sauce. Perhaps he was bothered by the drops of saké trickling down the pure white beard on his chin, for he was always rubbing at it with the palm of his hand. Sometimes he would put me on his lap and rub his beard against my cheek. Hating the smell of garlic, I would rudely push his pink face away with both hands.

One unforgettable incident took place on our return trip. We were standing beside a large pillar inside the old Shinbashi Station. Putting her large cloth holdall on the floor by my feet Mother said, "Now you stay here and keep an eye on the bag while I go and get our tickets," and disappeared into the crowd.

After a while she returned with the tickets. It was only when she said despairingly, "Where's the bag?" that I realized it wasn't there any more. Eventually a policeman and a station official appeared on the scene, and a large crowd of curious travelers formed a circle around us. I must have felt some measure of responsibility, for I started wailing—very loudly, I'm sure—and continued to do so, refusing to be consoled, as someone led me to the train.

This became one of Mother's favorite anecdotes, and she often told it even after I was grown up. Actually, she would say, apart from a few clothes and toilet articles, the holdall contained nothing but packages of unseasoned broiled eel, a speciality of Lake Inbanuma, which she'd bought to take back as gifts for people she knew in Yokohama. What could the thief have done, she wondered cheerfully, with all that fish?

Broiled eel seasoned with soy sauce is a common dish even today, but few people nowadays know or remember the special taste of unseasoned eel, or would think of asking for it at a restaurant. On the rare occasion when I'm served it myself, I'm immediately reminded of that incident in Shinbashi Station so many years ago.

The second time I saw Tokyo was in the spring of my third year at elementary school.

An exhibition of children's calligraphy, chosen from among entries from all over the country, was being held in Ueno. I think that mine was among them; but, whatever the reason, a group of us led by Yamanouchi Sensei went all the way from Yokohama to see the exhibition.

There were no more than ten or so in our group, including some parents. Although the principal of the school was himself in charge of the trip, it was actually more like a relaxed family outing. No one from my family came, but the girls, certainly, were accompanied by their mothers or some other older member of the family. One of the girls, I remember, was called Kato—I forget her first name. She was in my class, and I had always rather liked her. But there was another girl in the group named Miyazaki Chiyoko whom I liked a lot more and thought a lot prettier. Either way, it must have been a great treat for me to go on the same "study trip" with those two girls.

Yet, oddly enough, I don't remember feeling any pangs of puppy love, or sentimental yearning, for those two during the trip. I remember our going to Asakusa from Ueno and having lunch—seated in rows and on our best behavior—in a small private room in a well-known restaurant. But the most vivid memory I have of that day is of Kato-san's mother holding me on her lap as we sat in the horse-drawn streetcar.

The streetcar, a symbol of progress in those days, plied its way between Asakusa, Ryogoku, Kyobashi, and Ginza, leaving a trail of horse droppings in its wake. That I can still picture it so clearly may be because of Kato-san's mother. She must have been past thirty by then, but even to a boy's eyes she was unusually beautiful. Moreover—and this may have been the Yokohama style—her hair, her fingers, and her obi clasp glittered with jewels; and her slightest movement brought a whiff of some scent, accentuated by the warmth of her body, that reminded one of wisteria flowers.

The rickshaw ride from Aoyama to Ryogoku Station was too long to doze through; and I seem to remember that the ride on the streetcar from Asakusa to Ginza and Shinbashi Station was very long too. The streetcar must have picked up a lot of passengers en route, for I remember Kato-san's mother quietly lifting me from my seat and putting me on her lap. I think I squirmed, as if I disliked the move. She brought her face close to mine and told me about the places passing by outside. When I finally became still, so did she— pretending, I think, to have been lulled to sleep by the swaying of the streetcar. I felt a kind of bashfulness tinged with guilt, as though what I was feeling must be obvious to everyone around me, yet at the same time I was overwhelmed by an almost frightening happiness. Not that such abstractions honestly describe my condition: it was, essentially, a physical arousal in direct response to a stimulus. I was furtively indulging in vague fantasies, intoxicated by the warmth and fragrance of her body and the awareness of something unfurling within me under that gentle warmth.

Working it out carefully, I'm certain that this happened in the spring of my ninth year. Was I, then, unusually precocious? Or are such sexual awakenings a standard phenomenon among boys of nine? If so, it means that we parents are far too inattentive concerning sex as it relates to our own children. Most parents in fact tend, it seems, to ignore their own childhood experiences when they look at their children.

My father was an inveterate do-gooder and mediator. Of course, most people enjoy being generous when things are going well for themselves, and he, I suppose, was no exception. He was constantly rushing about trying to patch up quarrels between people, or bringing them to our house where he would sit before them playing the mediator. Presumably he liked the admiration and compliments that such acts of goodwill brought him. But if he felt he had been betrayed by his beneficiaries, he would become exceedingly bad-tempered and start shouting at Mother, innocent bystander though she was.

Undeterred by previous mistakes, he once picked up one of the foreign seamen hanging about the harbor and brought him home. He was a weak-looking man about whom we knew nothing, not even what nationality he was. He was young, but appeared to be suffering from some kind of illness. He was also rather dirty. "There'll be fleas all over the house!" protested my mother and the maid when told that he was to have a hot bath, fresh underclothes, and one of my father's old suits. Perhaps Father had it in mind to employ him eventually in his company, for he asked our doctor to come and see him, and also had him tutored in Japanese. With smug satisfaction, he watched his ward's health improve.

To have a foreigner living with us was an excitingly exotic experience for us children. We treated him like a new toy we'd been given to play with. He for his part behaved like a small animal unused to human beings, with eyes darting about uncertainly and lips in a perpetual made-up smile. He stayed with us for about six months, bringing in water from the well for the bath, clumsily sweeping the garden, and doing other chores. And then, one morning, he disappeared. We heard Mother saying mournfully in Father's room, "But I told you something like this would happen. . . ."

As Father left for his office that morning he was the picture of misery.

We constantly had various hangers-on living in our house. Relations, too, stayed with us from time to time; they, of course, could hardly be called "hangers-on." There was my uncle Yamagami Kiyoshi, for instance, Mother's elder brother who had come to Yokohama to work for the Yokohama Lighthouse Department. He was soon joined by a younger brother named Saburo, a civil engineer. Then my half-brother Masahiro arrived from Odawara, having found a job in the Yokohama Soda Bank. With these three additions we were, for a while, quite a big family.

Our house became much too crowded, so Father rented a nearby house that fronted on Yugyozaka and made my uncles and any other lodgers move in there. Their breakfast and dinner would be cooked in our house and taken over to them by one of the maids.

They were all afraid of Father and careful to stay on the right side of him. But at times when they knew he would be late getting home, they would keep all the Western lamps burning and under their bright light regale themselves with sukiyaki and saké, and become so rowdy that one wondered what they were up to. Sometimes the maid would join the party and could be heard screeching with delight, and Mother would find it very difficult to get her back.

And then my uncle Kiyoshi began showing symptoms of mental illness. One night he suddenly got out of bed—they all slept in the same room on futon laid out next to each other—and began urinating. There was great consternation, and he was immediately taken to a hospital. After a brief stay, he seemed to recover his normal state of mind and came back to the house. He started going to work again, but there, too, he had apparently given cause for doubt about his mental health. He resigned, and for a while remained in the house convalescing. But he continued to have lapses, and at times became violent. So finally he was sent back to his home in Sakura with someone to look after him. There, his lapses became less and less frequent until in time he fully recovered. He later moved to Tokyo, and ended his days there without mishap as a perfectly ordinary company employee and staid family man.

It so happened that his younger brother Saburo also came to suffer from the same kind of mental problems. For a while he seemed to recover and was able to work as a civil engineer, but his illness returned, and he died young.

Though no one else in the family has shown such tendencies, the fact is that on Mother's side I have two uncles who quite unmistakably suffered from mental illness. If this disorder is hereditary, then how can I be sure that someone related to them won't suddenly be the third in the family to show symptoms of it?

In my more vulnerable moments I am sometimes assailed by the fear that the same seed may lurk in my blood too. I comfort myself with the thought that, so far at any rate, neither I nor those around me have given cause for any concern. Even so, looking back on my own childhood and youth, I can't help wondering whether there weren't times when the illness betrayed itself in brief flashes.

In the autumn of my ninth year, we moved to a house at Aka-mon-mae in Minami-Ota ward, and I changed schools again. This time, the school was near our house, and if I ran I could get there in two or three minutes. The district called Akamon-mae was small and extremely quiet, its few houses forming a perfect square. Through it meandered clear streams flowing down from the hills in the northwest, and every building had its own miniature bridge connecting it to the street. Ours was a corner house facing the street that went past the main gate of the temple we called Akamon, and because the house stood on a corner it had water running along both the side and the front of it. No foreigners lived in the neighborhood and I had no friends of mixed blood, so the atmosphere was totally different from that of the places I had lived in on the Bluff.

Our house stood by a large crossroads. On the street going north there was an inn known for its hot mineral baths. Going south, you soon came to the buildings of the elementary school I now attended. Next was a temple called Fumon-in, and then quiet residential sections with houses fronted by a continuous line of hedges. A little further on you came to Hatsune-cho, a somewhat livelier section with a large wholesale store standing on the corner. The son of this establishment, I heard, was Mori Sannosuke, a star actor of the "*soshi* [political activist] drama," then nearing the height of its popularity.

Another prominent figure living thereabouts was Ito Chiyu, also a *soshi*, who had an elegant house on the other side of the crossroads from us. It stood with its back to a hill we called Heitai-yama [Soldiers' Hill]. Its front wall was made of old ship's planks, and was overhung by a tall pine tree growing there. It may well have been where he kept his mistress.

Near our house was a rickshaw station, and one morning as I was walking to school with my school bag slung over my shoulder, I saw a group of rickshaw men and neighbors standing outside the station solemnly engaged in some kind of gossip. Just before dawn that morning, it seemed, someone had broken into Chiyu's house with the aim of catching him there in bed with his mistress, and Chiyu had been seen running out of the place in his nightclothes. The incident was being mulled over again and again by the group.

Chiyu in those days owned a theater in Kumoi-cho called the Kumoi-za. His reputation as a *soshi* had reached even us children, and though we didn't know what a *soshi* was, the word suggested something frightening and dangerous. Some years later, I heard him recite one of his political tales, but I never saw him during the time we lived in the neighborhood. Perhaps he moved away as soon as the neighbors started talking about his amorous liaisons. It says something about the neighborhood that anything so trivial could have caused such general concern for its reputation and moral health that Chiyu felt compelled to leave. You might have called it clean-minded, or strict about conduct; it was certainly quiet and orderly.

The Midori-ya Variety Store

No matter how old I become, in talking of my parents I revert to childhood. I portray them to others as their child—which means, inevitably, in as favorable a light as possible. I wouldn't actually lie to protect them, but I find it difficult nevertheless to describe their worst failings and absurdities.

To the young people of today, who well before they are twenty are used to being critical of their parents, this sentiment may seem ridiculous or incomprehensible. But the old-fashioned sense of being the same flesh and blood is not some kind of scar left by a wound inflicted on us by our parents; rather, it is the unavoidable sense of shared responsibility that comes from sharing the same blood. In other words, Father's weakness for drink and his failings as a man were undoubtedly distributed in some measure by heredity among his children; and watching him as he lurched through life we felt ashamed, for it was like watching ourselves.

Father was always a heavy drinker. To this day, we children retain anguished memories of the days when he was half-crazed by drink.

His bedroom upstairs was a Japanese room, but in it was a large Western cabinet, on one of whose shelves stood an array of bottles containing various kinds of imported liquor. When he'd gone to bed and was ready for sleep, he would invariably have moved these bottles from the shelf and lined them up on the floor behind his pillow. I often woke up during the night; and during those moments of wakefulness I would catch a barely audible sound, eerily like the sound of a cat enjoying its meal, coming from his bedroom. It was of course Father, who was lying on his stomach sipping mixtures of gin and brandy or something. He did this whenever he found himself awake—two or three times a night.

"They talk of men who can drink a whole magnum," Mother would say sadly, "but that would be nothing to your father." By the time he set off for the office in the morning, he would already reek of alcohol.

Bicycles in those days were still a rare commodity, even in Yokohama. Father had one, though, on which he would ride to his office and rush about town. More than once Mother was told that he'd been seen on his bicycle pulling a whisky bottle from his pocket and taking a swig. That he had accidents was not surprising. Once he knocked down an apprentice geisha and had to pay her hospital fees. He also rode straight into shops—a tofu shop, for instance, and another time a grocer's—and had to pay for any damages. There were always bruises and scratches on his face and hands.

There were times when he would stay away for several nights, then, when he came home, sit down and as he drank regale us with accounts of his utterly idiotic exploits. He did this boastfully, showing not the slightest sign of remorse. Once he went aboard a foreign ship moored alongside the pier and spent a whole day and night drinking with the captain, the purser, and other ship's officers. He then went ashore with all these foreigners in tow and led them to one establishment after another in Omori, Shinbashi, and other such places. It was a drinking spree lasting several days, during which they didn't have even one proper meal. At last they returned to Yokohama, and as he stood on the pier watching the ship sail out of the harbor, he coughed up blood.

He had apparently coughed up blood a number of times before. I think it likely now that his ulcers were already turning into cancer. Dr. Komiya, who took care of us, said to him: "I have my conscience as a doctor, and if you don't stop drinking, I won't come to this house again."

Father was then barely forty, the prime of life for a man. During the period stretching from our Yugyozaka days to our time in Shimizu-cho, his company had prospered; his circle of acquaintances among foreigners doing business around the harbor had continued to grow; and he enjoyed a reputation in the pleasure quarters as a man who did things with style. I shouldn't wonder if all this success had gone to his head. Besides, he stood five foot seven—tall for his generation—and had a robust physique. In short, he was in no mood to listen to the doctor's warning.

Mother didn't dare breathe a word of complaint. If, while he was eating and drinking, she so much as suggested disapproval on her face, he would fly into a rage and knock over the small tray table on which his dinner stood. On one occasion he caught me tugging at Mother's sleeve and looking enviously at some side dish he was having with his drink. He immediately picked up his table and threw it into the courtyard, shouting, "I can't enjoy my drink! Why can't you give the children the same things to eat? How can I eat the stuff with them staring at me?" If something irritated him when he was dead drunk he would force Mother to sit there for an hour or two, continuing to drink as he muttered the same old criticisms of her or made disparaging remarks about her relatives. If Mother objected, he would order her to leave the house and not come back; and sometimes he completely lost control and attacked her physically.

We enjoyed having him around when he was only a bit tipsy and in a good mood, but as soon as we saw signs of change in his condition, darkness would descend on us, like a power failure in a typhoon. I didn't fare too badly myself, as I was only ten or so at the time, but it was different for my half-brother, a slender, handsome young man. "Masahiro, come here," Father would say ominously. Then, once Masahiro was seated within range of his boozy breath, he would proceed to berate him at length. "The trouble with you," he would begin, "is that you're a feeble, effeminate fellow. . . ." In the course of one of these sermons he became very angry—why, I don't know—and even began demanding that Masahiro commit harakiri. I remember watching Masahiro—who actually did look rather like a kabuki actor playing female roles—and seeing his face turn pale and tearful.

There were, in fact, swords at hand in the house if one had wanted to use them. I remember Mother in moments of panic rushing about in search of a hiding place for them. Once, after an absence of ten days, Father suddenly appeared with some hangers-on in tow, including his mistress, a geisha called Okoto who worked in Kannai, the pleasure quarter, and the madam of a teahouse he frequented. The first thing he did on entering the house was order Mother to have food and drink brought in for himself and his guests. A coarse, rowdy party ensued, and when at last it ended and the visitors had left, Mother ventured a brief complaint. In a rage, Father went and fetched a sword from somewhere and, unsheathing it, flourished it in front of her. "I'll cut you down!" he shouted, as though he meant it. Mother rushed out, in her socks, into the back garden with my little sisters, then went outside through the back gate, where she stayed until midnight, crouching beside the wall, with her arms around the girls.

Father meanwhile went on drinking heavily. "You are boys, so you'll stay with your father," he kept telling us loudly. "Don't you dare go chasing after your mother! If you leave the house now, I'll never let you back in." There was nothing we could do except sit there and wail.

When at last he was in his bedroom upstairs, apparently asleep, we sneaked out of the back gate to look for Mother. It was so late the whole neighborhood must have gone to bed, but Mother stayed there with her arms wrapped around us, holding her kimono sleeve up to her face and weeping bitterly, like a figure in a traditional kabuki "lamentation" scene. "Oh, why did I marry such a frightening man!" she kept saying. "If only I didn't have you children. . . ."

I suppose the only way she could bring herself to go back, the only way she could deal with her feelings, was thus to cry her heart out, with her children trying to console her.

Even now I can see Father's tyrannical figure and Mother's weeping face, the images so clear I feel I could draw them. The memory of her weeping is particularly vivid, and I can recall the smallest details: the teardrops running down on either side of her small nose, reaching her quivering lips, then disappearing inside them as she bewailed her lot; or the creases on her pale brow—how can I describe that look?—as she let us see the anger that she couldn't reveal to her violent husband.

Naturally enough, we children came to feel hostility toward him, and with no hesitation whatsoever we sided with Mother. Nevertheless, whenever in her anguish she let slip the words, "If only I didn't have you children. . . ," we were terribly hurt. Somehow we felt we owed her an apology for having been born; it was a miserable feeling, and all we could do, at a loss for anything better, was cry with her.

I could go on forever telling stories about Father's mad drinking and the suffering it caused Mother, but they would differ little from those I've already told. His career was ruined because of it, and it finally gave him the chronic disease that kept him bedridden during his later years. Yet, in all fairness, he was not always mean and quarrelsome when he drank. At the teahouses he frequented he was apparently liked for his high-spirited ways; even at home he could be very cheerful when drunk, and sometimes would entertain his children and the maids by clowning around all evening before finally lying down peacefully and going to sleep.

Sometimes on such evenings, when we were really sure he was in a good mood, we would gather expectantly around him as he sat drinking and eating. "You'll get a prize if you can get me down on my back," he would say, and we would try to get a stranglehold on him from behind and pull or push at his head with our hands. Soon father and children would be locked in combat. My cheeks rubbed painfully against his bristly face, and there was that overwhelming smell of drink mixed with a heavy, masculine body odor that is as inextricably linked in my mind with Father as tears are with Mother.

The one time that I saw him in a cheerful mood for a whole day was when he and I went plum-blossom viewing in Sugita. Whenever we came across a tea shop, we would sit down on a bench outside and he would have some saké—a bottle here, a couple of bottles there. After several such stops he was completely drunk. In those days it was not uncommon to see drunkards staggering about in public in broad daylight, and still less uncommon to see them on festive occasions such as plum-blossom viewing. Even then, though, Father's condition was enough to attract attention. I was only a young, undersized boy, confused and embarrassed, faced with the responsibility of taking this blind-drunk father home.

When we came out of the Isogo underpass he immediately lay down on a grassy strip by the seashore and went to sleep. I sat beside him and watched the sea at sunset, utterly forlorn. After a while, a rickshaw man came up and asked if he could help. I gave him our address, and he lifted Father into the rickshaw, then put me in after him, and thus we went home. By now, my memory of Father that day has become a rather precious one. And recognizing in retrospect the streak of helpless abandon in him, I find myself wishing I'd been old enough at the time to drink with him.

He hardly ever went out with his children; but I remember one other time. It was a summer evening. I was sitting about in the house when Father, dressed in a kimono of fine linen or some such material, came and to my surprise said, "Let's go out for a walk, Hide." We walked for a while along the main street of Isezaki-cho, mingling with other strollers out to enjoy the cool of the evening. When we came to a bookshop Father stopped and said, "Buy yourself something." So I chose the latest issue of *Boys' World* and a copy of *Boys*, which had started publication by then.

We crossed Kane-no-hashi and entered the Kannai pleasure quarter. In front of the entrance to a certain teahouse, Father stopped and said to me, "You can go home now. Just say that as we were walking I happened to meet a friend from the company, and decided to go off with him. There's no need to say anything else. Right?"

But it seems that when I got home I gave Mother an accurate account of everything that had happened. Some days passed without incident, and I forgot all about the walk. Then one evening Father, as he sat sipping his saké, suddenly said to me in a voice full of anger, "I thoroughly dislike fellows like you. If you were a real man, wild horses wouldn't drag a secret out of you. A miserable blabbermouth, that's what you are! Get out of here, I can't stand the sight of you!" Egocentric and impulsive, he was beyond the control of reason. "Samurai" aphorisms learned as a child were authority enough for his outbursts and his tyrannizing of the household. Passing in the pleasure quarters as an easygoing, liberal man, at home he sought to be the unbending disciplinarian; he was two different men in fact— the one outside and the one at home—and which of them was our real father we children could hardly be expected to know.

The business venture I am about to describe was one matter, at least, on which he first consulted Mother. What possessed both of them to become involved in such a thing, I still don't know. Father's company was doing very well, and he hardly needed more money. Even so, one day carpenters suddenly descended on us and proceeded to make extensive alterations in the front part of the house. What emerged in very short time was a variety store with a blue shop curtain hanging over the new entrance. The letters on the curtain said "Midori-ya."

Our neighbors, apparently, could hardly believe what they saw. As I said earlier, the whole area around Akamon-mae was a quiet residential neighborhood. Moreover, our house had small, clear streams running in front and alongside it, and to get to our outer gate from the street you had to go over a small bridge about three feet wide; so that even after the outer gate was torn down and an extension built onto the house so as to bring the shop front closer to the street, a potential customer still had to go over the bridge just to see what kind of merchandise was being sold.

The house next door to ours on the south side was the residence of a big wholesale cloth merchant named Ogushi. It too had a small bridge in the front and was surrounded by a black wooden wall. The houses that came after it on the same street and those that stood on the quiet street going toward Akamon were all similar private residences surrounded by walls or hedges and with outer front gates. The only buildings in the entire neighborhood that were different were the rickshaw station not far from us and the few little shops near Hanabusa-cho—one selling cheap candy, another baked sweet potatoes, and another fancy goods. As for pedestrians, there were hardly any, and it wasn't surprising that our neighbors should have wondered whom my parents had in mind as customers when they opened the store.

Father was dead serious about the new venture, however, and put a lot of money into it. The name "Midori-ya" was chosen, Mother explained to me, because the section of Odawara Father was born in was called Midori-cho. "Your father is determined that you should become a businessman," she said. "He opened this store because he thought it was important for you to start learning basic things about trading now. So, you see, minding the store is more your responsibility than anyone else's; and when you're not at school or doing homework, you're to practice the abacus, get to know the merchandise, and so on." Mother's words left me quite unconvinced. But there was a pleasurable sense of novelty and anticipation in being in such a radically altered house and so much more exposed to the world outside.

This, then, is how the Midori-ya Variety Store in Akamon-mae came into being. I heard Father say once that he invested three thousand yen in it. A more unpromising and amateurish venture would be difficult to imagine. In nearby Matsukage-cho there was an establishment called Matsu-ya which dealt wholesale in domestic and foreign goods; and it was to this Matsu-ya, I am told, that Father entrusted the whole job of laying in the stock.

On the day before the opening, seven or eight senior and junior employees of Matsu-ya descended on us and with kimono sleeves tucked up worked day and night putting the merchandise on display and attaching price tags. From the way they worked, you would have thought they were opening up a new branch of their own. On top of all this bustle there were the visitors dropping in to congratulate Father, drinks being served to them and to the Matsu-ya employees, and gifts from' well-wishers being delivered. By evening the festive mood had reached a feverish pitch which persisted into the early hours of the morning.

For the first three days customers were given lottery tickets with their purchases, and during this period a fair number of them came over our little bridge to look around the store and buy things. A senior Matsu-ya employee took care of the store for us for these three days, which allowed Mother and us children to sit in the morning room and surreptitiously watch the goings-on in the front. "Here comes another customer," we would say happily, or "That's one more sale!"

But as soon as we stopped giving away lottery tickets the steady flow of customers ceased. On those rare occasions when people did come in, Mother would turn speechless with embarrassment, and if we children happened to be minding the store, we'd run away to the back of the house and call one of the maids. In time, however, we got used to sitting in there, and though we were certainly making no money, the shop curtain saying "Midori-ya" continued to be put up over the doorway every morning without fail.

In the days preceding the opening of the place, the young rickshaw men from over the way had come every morning before we were up to sweep the little bridge and the street in front of our house, then sprinkle water over the swept area. And now, every morning at opening time, they would again come over and put up the shop curtain for us.

One morning, as Father was about to get into the rickshaw to go to the office, he paused, turned around, and stared intently at the dark blue curtain. The characters for "Midori-ya Variety Store," in white on a blue background, were reproduced from his own original calligraphy. There were seven characters in all, very large, each occupying one of the seven panels formed by the slits in the short curtain suspended across the top of the doorway. Immediately on returning home that evening Father ordered my half-brother to get out the ink stone and make him some ink. Then with a huge brush he wrote and rewrote each of the seven characters on separate pieces of paper until he was satisfied. "Send these to the dyers," he said to Mother, presenting her with the final copies, "and have them make us another curtain." She tried to dissuade him, saying it would be a waste to discard the one they already had, but he wouldn't listen. "Those characters somehow don't sit right," he said. "They bother me every time I look at them. So do as I say."

He was the quintessential "samurai in trade," the very type that was such a figure of fun on the popular stage at the time. Quite likely, the young rickshaw men from across the street, and the Matsu-ya employees, and the various tradesmen who regularly came to our house saw us as a rather scatty, comical family. Quite likely, too, there were people saying behind Father's back: "Things are going well for him now, but he'd better watch out. . . ."

Often, on coming home from school, I would hear the sound of a samisen and happy laughter coming from the morning room, with no one left minding the store.

On these occasions, my younger sisters were being given dancing lessons by a teacher who came to our house a few times each week. It all started, apparently, at the urging of my half-brother Masahiro who, having grown up in the pleasure quarter of Odawara, was not merely accomplished in the arts of dancing, singing, and samisen playing but took a real pleasure in them too. The dancing lessons could not of course have been arranged without Father's consent, but I have an idea that Mother backed up my brother's idea from the start, as a temporary relief from worries about her husband's dissipation and the future of the family.

The dancing teacher was an attractive older woman who looked as though she had once been of the demimonde. She was first introduced to us by Mrs. Kondo, a neighbor of ours. Rumor had it that Mrs. Kondo's current patron was the chief priest of Fumon-in temple, but previously she had been the mistress of a rich foreigner; she'd had a child by this foreigner, and when the time came for him to return to his home country he had left her with a guarantee of lifetime support for the child, including the cost of a decent education, so that she herself was now living in great comfort.

The child by now was a young woman of seventeen or so, a beauty of the Queen Elizabeth type.[9] We felt close to her, and used to address her familiarly as "Otei-chan." Otei-chan never wore Western clothes, but was always dressed in a kimono with long sleeves, with a wide sash that looked very good on her because of her height. "If only," some people would say, "she wasn't half white. . . ."

She was lively by nature, and whenever she came to see us Mother would forget her woes and laugh out loud, so that the whole family would soon cheer up.

Otei-chan had one younger sister, whom we called Fumi-chan. She and I were in the same year at school. Temperamentally, she was rather reserved, the exact opposite of Otei-chan. Her father, we were told, was Mrs. Kondo's Japanese patron; and one felt somehow that there was indeed a touch of the priest about her. But we were the same age, and played together a lot, and I developed a sort of puppy love for her.

She hardly ever spoke to me, however, when she came to our

9. The perceived likeness is presumably based on a highly flattering portrait of the English queen the author had seen somewhere.

house with her elder sister. Even when we played together, she maintained her distant manner—except once. It was a moonlit evening, and a large group of us were playing hide-and-seek. Fumi-chan and I hid together in the shadow of a neighbor's wall, and we remained crouching beside the wall even when the rest had gone, very close to each other, conscious of each other's breathing, knowing full well that the game was long over.

Whenever I read Ichiyo's "Child's Play," I can't help thinking how very similar that world of children growing up in Asakusa at the time was to the children's world of Yokohama. That even now I can recall those two sisters with such vividness would suggest that I had already begun to feel unmistakable feelings of attraction toward members of the opposite sex. Where Fumi-chan is concerned, though, my only clear-cut memory is of that moonlit evening.

She went into hospital just before we were due to graduate, and died there. Perhaps she had a chest ailment, for there had always been an air of fragility about her.

I think that Otei-chan was secretly in love with my half-brother Masahiro and that she was hiding it behind her lively, carefree manner. In matters of love, she was a typically innocent Japanese girl, who from shyness and fear of what others might say affected an air of gaiety that was far from her real feelings. Such, at least, is how Mother, and even the maids, seem to have seen it.

For a time, a niece of Mrs. Kondo's named Takeko was an eager rival of Otei-chan for Masahiro's attention. She was always heavily made up, and strove to give the general impression of a voluptuous temptress. According to Otei-chan, who wasn't above talking about Takeko behind her back, she was much taken with an actor named Ichikawa Shiko, and in feverish pursuit of him would send presents or visit him in his dressing room at the theater. People were ready enough to believe such stories, for she was perceived as that kind of person, and her reputation in the neighborhood was not good.

Be that as it may, I myself was somewhat resentful of Masahiro at the time. All the attention he was getting seemed to have gone to his head, and he undoubtedly took a certain pride in his own good looks. One night, he went out with Otei-chan dressed up as a woman. He wore makeup, a woman's kimono and clogs, and, because it was February and still cold, a combination hood and veil of the kind in fashion then. Dressed thus he left the house to the cheers of my mother and the maids. Several hours later, he came home looking quite pleased with himself, reporting with ill-disguised pride that in Isezaki-cho, with Otei-chan at his side, no one seemed to have the slightest doubt that he was a woman. Such antics, including a tendency in his cups to show off his artistic accomplishments, seemed to make him all the more attractive to women, but they certainly didn't sit well with Father, who when very drunk himself would give vent to his accumulated anger, cursing his son for his effeminacy, and even, as I've said, ordering him to commit harakiri.

But in spite of his delicate good looks and gentle ways, Masahiro was actually a very stubborn man. In all the years he'd had to live without a father, he had acquired a spirit of defiance. Repeatedly, when being lectured by Father, he threatened to go away and be independent; and eventually, after one huge quarrel, he did just that. He rented an upstairs room in the house of a stockjobber, from which he went daily to his place of employment, the Soda Bank. The stockjobber had a daughter by the name of Oyae. He had an affair with her, and she was soon pregnant.

The Indiscriminate Reader

Before long I acquired a new relative, an elder sister-in-law. In other words, my half-brother got married.

I shall say something later about the circumstances surrounding the marriage. First, though, it should be said that for a boy of nine or so just coming to a new kind of awareness, the sudden inclusion in his immediate family of a pretty young woman was rather unsettling, both physiologically and mentally. Morning and night, she dazzled me with her presence; and I soon found myself acutely aware, as never before, of my own and other people's physicality. Though I was always excessively shy with her, I would watch stealthily every little detail of her behavior toward my half-brother, with its coquettish smiles and pouts; and when, during a meal, she filled my bowl with rice after she had filled his, I would gaze at her pale fingers with a special fascination.

Although Oyae was only present in our household for half a year, she was one of those who helped me, her little brother-in-law, take another step toward maturity.

Actually, this sister-in-law who appeared to me the personification of full womanhood was not yet seventeen. I have no idea what sort of schooling she had had. She certainly showed no sign of ever having been given training in the traditional responsibilities such as housekeeping, or even in a woman's proper deportment. Every morning when she got out of bed she would disappear into the washplace adjoining the bathroom and stay there seemingly forever. Finally, she would emerge with the kind of makeup on her face that made everyone gape at her; and her kimono would be different every time.

What with opening the shop, getting Father ready to go to the office, and sending us kids off to school, mornings were frantically busy, especially for Mother and the maids. But even after some months with us my sister-in-law remained outside these frantic goings-on, wandering about with not a hair out of place like a newly arrived bride waiting to be shown where to sit. To serve Masahiro at the breakfast table, and to see him off as he left for the bank, seemed to mark the limit of her capacity for young-wifely behavior.

True, she hadn't lived in our house long before her belly was noticeably large, and she must have found it hard to move about, this being her first pregnancy. Moreover, even we children could see that Mother, because she wasn't related by blood to Masahiro, was all the more consciously protective of his wife.

Father, who would normally have treated someone like my sister-in-law with great severity, was uncharacteristically silent. That he didn't censure her for her untimely pregnancy was understandable, for he had formally acknowledged that she was pregnant when he agreed to take her into the house after the wedding; but he also kept quiet about all kinds of other things that he obviously disapproved of. Either way, so far as we children could see, Oyae never became the subject of serious friction while she was living with us. It would seem, however, that there was controversy enough before she came.

In the days leading up to the marriage, Father had been involved in acrimonious discussion about conditions with the other party, and on several occasions had flown into a rage, so that when the negotiations finally ended and it was clear that he had been defeated, he was emotionally spent. The pained silence he maintained while

Oyae was living with us was, as it were, a form of indemnity paid to the victors.

I have described briefly how one day Masahiro, announcing his decision to become independent, had resolutely left our house for a rented room in Motomachi. This spirited act, however admirable in itself, eventually resulted in his landlord, the stockjobber, paying Father a surprise visit with some very unwelcome news.

The stockjobber, Yamada by name, looked like a gambling boss. He held his long silver pipe at a jaunty, sideways angle; over his kimono he wore a haori of fine cotton with heavy stripes, and the obi of thick, expensive stuff tied casually around his waist was also city-smart and menacing. He was, in short, an altogether different type of man from Father. He was heavily built, too, which seemed to make all the more credible the rumor that he was generally feared even by his fellow stockjobbers.

This, then, was the father of the girl Masahiro had made pregnant while living in their house, and he presumably came to find out what Father was going to do about it. Father's natural response to aggressive behavior in another was to be doubly aggressive himself. The confrontation between the two must have been like two angry bulls charging at each other—no quarter given, a fight to the finish. I have vague memories of various dubious individuals coming to the house to try to browbeat Father or offer to intercede; and I seem to remember that toward the end of the whole confused affair, women looking suspiciously like teahouse madams would drop in when Father was out and harangue Mother.

It is hard to imagine people today making quite such an issue of a similar matter. But in Meiji society, where there was so much generally shared concern and uniformity of opinion concerning sexual morals and family responsibility, a person in Father's predicament risked serious public censure if he was seen as ignoring his duties as the young man's father. He must have worried, too, about possible repercussions at the Soda Bank where Masahiro worked, or within his own business circle. He had no choice, then, but to give in to Yamada: to permit his son to marry the girl, and have them both live in his house. For a man so full of stubborn pride, the capitulation must have been acutely painful. But it was not merely his pride that was hurt. Besides paying for the bride's trousseau and the wedding, he paid Yamada substantial sums to cover various expenses supposedly incurred by him.

Whether the actual ceremony as well as the reception took place at our house or not I don't recall, but I do remember that it was the height of summer. About four rooms upstairs were reserved for the guests, while downstairs the teahouse madams together with young male underlings recruited from various places were busy getting trays of food ready to take up to them. We children were excited by the spectacle of so many people working around the kitchen, and stared in wonder at all the delicacies being arranged on dishes. The more often Mother told us to go outside and play, the more determined we became to stay and watch. And when evening came we took turns sneaking upstairs to peek at the bride and at the merry-making in the brightly lit rooms.

Normally, Otei-chan the Eurasian would come and help on such festive occasions, her high spirits spreading cheer among those of us congregated in the kitchen or the morning room. But that day she did not appear. Nor was her mother, Mrs. Kondo, among the guests upstairs. The fact of the matter is that by then Otei-chan had already drifted away from us; and the reason, quite obviously, was that she had been hearing things about Masahiro and his landlord's daughter. I was too young at the time to be able to put myself in her place; but in later years I would wonder if she wasn't crying by herself somewhere that night—an idle fancy, perhaps, which first occurred to me when I was about the same age as Masahiro was that night.

I suspect that the pleasant modern custom whereby bride and bridegroom go off on their honeymoon directly from the reception did not yet exist at that time. Competition to keep up with the latest fads from Europe and America was nowhere keener than in Yoko-hama—where people sneered at the "hick" bureaucrats of Tokyo and their frightful Western suits, and where it was the height of smartness to wear Western clothes made for you in Chinatown—but even there I doubt whether the institution of the honeymoon was known as yet.

Everything, then, took place in the house. And by sheer chance I got to see what went on between the bride and the bridegroom on their wedding night.

I normally slept upstairs, but that night, because of the party, I was made to sleep downstairs in a room on the far side of the court-yard. A large mosquito net was hung up in the ten-mat room, and inside it three quilt beds were laid out in a row. I slept in one of the end beds.

What woke me up I couldn't say, but I found myself suddenly awake. Though it must have been very late, I could hear the laugh-ter of lingering guests and the sound of tables being hurriedly cleared. For no particular reason I looked around me. The bed next to mine, the one in the middle, was unoccupied and exactly as it had been when I got into bed; but I could see someone lying in the one beyond.

It was not pitch-dark, and I realized immediately that I was looking at part of the bride's white face. Almost simultaneously, I knew why I couldn't see the whole of it: it was partially hidden by my half-brother's head. To say that the sight of the two pillows placed next to each other on the same bed was a big shock to me would be no more than adult hindsight; whatever immediate reac-tion I might have had, I was not shaken in the way of an adult who experiences what we call "shock."

While the scene made an indelible impression on me, it doesn't seem to have induced any sexual imaginings with a corresponding physical response. What blunted the possible effects of what I was seeing, I think, was the initial sense of wonder at the fact that this was the way a man and a woman slept together. And beyond my watching them with eyes instinctively half-closed, and the excitement I felt at seeing something that I thought I shouldn't be seeing, I don't appear to have been sexually aroused by it.

It may be, of course, that I was only half-awake and that my senses were dull. Even so, I can still remember fairly clearly certain details of my experience that night: holding my breath till I thought my chest would burst; the dimly seen figures of my half-brother and his bride in some subtle way changing position; the gentle undulation of the mosquito net extending to where my head lay. And the total effect was not of witnessing some ugly physical activity, but of seeing through my eyelashes something precious and beautiful enacted by two ghostlike beings. What helped give the scene an illusory quality, I suppose, was the appearance of the bride on her wedding night, with her elaborately coiffured head perched gingerly on a small, hard Japanese pillow. Even now I can appreciate how fortunate I was that this crucial thing, observed in my childhood for the first time, should have seemed so beautiful.

But to go on with the story of their marriage: Masahiro, denied the loving care of real parents and acquainted from early childhood with loneliness and misfortune, had entered on a relationship that was from the first fraught with confusion. That it was ever a happy marriage is very doubtful.

For in spite of all the fuss that preceded the marriage, Oyae went back to her parents in Motomachi after living in our house for only about six months. She did so, moreover, without saying a word about it to Masahiro. One day, while he was at work, she left the house telling everyone she was going out to do some shopping, and never came back. Masahiro of course went to try to get her to return, and there were repeated comings and goings of intermediaries between Father and Yamada. But it all came to an end when a man representing Yamada appeared at our house to collect everything Oyae had brought with her on her wedding day.

"Perhaps you'll understand by now," Father said to Masahiro, "that the Yamadas always saw you as a gullible, rich man's kid. It's your stupid preening and playing the lover-boy that got you into this mess."

We overheard him saying this, and even we, children though we were, thought his comments terribly unfair. Masahiro came running down the stairs as if he were being chased, and sitting in a corner of the maids' room cried for a long time. For two or three days after that the house was so quiet that even the clatter of crockery seemed muted, and for us children, robbed of the familiar figure of our beautiful, big-bellied sister-in-law, life wasn't as much fun as before.

Father continued for some days to hurl abuse at Masahiro: "Look at you," he would say, "falling in love with a woman who doesn't even want you!" At such remarks my half-brother's face would suddenly turn deathly pale, while Mother's face registered pain as though it were she who was being abused. But it was a matter that went no further than between father and son; in time, Masahiro seemed to get used to being a bachelor again, and Oyae became a dimly remembered, shadowy figure for us children.

Thus Masahiro's marriage came in the end to seem merely like a brief, bad dream. Not, I think, that anything like real love had ever existed between the two. Masahiro was to show no sign of regret later over the parting; on Oyae's side, there was no mention, even, of a baby being born; and there was no indication at all that the two ever met again after her departure. Indeed, both of them showed so little concern that Mother, who had gone to such lengths to protect Oyae and respect her feelings, must have felt that she had been wasting her energy. Either way, the affair seemed to leave her completely at a loss.

She once grumbled mildly to me: "You know, the trouble with your elder brother is that he's really still a child. He's not so different from you—it's just that because he was brought up by strangers, he *seems* more adult. The mistake he makes when your father lectures him is to react like an adult instead of taking it like a child." This seemed strange coming from Mother, who herself at times found

Father's tyrannical ways so unbearable that she would let her pain be apparent to us.

She continued to care deeply for her stepson, however, and to shield him whenever possible from Father's temper. And we children remained as always adoring of our half-brother, regardless of Father's moods.

It was around that time that I started avidly reading things unrelated to school work. I also learned to send samples of my own writing to boys' magazines, and together with my school friends started what you might call a coterie magazine, which we printed with a hectograph. At home, when I wanted someone to talk to about this budding literary interest, there was no one I could go to but Masahiro. It was he I showed my writings to, and he who first got me to compose what amounted to a haiku by saying, "Look, why don't you try putting down whatever's in your mind in seventeen syllables?"

Unfortunately, one of my early efforts at haiku composition was the cause of a very unpleasant experience.

At elementary schools in those days, essay assignments were referred to as "descriptive writing" or, more commonly, as composition. The style that we had to write in was the so-called "literary" style which was basically classical in cadence and grammar, and the subjects preferred were the likes of "Plum-Blossom Viewing with a Friend One Day" and "Feelings on the Occasion of His Majesty's Birthday."

In one such essay I included a haiku I'd written. The teacher, Mizutani Sensei, was an amiable, balding man, a very conscientious teacher much admired by his pupils. One day, though, as he took his place in front of the class, his face was flushed with anger, and holding up my essay he began to bawl me out. What he said in essence was that an essay should express one's own true feelings, and in one's own words; to insert someone else's poem as though it were an original piece of work was a disgraceful thing to do.

I wanted to say, "But Sensei, you're wrong—I wrote that haiku myself"; but looking at this usually gentle man, now so adamant, and red to the tips of his ears, I found myself unable to utter a single word in my defense. I suppose I was by nature something of a blubberer, for all I did was shrink into my chair and cry. After this bitter experience I determined never to show my haiku to other people.

Around that time, I picked up a new habit. There was a lending library in a little house just outside the rear gate of Minami-Ota Elementary School. The gate was reserved for use by the girl pupils, so every day after school I would go out through the front gate and walk right around the school to the girls' gate in order to visit the library.

Since the man who ran the library was the school janitor, I was already known to him when I started going there, and he knew my family too. I would put my school bag on the floor in the gloomy little room where the books were kept, sit down with my back against a wall, and read a whole book through before I went home. I enjoyed the routine so much that it became a necessity.

As to why I didn't read at home, the answer is simple: had Mother or my half-brother caught me reading the sort of books I was in fact reading there in that gloomy room, they would have been very cross. *Otama the Bicycle Woman*, *Iwami's Heroic Exploits*, *The Lightning Kid*, *Tamiya Botaro's Vendetta*, *Omatsu the Demon Woman*—they were all cheap, sensational stories written in the style of the raconteurs who performed in the variety theaters; but whatever I found on the shelves, I read. The books themselves, known as "Osaka printings," looked bulky but any one of them could be read in an hour or an hour and a half at most. In about six months there was nothing left on the shelves for me to read.

I was able, then, to indulge in the continuous, indiscrimate reading of dreadful books without anyone in the family knowing. That it had a bad influence on me is beyond question. Had my parents or Masahiro ever found out about it, I am sure they would have shuddered at the thought of the potential harm to me. The books really *were* that bad—and besides, family concern about the reading habits of children was quite intense in those days. Nevertheless, I managed to read a great deal of the stuff undetected.

The lending library was succeeded by secondhand bookstalls at fairs, where I rummaged around for things like Kuroiwa Ruiko's translations of foreign romances and Oshikawa Shunro's adventure stories. Next, I quickly acquired a taste for the Imperial Library reprints. I read voraciously, like a silkworm munching through mulberry leaves. I never had enough money to buy all the books I wanted, and one attraction of the Imperial Library series was that each volume contained as many as five or six hundred pages. Actually, there was another attraction too, which was that works by such authors as Chikamatsu and Saikaku[10] in the series were for the most part the first modern reprints, and therefore unexpurgated. This meant that around the age of eleven I was for some days immersed in an unexpurgated edition of Shunsui's *Umegoyomi*.[11] I was such a relentless reader that I would finish even a work like *Taiheiki* [the medieval military chronicle] in the course of a few nights. "Haven't you gone to sleep yet?" Father would shout through the door as I lay in bed with bloodshot eyes, reading until all hours of the night.

I was finally caught reading *Umegoyomi* by Father, who promptly tore it out of my hands and, dragging me around behind the bathroom, threw the book into the wood-burning furnace. Tears filled my eyes as I watched the peeping white thigh of Yonehachi and the seductive figure of Adakichi [two women rivals in love] being consumed by the flames.

Considering our extravagant family style and my own tempera-

10. Chikamatsu Monzaemon (1653–1724), the most famous of Edo-period playwrights, was often erotic, and Ihara Saikaku (1642–93), the great writer of fiction, could be fairly obscene.
11. Tamenaga Shunsui's (1790–1843) *Shunshoku Umegoyomi* (Plum Blossoms, the Harbinger of Spring Colors) is a novel about three women who compete for the hero Tanjiro's attention. Though only moderately erotic, it was certainly no fit book for any properly brought-up boy to read.

ment, I hardly think that my life during that particular period in my boyhood was on a desirable course. Not that my parents had in any way become lax about their children's education; they were as strict as ever about our daily lessons, not to mention our manners, speech, dress, deportment, and play. Father even—presumably believing it to be a necessary part of a child's education—made a point of having us carry water for the bath, and go on distant errands, even though there was no shortage of help in our house. Sometimes his orders struck us as arbitrary and bizarre, with no ascertainable purpose or reasonable chance of execution. Either way, his efforts to teach us the meaning of hard work were just as energetic as before.

The evening tutorials in the Chinese classics that I used to go to in our Yugyozaka days were continued after our move to Shimizu-cho. Now, though, they were reduced to once a week on Saturdays, since walking to the tutor's house from Shimizu-cho amounted virtually to going from one end of Yokohama to the other. At first I went conscientiously to Oka Sensei every Saturday evening and read through passages in a mechanical fashion; but when the review sessions with Father, which had been occurring less and less frequently, finally ceased altogether, I decided to play truant. Come Saturday evening, I would leave the house ostensibly to go to Oka Sensei's house but in fact to wander about Isezaki-cho, where I would go into theaters like the Kiraku-za and Nigiwai-za and watch a single act from the standing area. On occasion I would even sneak into a theater playing the Genji-bushi drama that was extremely popular at the time.

I can't recall now exactly how Genji-bushi music went, but it was a kind of variety show related to Naniwa-bushi drama, and its special feature was that all the performers were women, the so-called "drama" being little different in intent from the modern stripshow. For a while it enjoyed an unrivaled position among such shows, but it was eventually banned by the authorities. The performers would enact scenes taken from the kabuki repertoire, but neither dramatic content nor acting was a major concern of the genre, so it had little power to sustain interest, even for boys like me who went out of vulgar curiosity.

What really did begin to interest me at about that time was the orthodox theater. Indeed, I was quickly to fall madly in love with it.

The general feeling in those days was that you were extraordinarily fortunate if you went to the theater even once a year. It was correspondingly exceptional that a mere schoolboy should be given permission by his parents to go and see a play simply because he wanted to, and I didn't of course dare breathe a word to them about my new passion. Yet, for all that, I was able on Saturday nights to visit one or another of the theaters in Isezaki-cho, though only for an act at a time. On Sundays, too, I would sometimes sneak away to Isezaki-cho and watch a play from the gallery.

How was I able to pay for all those visits to the theater? It was commonly held in those days that money was something a child should not have; so that unless it was to be spent in an obviously justifiable way, there was no hope of my being able to wheedle any out of Mother. In one part of our house, however, there existed another source of pocket money—the cash box in the Midori-ya Variety Store, from which I would freely take silver coins as needed. I say "freely," but of course I did it only when I thought no one was looking, and not to be caught required both cunning and adroitness on my part. My morals were clearly, at that point, in a very perilous state; indeed, when I think about all the clever, underhanded things I used to do then with no sense of wrongdoing, I feel quite queasy.

✣
A Fight

Despite this scheming mind of mine, I was generally thought to be an open, nicely behaved boy. "He always looks so neat and tidy," people used to say to Mother. And probably because I was diminutive and had deep dimples in my cheeks, female visitors, when I presented myself, would say, "What a darling little boy you have!" The adults around me all seem to have been utterly blind to the bad habits that were taking root inside me.

Thinking about the people who visited us and their behavior in my presence, I realize that the pretty women guests left a far deeper, more complex impression on me than the men. Possibly a little girl would have remembered the male guests in greater detail. What is certainly true is that in Japanese households, in a feudalistic age of mindlessly strict discipline, there seems to have been an incongruous tendency for adults to talk carelessly in front of children about the most unlikely things.

Listening to talk between our parents and their guests, we would often draw inferences with a perspicacity beyond their imagining. "They're only kids," they told themselves smugly, "they wouldn't understand." In this, they were being comically naive. We couldn't of course be expected to know the precise meaning of their private language; but in the voracious appetite of growing children a mysterious mechanism seems to be at work. It's not unlike the digestive process of a Venus's-flytrap: catching snatches of adult conversation here and there, they proceed to absorb them into their systems, the nourishment they thus receive imparting a kind of understanding quite above the ordinary.

A couple of episodes will illustrate what I mean. They are experiences, of course, from my own childhood and may well say nothing about families in general, or about other children. But it seems that the notion of children as "just kids" and the resulting carelessness of adults in their presence are fairly widespread phenomena.

I knew that a certain visitor was the madam of a teahouse somewhere. Perhaps she came to pay her respects on the occasion of some festival, but I can't even remember what time of the year it was. I knew who she was, all the same. This was the period when Father was playing around a lot, often staying away from the house for days, then finally coming home reeking of alcohol and surrounded by women, and she was one of them, I suppose.

She was chattering away at Mother, the gifts she had brought us deposited on the tatami at her side. Father of course was not at home. She mentioned the name "Okoto" several times. Okoto was a woman Father kept somewhere, and I gathered that the madam was relating a series of slanderous rumors about her. All of a sudden her voice dropped in a peculiar way and she said: "And do you know, I'm told that in the days when she was still working in Kannai she had the reputation of being very good in bed—even knew just the right moment to cry out, they say." And she gave a lewd laugh. Mother, who was suckling my baby sister at the time, blushed with embarrassment and, saying nothing, hung her head and stared at her own bared breast. I was sitting close by. Why I was there, I don't know, but the one thing I'm sure of is that both Mother and the guest were quite indifferent to my presence.

Another conversation I heard took place, I seem to remember, on a Sunday. We had a female visitor who sat in Father's room talking incessantly all through the afternoon. Her name was Togashi, and her husband was a senior clerk in a Yokohama—"Hama," as people used to say—trading company. The two of them frequently visited us together bearing gifts of imported novelties, but that day Mrs. Togashi, a young woman, came alone. Saké had been served with the food, and as she shared a bottle with Father she began talking animatedly about her married life: "I do envy you two with all those children. I want one so badly—I've tried everything to have one, but nothing has worked so far." When Father responded with some kind of joke, Mother joined in the laughter and said, "You do say such silly things!" But then I heard Mrs. Togashi say a bit shrilly, "But it's true, believe me! We simply can't do it right. Just when I'm getting into the mood he's already finished." This time Father, emboldened perhaps by the saké, must have made some fairly crude comment, for I heard Mother say with some displeasure, "Stop it, now! You may think it's funny, but you are after all talking to another man's wife." However dimly, I understood the drift of what was being said.

I was not in the room myself. I was sitting at my desk, at some distance, and yet I was able to hear them. The fact that I can still recall such fragments of the conversation, both on this occasion and when the madam of the teahouse was visiting us, must mean that they made a strong impression on my mind. I didn't, of course, understand in any ordinary sense of the word. The thing at work in me was something that precedes normal understanding.

It seems to me that in this respect what we may call the critical period in a child's development does, in fact, occur before understanding. I was already at the time secretly reading works like *Umegoyomi*, Chikamatsu's plays, and Saikaku's stories. In those days books such as *The Complete Puppet Plays of Takeda Izumo* [1691–1756] were readily available, too, and I read them avidly from cover to cover, with no notion of their literary worth. Thus when I heard snatches of what the madam of the teahouse or Mrs. Togashi was saying, I could pick up the gist of their private conversation. To be so unaware of such a capacity in children, and thus so indiscreet in their presence, adults must have forgotten the days when they, too, were hungry "Venus's-flytraps." Or are there, perhaps, individual differences far greater than one imagines in the hidden development of children's sexuality?

Probably the main reason why people immediately took me to be a "good boy" was that I was always neatly turned out. Father was extremely strict about personal appearance, and was always admonishing Mother to be mindful of her toilet and dress, and not to be "like one of those slovenly women." Even after she'd had several children, the first thing she did on going into the kitchen early in the morning was to stand under the skylight, mix white makeup powder with water in her hands, and apply it to her face. Then she would smooth her hair down with a wet comb before starting work. She maintained this habit for a long time—even after she had become old.

We children, therefore, hardly ever saw Mother as she was when she got out of bed, her face frowzy and nightclothes in disarray. Whenever I picture her in my mind, I see her as a nice-looking woman, neatly dressed and wearing light makeup even in our poorest days. Some people, I suppose, would have called her vain, but as far as Father was concerned, a properly brought-up woman could do no less. Yet, careful though she was about her appearance, we rarely saw her linger in front of a mirror to put on lipstick or fiddle with her hair; this, I think, would have come under the heading of "slovenly" in those days.

We boys had to wear kimonos of dark blue cloth with white patterns on it, and sashes that were black and soft. We were never allowed to appear in any other kind of kimono. When we went to school, we had to wear a duck-cloth hakama over the kimono. Father himself taught us how to put it on, and if any of us was caught going about with the cords of his hakama hanging loose, he would be scolded by Father—or, for that matter, by Mother. As a consequence of such childhood training, I was, until quite recently, in the habit of pulling the sash around my kimono, or the belt around my trousers, as tight as it would go; I felt uneasy otherwise. Nowadays, the looser the sash or the belt the better.

The rules of behavior and dress I was taught as a child were unnecessarily strict; *now*, on the other hand, I worry whether I'm not letting myself go in my old age.

Being a "nice child," I didn't get into fights outside. But at home, when Father wasn't there, there was no telling what I would do. My habit of pilfering from the cash box in the family store lasted a long time, and judging from the fact that I was never punished for it, it may be that neither of my parents ever found out.

Actually, "punished" is not quite correct, for I was once caught in the act by a maid called Sada. Sada was the daughter of a fisherman in Negishi. When my younger brother was ill, he had been put out to nurse with her family, and I myself used to go there in the summer to swim, so that in one way or another her family and mine were closely associated, with a degree of personal warmth between us. This Sada, then, happened to see me in a dark corner of the store just as I'd got the loosely hinged, old-fashioned cash box on its side and was trying with the aid of some implement to coax a silver coin out of it. "What do you think you're doing, Hide-san!" she cried, goggling. "What will your mother say when I tell her!" I jumped up in a rage and confronted her, making as if to hit her. "Go ahead and tell her!" I shouted. "Go ahead if you dare!" With some parting remark at me over her shoulder, she fled to the inner part of the house.

Perhaps because of this incident, I bullied her a lot, in the way unruly boys are apt to do. Mother was always very concerned lest we mistreat the maids, but once, perhaps when she was out, I lost my temper with Sada over something she said or did, and chasing her into a corner of the corridor began hitting her on the head and face with a book I happened to be holding. Her back against the wall, she slid down to the floor and, covering her face with her hands, sat quite still for a while. I watched her, thinking that as usual she was pretending to cry, so for good measure I gave the top of her head one mighty final blow. At that, she uncovered her face and lifting her head stared straight at me. Blood was trickling out of her mouth. She hadn't been shamming, she really had been crying, and the mere thought made my hands go numb. She looked at me steadily, her eyes filled with bitterness, and kept repeating between sobs: "Don't ever forget this—just you wait and see—not even you can stay at home forever, and when you leave home, someone is going to do to you what you just did to me."

I have never felt my own wickedness so acutely as I did then. I felt a kind of dread, too. Sada had curly hair and a mole in the middle of her forehead. Some years later, what she said would happen to me did in fact occur. Carrying a peddler's chest on my back, I would be turned away from one door after another; and picking up discarded sandals with broken thongs I would put them on my feet and wander about like a stray puppy in search of food. Sometimes, overcome by dejection as I walked and unable to keep my head up any longer or stop the tears, I would seem to see Sada's face on the ground below me; I would wonder if she was married by now, and seriously think about what I would say and do if I were suddenly to come across her somewhere. And in my heart I would ask her to forgive me.

I said earlier that I never got into a fight outside, but that wasn't exactly true, for I did once.

I don't remember his name, but he was a year ahead of us at school, and his father owned a baked potato shop in Hanabusa-cho. He had earlier had to go back and repeat two of his years at school, so he was enormous compared to a little fellow like me. Whenever he appeared among us, he cut a menacing figure—an eagle swooping down on a flock of sparrows. We thoroughly disliked him, but he was so strong that all we could do was scatter whenever his shape cast its shadow on our group.

One day, as some of us were going home, he showed up in front of us and blocked our way. My companions fled as soon as they saw him, but I wasn't quick enough and was cornered. The thought that I had no hope of escape made me blind with desperation. I think he poked me hard two or three times. My school bag was slung over my shoulder, but I hadn't yet put in it the sack containing my sandals, which I was carrying in my hand. They were the regulation sandals for wear inside the school, made of leather with heavily studded soles more or less like workmen's boots. Suddenly, I jumped up and hit him in the face with the sack as hard as I could. Unprepared for such violence from a runt like me, he let out a fearful howl of pain and covered his face with his hands. He was shortsighted; the glasses he wore were hanging from one ear, and I could see blood trickling down both wrists.

Scared out of my wits, I ran all the way home and sat cowering in a corner. As might be expected, the woman from the baked potato shop, whom I knew slightly, soon came dragging her son behind her and started yelling at Mother. In spite of his size the son was bawling his head off. Not all the blood had been wiped off his face, and his myopic eyes looked as though they'd gone blind. "What if he loses his sight?" the woman kept shouting. Hearing the noise, the young men from the rickshaw station across the street came over and, quieting the mother down, put her and her son in a rickshaw to take them to an eye doctor. Mother rode after them. How the matter was resolved I don't remember, but I do remember vowing to myself never to get into a fight again.

My first experience of an encounter involving physical force being what it was, I never engaged in one again. Another restraining factor, of course, was that being so small I knew I wouldn't stand a chance against any opponent. I must admit, however, that there was one incident where I almost did commit an act of violence. It happened much later, when I was a grown man. I was working at the time in the domestic section of the *Tokyo Evening Newspaper*. It was late in the day, and I was on an urgent errand. I had to change streetcars at the stop in Kasuga-cho, and every car that came was absolutely packed. Finally losing patience, I jumped onto the step of the last car and hung on to the rail. The conductor stared at me angrily and in a voice hoarse from shouting ordered me repeatedly to get off. I knew that he was only doing his duty, but the car by then was going at full speed and there were others hanging on too, so I decided to pretend not to hear and brazen it out. Whereupon he reached out for my right hand, which was holding on to the rail, and began painstakingly to pry it open, finger by finger. With no means of resistance, I tumbled to the ground. This was just at the beginning of the Tomizaka slope.

It was clear that he was in the right and I was in the wrong, but the thought of the abject figure I must have cut and of all those passengers laughing at me made me fighting mad. I picked myself up and started chasing the car. The slope was steep, and though the thing had slowed down, I was soon out of breath. I struggled on for a bit, but it was a humiliating, pointless exercise, so eventually I gave up. And thinking back on it now, I'm glad I failed to catch up with it; in such a state, who knows what awful thing I might have done? Apart from this incident, though, it never occurred to me to use violence on someone else—except, that is, the younger members of my family, whom I did sometimes take a swipe at. But that wasn't fighting; rather, in its roundabout way it was a sign of affection. And even that ceased as we grew older.

I fancy that individual tastes and predispositions are formed rather earlier in our lives than we think—in fact, long before we are adults. All the girls who attracted me most at school or in the neighborhood or walking along the street seem to have been of a type: slender, dark-skinned, and curly-haired.

I was not a very manly boy, and was often called a crybaby by Father and my playmates. I don't think I really cried all that often, though perhaps my eyes did moisten rather easily. Admittedly, there were no end of times when the pages of some classic or other got soaked with my tears, and at the theater I would cry until my head ached. Presumably I was unusually subject to adolescent emotionalism. I also seem to have had a great capacity for daydreaming. I loved to place myself in some imagined situation, then let my fantasies play themselves out. That is why I liked house-sitting, a chore normally much disliked by boys. Sitting there in a large house with only one or two other people about, I could daydream to my heart's content.

No matter how much I liked a girl, I never approached her on my own initiative. I was a timid boy. If I came across her on the street I would pretend not to have seen her, and go home with a strange fluttering in my breast and a memory of her fragrance as she walked past. Back home, I would create a setting for her in my daydreams wherein we could play happily together. Such fantasies were my constant companions on distant errands.

Almost certainly, this habit of mine received additional nourishment from my avid reading of Edo literature and my surreptitious visits to theaters in Isezaki-cho such as the Hagoromo-za, Nigiwai-za, Kiraku-za, and Kumoi-za. The so-called *soshi* drama was popular around that time, but kabuki was my real favorite. Both the Hagoromo-za and Nigiwai-za offered such traditional fare. I was particularly fond of an actor called Nakamura Tamanojo, who performed at the Hagoromo-za throughout the year, and another actor of the same troupe called Dando. I must have seen just about every one of that troupe's productions.

Luckily, Grandfather from Sakura came to stay with us every two weeks or so around then, and under his wing I would go to the theater almost every other Sunday. We always took a large lunch box with us. He happened to like the Nigiwai-za better than the Hagoromo-za, so I, too, ended up as a fan of the former.

The Nigiwai-za at the time was commonly referred to as the "handkerchief theater," a term derived from the phrase "handkerchief women" then in fashion in Yokohama. A boom in exports of raw and habutae silk had encouraged trading companies in the concession to begin exporting silk handkerchiefs in large quantities. As a result, countless small subcontractors engaged in hemming and embroidering handkerchiefs had sprung up in the back streets of Yokohama. The "handkerchief women" were a species of female personnel employed at these establishments. As a perquisite of their employment they were given silk handkerchiefs, and they developed a fashion of folding these into triangles and wearing them proudly around their necks when they went out. The handkerchiefs came in various colors—red, purple, blue, pink—and with their kimono collars thus brightly adorned the women would take their evening strolls along the city streets, often mingling with groups of young layabouts. The term "handkerchief women" thus had a disreputable ring to it.

They were, even so, in the mainstream of the economic life of "Hama," engaged in very competitive work; they had money to spend, and they were wild spenders. The pit at the Nigiwai-za was always a sea of red, yellow, white, and purple handkerchiefs. They all had their favorite actors and would root for them with weird cries whenever they appeared. Talking of this or that actor, people would casually remark that a certain "handkerchief woman" had exclusive rights to him. The atmosphere of the theater being what it was, even a boy like myself had misgivings about going there, but Grandfather enjoyed it thoroughly, and would spend the whole day watching the stage with saké cup in hand and eyes creased with pleasure.

I say "the whole day," but with the Yokohama theaters of that time it was more like a whole day and night. The curtain would go up at eight or at the latest nine in the morning, and the day's program would end at about eleven at night. Thus the people who wanted to take in the formal opening of the day's program included some who would have breakfast, lunch, and dinner at the theater. All plays without exception were shown in their entirety. A play by Chikamatsu or Takeda Izumo, for example, would be performed exactly as it appeared in the full version printed in their complete works. The performances as such had their failings and idiosyncrasies, of course; but seeing all those plays in their entirety did give me some sense of dramatic development, of how plays and stories might be structured, and thus, I think, provided me with some kind of foundation for what I was to do later.

There were skillful actors performing at the Nigiwai-za: Ichikawa Kosha—highly popular, too flamboyant, but with a style all his own—Arajiro, Shiko, and Eisho. The characters they brought to life for me have stayed in my memory in all their original vividness. Some decades later—in 1942 or '43, I think—I heard or read somewhere that these old actors were performing at the Kotobuki-za in Honjo. I longed to see them again, but before I could do so the theater was burned to the ground in a wartime raid.

Reduced Circumstances

I doubt if even in downtown Tokyo the old expression "*annya-monnya*" [meaning something like "not much aware of one's surroundings"] is much used today. But when I was a child people were always saying, "I'm afraid this child really is still *annya-monnya*," or "Won't you ever stop being so *annya-monnya*?"

By the time they're thirteen or so, young people today are clearly in the pre-adult period—and occasionally even make the columns of the newspapers by killing themselves, say, or joining in a "love suicide." Even if they're not that type, they look at their parents with critical eyes, and are generally knowing about grown-ups; whatever else they may be, they certainly aren't *annya-monnya*.

Applied to us Meiji children, though, the term seems to have been exceedingly apt. It wasn't that we were pigheaded and refused to understand; in a sense we were worse—we were simply unaware.

I myself was a good example. In the course of a year or so after I had turned twelve our family fortunes underwent a drastic decline. Father's drinking was becoming steadily more frenzied and Mother's life more miserable. Young though I was, I should at least have sensed that as a family we were facing some kind of crisis. But I noticed nothing untoward at all.

The day finally came when Father suddenly informed me that we were ruined, that I had to quit school, and that I must leave home and apprentice myself somewhere. Until the very moment he told me all this, I had known nothing. I had never dreamed the family could be so fragile. Thus my recollections of that critical year are made up of scattered incidents that only became significant later as a result of bitter comments made by Mother in retrospect and of perceptions attained naturally through changed circumstances. What more, indeed—though I hate to sound so helpless—could have been expected of a boy still in his *annya-monnya* stage?

I can't say exactly how old I was when it all happened, but I'm certain that my family's headlong descent into disaster occurred roughly during the year or year and a half before I became thirteen. And I can see now that that was when my precious *annya-monnya* days came to an end.

Of all the things that struck us children as rather odd when Father, without our knowledge, was heading for bankruptcy, the oddest was seeing a succession of strange men in the middle of the night carrying pieces of furniture down the stairs and out to the back of the house.

We were of course awakened by the noise. Holding our breath, lying rigid, we watched with half-closed eyes the unfamiliar adult figures and their shadows moving about in the lamplight.

But what we saw said nothing to me about the state of our family. The scene repeated itself a number of times. On nights when such visitors were due, our beds would be moved to a room downstairs and our parents would tell us to go to sleep at once, as though they wanted to get us out of the way.

I presume that by then both the family and Father's company were faced with imminent ruin. The slump in the company's business was due above all to the outbreak of the Russo-Japanese War. The actual declaration of war came on February 10, 1904, when I was twelve, but even before then there had been signs of growing uneasiness about maritime safety, and of economic disorder, and more and more trading companies in the concession were closing down. For Father's Yokohama Pier Company in particular, which depended for its business on foreign ships using the pier, the sharp decrease in their number was a big blow.

Moreover, relations between Father and the titular president of the company, Takase Risaburo, had taken a turn for the worse, and mounting ill-feeling between them had finally led to a lawsuit being filed by Mr. Takase. Father's defense had been successful in the district court but not in the court of appeal, so he had taken his case before the high court. His fall, therefore, was preceded by much stubborn, wasteful, and protracted internal fighting.

Father and Mr. Takase had been brought together initially by a common vision of the commercial opportunities afforded by the newly opened port city of Yokohama. And though Mr. Takase was considerably above Father in age and position, they became close friends.

That they should almost overnight have become bitter opponents in a silly lawsuit was ultimately due, of course, to the slump in the company's business; but it would appear that it was their respective supporters and lawyers, who had their own axes to grind, who finally put them in a situation from which they couldn't extricate themselves. Added to this was Father's profligacy, which must have been distasteful to many and which was not excused by his being in a business that involved the entertainment of foreigners. I wonder, too, if Father, in his arrogant conviction that the success of the company since its inception was due to himself, had not begun to act as though Mr. Takase, who had provided most of the capital, did not exist.

At any rate, the latter lost all confidence in Father, and a head-on clash occurred when he raised questions about figures in the account books. A simple disagreement over figures might surely have been resolved without going to court and in the process bringing about the demise of the company. What happened, though, was that in the course of the confrontation with Mr. Takase, who was his usual calm and collected self, Father, who was his usual overbearing and excitable self, lost his temper and struck him in the face with his fist.

Mr. Takase was a leading Yokohama merchant and a figure much respected in shipping circles. He was not a man to cross lightly. "I shall not let him stay in Yokohama," was one comment he apparently made. "I shall see to it that he is utterly destroyed," was another. Father's uncivilized behavior, it seems, was reported in various Yokohama newspapers and caused quite a stir for a while.

Some people capable of acting as he did would later have regained their senses and sought to come to terms with the other party, either by apologizing directly or by asking a third person to seek an amicable solution. But Father wasn't one of them. He might privately regret an irrational act, but that only made him doubly stubborn and insistent on trying to justify it. This was the case with Mr. Takase. Mother was appalled when she read about the incident in the newspaper, and the next day rushed over to see Mr. Takase at his town house and apologize profusely to him on Father's behalf. Some days later Father heard about the visit. "So even *you* are trying to make me get down on my knees," he said, looking as though he might hit her, too. "Don't you dare meddle in my affairs!"

In those days Yokohama still retained some of the rough-and-ready character of an open port, and not a few men in business around the Bund seem actually to have approved of Father's ways. "An interesting fellow, that," they would say, or "Now, there's a real man for you." Thus even when Father hit Mr. Takase and became involved in a lawsuit, there were those who made a big show of rallying behind him. They did so, however, not so much out of genuine concern for his welfare as from a desire to see Mr. Takase humbled—some of them were his competitors in the shipping business—or to take over the Pier Company. Father, alas, was not the kind of person to see through such deviousness. Convinced that he was right, he continued his lengthy fight in the courts, spending all the money he personally possessed and more, and exhausting himself physically and spiritually in the process.

The Midori-ya Variety Store which had occupied one part of our house closed down sometime during this period. I don't remember the details, but I do remember seeing all the senior and junior employees of Matsu-ya who had come to help at the time of the grand opening return this time with carts to haul away the remaining stock. Even after their departure there were still canned goods and bottles of perfume left lying about the house. These were treated more or less as unwanted, useless objects, and were given away to visitors or carried off by the children for disposal as they saw fit.

My half-brother Masahiro was still with us and working for the Soda Bank, but now he made more trips back to his adoptive family in Odawara. Once, as he was about to leave for Odawara, I heard Father saying to him painfully, "Please try, Masahiro." He was asking him to get hold of some money. But Masahiro had no access to his adoptive family's assets, and aid from that quarter never materialized. In the end, Masahiro was to get in a jam, flee Yokohama, and disappear for thirty years. But that happened a little later.

Following the conventional pattern of impoverishment, our family came to depend for its livelihood on the sale of household furnishings, which for us children meant sounds heard in the middle of the night once every two or three months.

I am sure that the secondhand people Father dealt with came from somewhere far away. Concerned as ever about appearances, he certainly would not have wanted the neighbors to know; as for his own household, presumably only Mother had been told. And they never, of course, came in broad daylight, but in the middle of the night.

The very order in which he sold the furnishings was eccentric. He began by selling the contents of one upstairs room: "How much for what's in here?" he asked the dealer. In other words, he sold one roomful of furnishings at a time. Since the removal had to be done with the utmost secrecy, the dealer, accompanied by his wife and his young men, would arrive at the back door with a large, discreetly lit wagon after the entire neighborhood had retired for the night.

Without waking the maids, Father and Mother would go out to meet them, and soon the visitors would start carrying down wardrobes, wool rugs, framed pictures, tables and the like. Father, standing at the bottom of the stairs, would urge them, as though afraid of waking the neighbors, to go "quietly, quietly." Only someone who understands the reality of that world where the appearance of dignity was all-important can properly appreciate the mind of a man like Father as he made that plea.

Incidentally, there is a little story I was told about the second-hand dealer. One day much later, when we had reached rock bottom, he suddenly appeared bearing a small gift. How he found us I don't know, but he had come to express his appreciation for the business we had given him in the past. "Thanks to the very large profit you made possible," he said, "we've been doing nicely ever since."

That Father's way of doing business should have left such a deep impression on the dealer is a sign that even in those times his attitude toward economic matters was by no means typical. Indeed, people in those days were a far cry from those of our own extravagant age in their general tolerance of hard living and the restraint they exercised in household expenditures.

Take, for example, the way the children—there were six or seven of us—were fed at breakfast time even in a family like ours: the maid would break three raw eggs, never more, into a large bowl, add a fairly generous amount of soy sauce, beat the contents, then pour them in more or less equal portions over the rice in the seven small individual bowls. This often led to contention around the breakfast table: "She got all the yolk!" "You gave him more than me!" We all eagerly looked forward to the day when we ourselves would be able to pour a whole egg over our rice.

There was equal austerity regarding clothes. The mere mention of habutae silk brought associations of special occasions or exalted company. To be wearing even the most common kind of silk meant that you were "going out." In every household women strained their eyes at night darning socks or restitching pieces of kimonos that had been unstitched for washing and starching. Needless to say, all waste in the use of fuel and lamp oil was assiduously avoided. Walking past the rear of houses in a residential area, you would often see grains of cooked rice, saved when the cooking pot and serving tub were being washed, carefully laid out to dry in the sun on a large basket-weave tray beside the kitchen entrance or on the verandah. When the large paper bag in which she kept these dried white grains was full, Mother would mix them with diced rice cake and black soybeans, then "sugar-roast" the mixture. This was a winter-time confection which we called "hail," and we loved it when she made it for us.

Yet while preserving intact in their domestic lives these customs reminiscent, in their austerity and traditionalism, of the samurai style of life, people were at the same time ashamed of appearing poor to the outside world. In a sense, people in those days never thought to trace the causes of poverty to politics or the social system; poverty was a personal trait, and there was a strong tendency to discriminate against the poor as, by definition, inferior human beings. Thus families were scared to death of going under. Even if you were in real trouble, you tried to hide it and keep up appearances.

Perhaps my parents were typical of their times in this regard, for the fact is that Father, who normally seemed so headstrong, was altogether timid with the secondhand dealer, and Mother, for her part, revealed a quirky side of her own. She had not, after all, had a particularly coddled childhood nor—though not exactly hardened to the ways of the world—had she been kept in total seclusion in her young days; yet after the family went into decline she did things that would seem very strange by today's standards.

It seems finally to have dawned on her that domestic spending had to be drastically cut. With what was for her tremendous resolve she stopped the dancing lessons, sent all the maids home, and undertook to do all the household chores herself. Having taken these necessary steps, however, she then did things so contradictory and eccentric-seeming that she became a laughingstock among the neighbors. For instance, whenever the rickshaw men across the street saw her coming out of the house, one of them, from long habit, would immediately come unbidden to pick her up, and though she might only be going to buy a bunch of spring onions or bits of meat in the neighborhood, she couldn't bring herself to refuse. It was only to be expected that the neighbors should laugh at her behind her back: "She gets rid of all her maids, then goes out to buy groceries in a rickshaw!"

One incident became the subject of much talk among the rickshaw men. One morning, the ornamental hairpin Mother was wearing fell into the clear little stream that ran along the front of the house. It was probably the kind in fashion then, a round piece of coral mounted on a long gold pin. Standing on the bridge, Mother looked down and saw the pin glittering on the bottom of the fast-running, rather deep water. One of the young rickshaw men happened to be nearby, sweeping in front of our house, as was their custom, after having swept in front of their own place. He immediately dropped his broom and, rushing over to Mother's side, lowered himself straight into the hip-deep water and retrieved the pin. "Thank you so much," said Mother. "But please keep it. I want you to have it for going to such trouble." And so she gave away her gold and coral hairpin. This was probably before we became so poor that we had to sell our household furnishings in order to eat. Either way, for a woman capable of such strange, impulsive acts of generosity, the decline of our family must have been especially hard.

But in the end even Mother had to stop trying to keep up a brave front and begin making trips by rickshaw to the pawnbroker's house. On one occasion she took me with her. We were shown politely into the drawing room and served tea and cakes, so that my initial impression of "a pawnbroker" was not at all the standard one. Before long, several clothes chests were brought in from the storehouse and placed before Mother. Such chests often had family crests on them done in vermilion lacquer. The crest on these was hawk wings inside a circle. "But that's our crest!" I thought to myself, wary all of a sudden. The master of the establishment, his senior clerk, and another man who looked like a merchant of some kind opened the five or six chests and pulling out the clothes began examining each item minutely. The process took a long time, and eventually the floor all around us was covered with fine silk kimonos I recognized as belonging to my sisters and my parents. It was almost dusk when I heard the third man—he seemed to be a secondhand clothes dealer—say to Mother, "I'm afraid it won't work out the way you wanted," then proceed at length to explain and persuade. Without knowing exactly why, I felt my heart constrict when I saw the sorrow and regret on Mother's face.

On the way home she said, "They cheated me." She looked wretched, and I noticed that there were actually tears in her eyes. More than once she said, "You're not to say anything about this to your father. He would be very angry with me if he found out." I didn't understand then what had really happened, but she told me later. Hearing that Mother was badly in need of money, an acquaintance, Mrs. Togashi, sent over a secondhand clothes dealer whom she claimed to know very well. This man said to Mother, "Don't go on paying monthly interest to the pawnbroker. You'd be much better off if you were to sell all those clothes outright. Then you'd get a lump sum of money worth having." Easily persuaded, Mother agreed to the grand evaluation session that took place at the pawnbroker's. There, though, she was told that the clothes were worth no more than the money she had pawned them for, and that she owed interest to boot. So she left the meeting empty-handed, having watched helplessly as all those chests of clothes went for nothing.

I could go on indefinitely telling such stories, all of them humiliating, about our hapless circumstances just before the final ruin. One day, though, stands out in my memory, since I shall always remember it as our family's last day. "Last day" may be a bit of an exaggeration, but to me it means the day when I had to leave for good both the house in Shimizu-cho where I'd spent five or six happy *annya-monnya* years and Minami-Ota Elementary School, where I'd reached the upper-level fourth year. On that day, that whole section of my life, and with it my boyhood, came to an end.

It was February, and I was thirteen.

I was expecting that spring to leave elementary school and be admitted to middle school. I was somewhere near the middle of my class, but confident enough to assume that I would have little trouble getting in. The main building of the Kanagawa Prefectural Middle School in Kuboyama had just gone up, and whenever I saw it rising impressively in the distance I would proudly tell myself, "That's where I'll be going when I graduate."

At our school, those who lived nearby were permitted to go home during the lunch break instead of bringing lunch boxes, and I for one did so quite often. On that day in February, I was at home gobbling my lunch when Father suddenly returned. He came in through the back gate, which was something he never normally did.

I could see that he was dead drunk, on the verge of passing out entirely. He was wearing a frock coat. This, together with his trousers, hat, and shoes, was so dirty it looked as though he'd been sleeping on the ground. The look on his face was at once menacing and haunted. As he came in through the kitchen door he tripped and fell with a loud thud. Mother, who had been standing in the vestibule to greet him, got him up and with her arms around him almost dragged him into the house.

I must have sensed crisis coming, for I hastily left the table and, picking up the bag containing my school sandals, tried to sneak off toward the front hall. But Father called after me. Meekly I returned to where Father was now sitting. There were raw patches on his face and hands where he had scraped himself. Mother sat beside him, crying. I suppose she knew everything. She held her right kimono sleeve up to her face with the fingers of her left hand, a posture that had become almost customary with her when she wept.

Father's whole body reeked of alcohol, as though he had been bathing in the stuff for days on end. "Look here, Hide," he said, pausing for breath after almost every word, "you're the eldest son. Your father got beaten in court—understand? It's not just you who's got to go—none of us can go on living in a big house like this. You're the eldest son, you've got to be the first to go and find a job— all right?"

"Yes," I said simply. There was no other answer I could give. Besides, I hadn't grasped the full significance of what he was saying. So when he finished speaking, I picked up the sandals again and made as if to go back to school.

Seeing me, Father shouted, this time in the way he always did when drinking had got him in a bad mood: "Didn't you hear what I just said?" Then he added in a quieter tone: "You don't have to go to school any more. You're to quit school and go out to work. Now do you understand what I'm saying?" With this, he rose from his seat and groped his way upstairs.

It was only three or four days afterward that I was sent to work as a live-in apprentice at a seal-maker's shop in Sumiyoshi-cho. The family who owned and lived at the shop were named Kawamura, and they'd been introduced to us by Otei-chan's mother, Mrs. Kondo, who was related to them. When she came to take me there Mrs. Kondo said consolingly, "The master's a kind man, and his wife is a cousin of mine, so there's absolutely no need to worry about how you'll be treated." But the fact that someone we knew was closely connected with my employers-to-be made the prospect of working for them all the more hateful. If I had to work, I wanted to work for strangers, somewhere where no one I knew would ever catch sight of me.

What I found still more hateful, however, was having to wear a striped kimono and stiff obi like all apprentice boys; I was never so sad as when I said goodbye to the dark blue kimonos with white splash patterns that I'd been wearing since I was a little child. The first time I had to take off the dark blue kimono and put on a striped one was when Mrs. Kondo came to fetch me. She and Mother stood on either side of me helping me on with my new outfit. "Why, it suits you very well!" exclaimed Mrs. Kondo with a cackle. At that moment, I felt like having a fit of temper the way Father always did. But when they'd finished tightening the stiff sash around my waist, all I did was go and stand in the corner of the corridor by the lavatory and cry my heart out. And as I cried I remembered how once I had chased the maid Sada into the same dark corner and hit her with a book.

A Slip of the Pen

The Kawamura Seal Shop was an unpretentious little establishment two houses down from the corner on the eastern side of a willow-lined street not far from Yokohama Park. Over the second story, hiding half the roof, rose a wooden sign on which were carved, in seal-style characters, the words "Kawamura Seals." Inside the shop, only the small, discreet shelves displaying the various materials for making seals—amethyst, ivory, agate, water buffalo horn—and small cases for carrying the red ink pads in, would have given the casual observer any clue as to the nature of its business. A glass sliding door—heavy-looking, as though to make entry difficult—stood between the street and the interior of the shop.

The floor of the shop, which was level with the street, was laid with Chinese-style tiles. Three or four chairs for their customers' use stood there, carelessly set out and uninviting. Beyond this cramped, square area was a raised floor laid with tatami mats, level with the floor of the living quarters at the back of the shop. On the raised floor to the right as you entered the place was a small red sandalwood desk, where the master occasionally sat, his chin resting on his hand. Arranged neatly on the desk were his favorite writing materials and a book of facsimiles of seals, as though to create the effect of a tea connoisseur or an artistic dilettante sitting in his study. The raised floor to the left was where the apprentices worked at their desks and where the occasional customer determined enough to pull open the heavy glass door and come in would be taken care of; all the real business of the shop was conducted here.

But of course I didn't see anything of this when, wearing my stiff new obi and shop boy's apron, and blubbering all the way, I was first taken there by Mrs. Kondo, for I approached the house by way of a back alley and entered it through a gloomy kitchen entrance half-obstructed by the next-door neighbor's storehouse. As I timidly followed Mrs. Kondo into the strange house, the coldness of the floor against the soles of my feet nearly provoked another fit of loud weeping.

The living quarters at the rear of such city shopkeepers' houses seem always to be dark, admitting little daylight, and strangely chilly. The room I was led into was no exception. The chest of drawers of inlaid woodwork, the staggered shelves in the alcove, the rectangular brazier—every item in the room had an air of neurotic neatness: even the small clock ticking away in the semidarkness seemed to be guarding the forbidding gloom and stillness against intrusion. I suspect that the shopkeepers' preference for such surroundings and the severe, introverted personality it reflects come from their always having to swallow their pride and adopt a humble, accommodating manner toward their customers in the shop in front, whereas back in their private quarters, separated only by a sliding door from where they work, they revert to the role of master of the household and its employees.

As for Mrs. Kondo, her behavior as she entered the room seemed to confirm her assertion that she and the mistress of the house were like sisters. She immediately plumped her portly self down on the thick cushion on this side of the brazier opposite the other woman, and without further ado launched into a conversation that both of them obviously much enjoyed. The conversation had absolutely nothing to do with me, but as soon as I heard the woman's voice I couldn't help thinking how mean it sounded, how different her whole manner of speaking was from what I'd been used to at home.

I learned later that, like Mrs. Kondo, who before Otei-chan was born had been the mistress of a foreigner, this cousin of hers had also been a foreigner's mistress or something of the sort. And so presumably when these two, with so much in common in their pasts, got together and started talking without restraint, they behaved as they had done in their youth.

When at long last the exchange of ripe feminine banter over the brazier had run its course, Mrs. Kondo began talking about me, occasionally lowering her voice. I was standing dejectedly in the dark corridor just outside the room. After a while she turned and, beckoning me with a jerk of her double chin, said: "Hide-san, come in and present yourself. Tell her that from today on you're dependent on their goodwill." Then, when I went in and gave a stiff bow, she said unceremoniously, "This is the mistress."

The mistress appeared to be about forty. Unlike Mrs. Kondo, she was very thin. Even with makeup on, her skin looked jaundiced and lifeless. Her hair was tightly drawn back into a bun, so that the thinning hairline seemed to have been charged with hitching up the corners of her eyes. Her teeth were a dingy yellow; she must have been very fond of tobacco, for she never once put down her long pipe. The first thing she said to me was: "You're terribly small. Are you sure you're thirteen?"

When we left my house, large bundles of my things in wrapping cloths had followed us on a rickshaw, and these were now carried in by my fellow apprentices. "What on earth have you brought with you?" said the mistress incredulously, then muttered something to Mrs. Kondo. Although the latter had come on my mother's behalf, she seemed only too ready to cooperate with her cousin, untying the bundles in response to her bidding and presenting each article for her inspection. Out came my quilts, my changes of clothing, my favorite reading matter, even the things I used to take to school—everything that Mother, sending her son away to work for the first time in his life, had packed in an excess of zeal.

"What is all this?" she demanded of Mrs. Kondo, mounting displeasure showing all over her face. "Are you trying to be funny? Why, it's like some stupid family sending off a bride! Look at these fancy bedclothes—what could his mother be thinking of? You've got quite the wrong idea! I said we were looking for an apprentice boy, not someone else's soft, spoiled kid to take care of!

"But it's all right," she wound up, with an unseemly display of nicotine-stained front teeth. "We've got the bedding that Masa-don[12]—the one this kid is replacing—used to use, so please just take these things back with you. And don't forget to tell his parents that we're taking him on as an apprentice, and it will be a good six or seven years before he's fully trained. Until then he's a working boy, and no more. Make them understand that!"

Mrs. Kondo said not a word in protest to this harangue, but grinned sheepishly, almost as though the mistress had some kind of hold over her. Even so, they seemed to get along very well together. The mistress sent the maid out to order some food for us, and in a while we were served sushi and thick miso soup. When it was time for the lamps to be lit, Mrs. Kondo quietly wrapped up those things of mine deemed inappropriate and carried them with her to the waiting rickshaw. "All right then, Hide-chan?" she said as she stepped up inside. "You've got to put up with it, understand? You've got to put up with it." And she went off, leaving my shadow at the end of the back alley.

The next day I was assigned a corner desk out in the front, where I was to work and tend shop.

That morning I saw the master for the first time, being presented to him as he and the mistress sat at the breakfast table. They couldn't have been more unalike. His slightly thinning hair was neatly parted, and he looked more like an elegant city man than a shopkeeper or a craftsman. He spoke quietly in a voice that had a

12. The suffix "-don," a friendly form of address for apprentices and other young working-class men, was added to the first part of the personal name, so that Hide-tsugu, for instance, would be called "Hide-don."

gentle, almost womanly quality. His wife, on the other hand, chattered away to him about my arrival the day before. His mind seemed to be elsewhere most of the time. When she had finished he said, "Is that so—I see—yes, indeed." Holding his chopsticks in one hand and raising the soup bowl to his mouth with the other, he looked at me over the rim of the bowl and merely said he hoped I was there to stay.

The three apprentices' desks were lined up next to one another along one side of the shop. On each were placed the tools used in carving seals. At the end nearest the living quarters sat Kura-don, whose apprenticeship would soon be up. The desk in the middle belonged to Masa-don, who had fallen ill and gone back to his family. Showing me to the desk beyond that, the mistress said to Kura-don, "This is Hide-don, the new boy. Make sure you're nice to him. You're his senior, so it's your job to take good care of him." Kura-don was deftly carving a seal, a clamp in his left hand, a knife in his right. He stopped for a moment and, still hunched over his work, turned his head toward me and said, "Nice to meet you."

Hardly any customers came into the shop. Since we were near Naka-dori with its brokerage houses, and the teahouses of the pleasure quarter inside the concession, someone from those places would occasionally come in to order receipt seals or the like, while the odd passerby might drop in to order a personal or legally registered seal; but that was about all we had in the way of direct dealings with customers in the shop. As for how it was possible for the master to maintain a shop on one of the principal streets in the concession, the answer is that he had in his employ two or three salesmen whose job it was to go around soliciting orders at big institutions like the customs house, the courthouse, the municipal office, and the main trading companies. When a very large order such as postmarks for the post office was involved, the seal-makers of the area would compete for it, and the master himself would go out to make his bid. Needless to say, such large-scale orders couldn't possibly be handled in the shop alone, so presumably the master had subcontractors working for him. In other words, the shop itself was a formality; and since so little business was conducted there, Kura-don and I were free to talk to each other, or to read or write, so long as the master and mistress weren't there.

The contrast between the home in which I had grown up and my new surroundings left me completely disoriented. As a first place of employment, the shop lived up to Mrs. Kondo's assurances, and was as relaxed and comfortable as I could have hoped for. Nevertheless, I was like a cat unable to settle in its new home, and found the house unbearably cold. As evening approached and, sitting at my desk, I looked through the glass door at the darkening street outside, my eyes—without my really knowing why—would fill with tears.

Perhaps because I had never lived with strangers before, my nose was offended by the smell of sweat that came from Kura-don and the cushion he sat on close to mine; my whole body was chilled by the familiar mustiness whenever I went into the sitting room at the back that got so little sunlight; while to go into the kitchen was to be more conscious than ever of the smell of strangers. What I disliked particularly was having to tidy up the master's and mistress's bedroom upstairs every morning. As I put the futon and the two pillows that lay side by side—the mistress's was of red lacquered wood—into the closet, I would turn my face away, with a boyish fastidiousness and intolerance, from the warmth and dust that escaped from them.

That this particular chore should have been assigned to me—there was, after all, a maid who could have done it—must have been because they saw me as just an ignorant, undersized kid. There was truly nothing I hated more than having to pick up those two pillows and put them away. It made me feel more slave-like and humiliated than sitting on a wooden floor eating cold rice, being scolded as I knelt beside a mop bucket, or massaging the mistress's legs and hips. To my boyish way of thinking it seemed the lowest possible form of work a person could be made to do.

The chore that regularly came after this was cleaning the lamps. Electricity can't have been widely available in Yokohama City at the time; most of the streets, and possibly large wholesale houses, hospitals, and the like, had bluish white gaslights, but I don't believe private houses ordinarily had even them.

Cleaning lamps was something we boys had been made to do at home, so I didn't find it so onerous now. But there was one more daily chore we had to do after breakfast: polishing the various chests of drawers and cabinets in the sitting room and anteroom. No households nowadays practice this custom with such time-wasting diligence, but it was a common routine in those days. Every morning, we had to rub the paulownia-wood surfaces endlessly, in a circular motion, with a folded yellow cloth. The results hardly ever pleased the mistress, and the patience the work required and its pointlessness were intolerable for a boy.

Some days after my arrival, I was sent out on an errand. It felt like my first taste of freedom, walking away from there. At the same time, I couldn't help feeling that this person dressed as an apprentice boy in stiff obi and apron was not really me, and to be seen like this by others on the street filled me with embarrassment. When I saw boys and girls of my own age hurrying along to their respective middle schools, I felt myself go hot all over. Envious and ashamed, I made myself even smaller than I already was and sought cover in the shade of the trees lining the street. I felt a sudden hunger for learning that I had never known before; the thought that I had fallen from the state where it was to be had for the asking was mortifying, and I gave in to a sense of childish self-pity.

My errand that morning was to fetch some dried horse mackerel from a shop on the riverbank by Minato-bashi. I made my way back to the shop holding in one hand the loosely wrapped paper package containing several of these dried fish, no doubt preoccupied all the while with thoughts about my situation. As soon as the mistress opened the package she looked at me closely, then back at the fish.

124

"Is this all you got?" she said. Perhaps I had dropped some on the street, or a dog had snatched a few and run off, but there were certainly less there than there should have been. "Not much of a shop boy, are you?" she said crossly, turning her back on me and walking out of the kitchen. "Can't even be trusted to do a simple errand!"

I've given the impression, I realize, that I have nothing but unpleasant memories of the shop and that I was an unduly sentimental and moody boy. But it isn't true that every day was of unrelieved unpleasantness. Admittedly, for a while after I parted from my parents I would go to bed feeling miserable and cry myself to sleep. But I was still at heart a child and very simple, and could be easily distracted from my homesickness. I quite enjoyed, for instance, the afternoon break for tea and snacks, when Kura-don and I would go to the sitting room in response to the mistress's call and, receiving with a show of gratitude our rations of hot cakes and salt crackers, take them back to our desks. In time, I even came to enjoy the meals of rice and miso soup that we ate with such solemnity in the kitchen.

Most important of all, though, was the kindness of the master, who never said a cross word to us. At first it was difficult for me to address him and his wife as "Master" and "Mistress," but I got used to doing so; and despite the times when I had to put away his and the mistress's pillows, I learned gradually to regard him with something approaching respect.

Mr. Kawamura wrote haiku under the pen name of Gochiku. He seemed to have many haiku-writing friends, for someone would often come in and ask if "Gochiku-san" was at home, or leave a scroll with haiku on it to be handed to him. These poems were by fellow members of the group the master belonged to, and were marked with corrections by their mentor. Sometimes, several of these friends would happen to come in about the same time, and there would be lively haiku talk lasting well into the night around the master's red sandalwood desk.

It was customary for us apprentices to work at our desks in the evening until the outer wooden shutters of the house were closed. With a manual of one thousand Chinese characters open beside me—in their ancient forms, and compressed into square frames for use on seals—I would practice writing out the characters; or with a piece of boxwood fixed in the clamp I would try to pick up the basic techniques of holding and using a carver's knife. One of my great pleasures while working like this was to eavesdrop on the master and his friends as they talked about poetry.

Mr. Kawamura was not of course dependent on haiku for his livelihood, but within his group he was a senior figure of some standing, and had even made his debut as a professional. Since he also conducted his business well and with dignity, and was a fine calligrapher and carver, his haiku friends, as even I could see in the way they spoke to him, regarded him as something more than the owner of a shop.

I have forgotten his name, but among the master's haiku friends was a trader in foreign goods to whose shop in Ogimachi I had gone two or three times on errands. He was a typical, bewhiskered Yokohama merchant, and nothing in his general appearance or manner suggested a taste for poetry. One evening, with a fine drizzle falling outside, he dropped in and sitting by the master's desk had a long conversation with him. From time to time, I caught them looking in my direction. I had my work lamp in front of me, with a spherical magnifying lens hanging on it. Focusing the shaft of light that came through the lens on my practice seal, I was working with a sharp-pointed knife, trying to pick out the tiny characters in relief. Like Kura-don, I was hunched over my work, but when I heard the master call out "Hey!" I raised bloodshot eyes and straightened up; whereupon the haiku friend, a quick little smile flashing between the pomaded ends of his moustache, made an unexpected demand: "Here—I've been told that you write well. It's raining tonight, so write something on the subject of rain."

I wondered how he and the master had got to know about my

writing. Not knowing what to say, I blushed and looked down. "The subject doesn't matter," the master said in an insistent tone, "just write about whatever you fancy. Do it right away, then show us what you've written."

As though my life depended on doing as I was told, I took out a pencil and started to write. What I wrote I have completely forgotten. All I remember is that I gazed out of the glass door and, watching the lights of the rickshaws and the shapes of passersby with oiled-paper umbrellas going to and fro in the night rain, somehow managed a descriptive composition in the literary style. Then, timidly, I walked up to the two men, presented them with my piece, and returned to my desk. They sat for a long time looking at it, close to each other, their chins resting on their hands. All the while I could feel my heart pounding. Neither said a word to me, though, and the evening ended uneventfully with the departure of the guest. I pulled the shutters to, then, curling up under the thin futon, went to sleep.

The next morning, however, I was called before the master. On the tatami in front of him lay an envelope addressed to my father in an elegant hand. Poking it toward me with the tip of his finger he said: "You are to take this home with you. It's all explained inside. And tell them someone from your family can come and pick up your belongings later."

And so I left the Kawamura Seal Shop by way of the kitchen door. I was horribly shocked by this sudden release from my apprenticeship. Yet at the same time, the happy thought that I was going home seemed to erase the constant sense of deprivation I had felt during the days I spent working there.

But I had never seen our new home. Mother had told me in a letter that they had moved out of the house at Akamon-mae, and had given me the new address, but that was all I knew.

Once, when I was sent to make a delivery at a bank in that general area, I had wandered about for a while to see if I could find the new house. But I gave up the search quickly enough, remembering what Father had said to me before I left home: "Once you take on a job, you are to stick at it no matter what happens." And turning to Mother he had added: "If he should stop by while out on an errand or something, you're not to let him in." So, rather than face an outburst, I went back to the shop without looking any further.

What troubled me most, therefore, was the thought of Father's anger on seeing me return as a dismissed apprentice. My heart full of dread at the prospect, yet unable to suppress the joy of going home, I searched for the house my family had moved to.

It was in a hollow lying below the hill known as Iseyama. You went part of the way down a gentle slope on the western side of the hill—on the other side from Momijizaka—then turned right and followed a narrow road to the bottom. There, cheap-looking rented houses, just beginning to form a neighborhood, stood dotted about among thickets and swampy areas. Beside the front door of one of these houses hung a nameplate that was unmistakably ours. Looking at the place, I could hardly believe that I had found the right one. Hesitantly opening the door, I stepped into an earthen-floored hallway so small that there seemed barely room for me to stand in it.

Looking about inside, I reckoned that it probably contained no more than three rooms. None of the familiar furnishings from our previous house was visible. There was no sign of Father, either. In the inner six-mat room I could see my little sister, who still needed diapers, lying on a futon. Beyond in the tiny yard was Mother, her back toward me, hanging washing on a drying pole. As if in a stranger's house I remained in the hallway and craning forward called, "Mother!" She turned her face toward me, away from the sun. It was so drawn that I hardly recognized it. Without smiling, she stared at me for a while. The pole she was holding fell from her hand and made a noise as it hit the ground. With no attempt to pick it up she stepped up onto the verandah, then, crossing the room with short, quick steps, came up to me and brought her face close to mine. "Did something happen, Hide-chan?" she asked; but she seemed already to have guessed. I put the master's letter down in front of her and, unable to say anything, burst into tears. "Come in," she said, apparently quite unmoved, and led me by the hand into the house. Then, with a touch of impatience, she said, "What are you crying about?" I was still feeling panicky, and looking around me kept on asking, "But where's Father?"

She explained that having lost his case he had various expenses relating to the trial, including the payment of a large sum in damages, and had gone to Odawara, his birthplace, on a fund-raising expedition. He would be away, she added, for quite a while.

At the time, I believed Mother's explanation and was secretly much relieved at Father's absence. But after a month or so I began to notice things that didn't seem consistent. Eventually I discovered that Mother, finding herself unable to tell me what had really happened, had told me an outright lie. It must have been extremely painful for her at the time. The truth of the matter was that after I was sent away to work, the high court had found Father guilty of falsification of private papers and embezzlement, and that he was now temporarily detained in Negishi Prison, waiting to begin serving his sentence.

If only during this waiting period Mr. Takase had relented and pleaded with the court for Father's release, or if Father had been able to reimburse the company for the losses it had incurred, he might not have had to serve his sentence. But he had always managed his affairs by borrowing rather than saving. As for his household possessions, he had sold them all in the course of a year or two; so that he was entirely without resources of any kind. And Mr. Takase, it seemed, having sworn to destroy Father and drive him out of Yokohama, would not be placated.

One memory that has continued to haunt me in connection with this whole affair is of the day my half-brother Masahiro and I said goodbye to each other at Sakuragi-cho Station. I had accompanied him all the way to the station to see him off. He got on the train and sat by a window close to where I was standing on the platform, his face looking unusually gloomy as I gazed at him.

I learned later from Mother that he went back to Odawara that day intending to sell some of his adoptive family's property and to help Father out of his desperate situation with the proceeds. It is possible that Father himself, swallowing his pride for once, had begged him to do this. But whether or not it was his own idea, he was going in full awareness of the difficulty of his mission. Haggard and downhearted, he said to me through the open window, "Hide-chan, you're going to have a hard time from now on." And as if he'd suddenly remembered something he pulled an envelope out of the inside pocket of his suit jacket and handed it to me. It contained the month's pay that he had just received from the Soda Bank. "Give this to Mother," he said.

That was the end of our short relationship as brothers. His attempt to sell property belonging to his adoptive family was discovered by some of their relations, who rallied in angry disapproval to frustrate it. Whether out of shame at his failure to help or a surfacing of accumulated resentment toward Father, he wrote him a postcard, the gist of which was as follows: "Though aware of how unfilial I am being, I have decided for reasons of my own to leave Japan. It is unlikely that I shall ever be able to see you again, so please think of me as no longer living." He never returned to Yokohama, nor did we ever discover his whereabouts.

In great consternation over Masahiro's disappearance my parents, with the aid of friends, the police, and private detectives, had inquiries made in all the likely places, but without any result. No one in Odawara had heard from him, and there were no indications that he had gone to Tokyo. They finally had to give up the search; and thirty-odd years were to pass before any of us ever saw or heard from him again.

Then one day, all those years later, he suddenly appeared at my house. I was living near Shiba Park at the time, and I suppose he had come across my name in some magazine or other and decided to seek me out. By then Father had long been dead, and Mother was

130

gone too. This is not the place to write more about him and that meeting, nor is it a story that can be told simply. For now, suffice it to say that my one and only elder brother disappeared completely from our lives shortly before Father went to prison.

Why—to retrace my steps a little—should someone as gentle as Mr. Kawamura have suddenly decided to send me home with a letter addressed to Father? The circumstances leading to the decision were not, in fact, given in the letter, being made clear some time later in a conversation Mother had with Mrs. Kondo.

What had happened was that two days before that rainy evening—the evening when the master and his guest ordered me to write a short essay on the subject of rain—I had committed a horrendous blunder.

It was daytime, and the mistress was having her hair done by her regular visiting hairdresser. I was sitting at my desk, and could see the two women quite clearly through the glass door separating the shop from the living quarters. The mistress was seated in front of her dressing table and the hairdresser stood behind her, vigorously dragging her hair upward with a comb.

I suppose the mistress's face had always held some kind of fascination for me. Now, each time the hairdresser applied her fine-toothed bamboo comb to the thinning hairline and with all her strength pulled it back through the hair, the normally sallow face would turn red and the corners of the eyes and the small nose would be hoisted up to the limit, the whole face stretching and elongating like soft, glutinous candy; it was a wonder she didn't topple over backward. I found the sight intensely funny. On an obscure impulse, I opened the notebook on my desk and began busily sketching her contorted face, darting glances at her all the while. It need hardly be said that if I could watch her through the glass door, she too could watch me out of the corner of her eye, but with no such thought in my head I put the notebook away in the desk drawer and totally forgot about it.

The next day, the mistress sent me out on some errand or other, then looked in the drawer and found the sketch. In a rage she showed it to the master. "That's a dangerous, wicked boy," she said. "You must get rid of him at once." The master refused to take her seriously at the time, but that evening, when he happened to mention the incident to a visiting haiku friend, the friend said: "You need to be a bit more careful with a clever, cocksure kid like that." And they hit upon the idea of seeing just how clever I was by giving me a difficult test.

I would have done better, I suppose, not to agree so naively to their demand and rack my brains writing my little piece, for in the event it made me look even worse in their eyes. "You never know what a kid like this will do next," said the haiku friend, apparently.

Looking back on the incident, I can't help reflecting that by punching Mr. Takase's bald head, Father not only put an end to his own career but pushed his wife and children onto the path to sorrow and destitution; while I, by sketching a subject that fascinated me—the mistress's long, thin face—and in consequence unwittingly committing a fatal literary error, ended up roaming the streets in search of a succession of jobs to support us.

1. The author's father

2. The author's mother

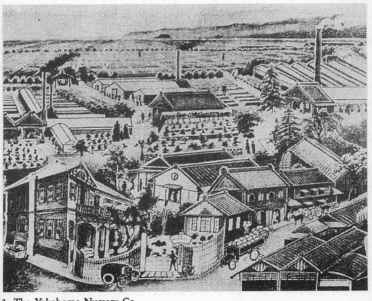

3. The Yokohama Nursery Co.

4. Negishi Racecourse

5. Banners advertising the attractions of the Nigiwai-za theater in Isezaki-cho

6. The Bund, with rickshaw men waiting outside a hotel

7. The shops on Benten-dori, catering mainly to foreigners

8. The Onoe-cho district, with a church visible on the left

9. Kane-no-hashi bridge

10. Yoshida bridge, not far from Yoshikawa's last residence in Yokohama

11. The main pier

12. Yokohama dockyards

13. The author around 1910–11

14. Yoshikawa with his younger brother Sosuke, working as apprentices for Mr. T (seated)

15. Women in the Yoshiwara pleasure quarter, Tokyo

16. The author at a *senryu* gathering (third from left)

Red Brick

B ack at home after that very brief spell of living with strangers, I took advantage of Father's absence to spend much of my time browsing in bookshops during the day and poring over books all night long, blissfully unaware of the extent of the suffering that Mother hid from us in that small house.

She never said a cross word to me about my conduct. Indeed, she would commend what she saw as my new ways by making such remarks as: "You really have changed! Going out into the world and earning your keep with strangers was good for you after all."

Unlike the places we had lived in before, our new home was a rented house the size, as they say, of a cat's forehead, and lacking a maid to help her Mother was constantly on her feet. Naturally, I was expected to sweep the floors, carry water into the kitchen, and rush to do errands for her whenever I was there. It was my willingness to help, no doubt, that led Mother to believe I'd changed for the better. Actually, though, what made me so willing was the novelty of living somewhere without Father around shouting at every little mistake I made, such as using my chopsticks in not quite the right way. It was the pleasure of living in a house without Father's severity but with Mother's love that gave me whatever enthusiasm I was able to summon up.

How Mother managed to make ends meet during the months

that Father was away is hard to explain. It was around that time that I paid several visits to a pawnbroker on her behalf. I would take with me, say, a small box containing various kinds of tortoiseshell hair ornaments that Mother had apparently worn in the early years of her marriage. I still haven't forgotten how I blushed and felt my knees shaking as the pawnbroker stared alternately at me and the box. In those days, the state of mind in which a person went to a pawnshop, and other people's attitude toward him, were quite different from what they are now.

At other times I would be sent to see people we had known with a letter from Mother asking them to give back the money she'd once lent them. In the past, without Father's knowledge, she had often obliged friends—or even carpenters and tradesmen with whom we dealt—who came to her for loans. So now she wondered in her letters, in the politest possible language, whether they would be so good as to repay her at least in part. Her appeals were hardly ever heeded. On some of my visits I was received with a cold indifference I hadn't encountered before, and I became reluctant to go, even for Mother's sake.

Even so, there were occasions too when to my surprise I would be given not only an envelope with money in it but a box of confectionery to take back with me. Our joy at such times was boundless. I could read in Mother's face immense relief at the thought that for some days to come we wouldn't be short of rice. If I remember correctly, rice at the time cost sixteen or seventeen sen a *sho* [1.8 liters]. China rice was three or four sen cheaper, and ordinary or pressed barley was a little cheaper still, so after our downfall Mother used to cook a mixture of seven parts white rice and three parts barley.

With a number of growing children to take care of, Mother had found herself suddenly living in a small house in a remote corner of Tobe with no ready means of support. She was totally without experience in coping with real poverty, and that initial step of mixing white rice with barley must have been a tough one in its way.

She bore, altogether, ten children. I was the eldest son, aged thirteen, and after me came Kino, the eldest daughter, aged eleven; Kae, the second daughter, aged eight; Sosuke, the second son, aged seven; Hama, the third daughter, aged three; and Chiyo, the fourth daughter, born that year. Three girls—Kiku, Kuni, and Sue—died before they were weaned, and a third son, Susumu, was not yet born. And yet she was only thirty-eight at the time I am writing about, and nice-looking, all the more so because of her fair complexion, which stood out in that poor neighborhood.

But she gave up her long-standing habit of lightly making up her face first thing in the morning. The minute she got out of bed she had to rush about, her baby on her back, getting three children ready to go to elementary school. After that came the family washing and then, until late at night, the sewing she took in to make a little money. And while she did all this, she had to nurse the baby too. Sharing the light of one lamp with her I would, unperturbed, read Edo-period novels and translations of foreign novels. To have me beside her as she worked under the lamp in the late hours was probably a comfort to her. For me, those evenings spent in the light of the lamp were hours of quiet, gentle pleasure, however hard they may have been for Mother. Father wasn't there to shout, "Haven't you gone to sleep yet?" nor was Mother one to threaten me with, "What's that silly thing you're reading? Here, show it to me!"

I started assiduously sending my literary efforts to various magazines. My first encouragement had come around the age of eleven, when I was awarded the silver medal for a short prose piece I submitted in a competition held by the magazine *Boys*. After that I set my eyes on magazines such as *Boys' World*, *Girls' World*, *Postcard Literature*, *Women's Literature*, *Middle School Writing*, *Middle School World*, and *Young Writers*. In the end I was even submitting poems to *Bookcase* and *Morning Star*. But almost nothing of mine, either in prose or in verse, was published. I was particularly unsuccessful with *Myriad Morning News*, which published a short story once a week and to which I sent a number of stories written with great earnestness. The best I did there was an honorable mention. Nevertheless, I was secretly rather proud of the several prizes I got from *Young Writers*, *Middle School World*, *Postcard Literature* and so on for my efforts in classical and modern verse forms, and in prose. I realized from the names and addresses listed in these magazines that some of those who had submitted compositions went to my school or lived in my neighborhood. We soon got together and began printing by hectograph a pamphlet which we circulated among ourselves; we also pooled what little cash we had to buy a simple mimeograph machine on which we printed a kind of coterie magazine. When I left school, my association with these friends simply came to an end. We called ourselves "The Literature Society" and our magazine "Wild Roses." Typical of the sort of things I wrote at the time was a piece I entitled "Observations on the Writings of Omachi Keigetsu"; just to think about it now makes me break out in a cold sweat. And we all gave ourselves pen names; not to have one somehow took away that literary feeling. The one I chose for myself was Kaho [Misty Peak], and I had no compunction about using it when I sent in pieces to magazines—though when I sent something to a girls' magazine, I would give myself a woman's name.

The one literary monthly we had in Yokohama was called, I believe, *Moshiogusa* [Seaweed, meaning miscellany]. There were also various poetry groups that had ties with the literary columns of such papers as the *Yokohama Trade News* and the *Yokohama Morning News*. In the haiku field there was a man called Matsuura Io—possibly of the same school as the celebrated Kyoshi—who was active as a judge of haiku and who used to send me notices of small get-togethers. On one occasion I entered a haiku contest held by the *Trade News* for its special New Year issue and was placed first. I was quite taken aback when I received the prize, for it turned out to be a large case containing four dozen bottles of beer. There was also an occasion when I decided to accept an invitation from Mr. Matsuura to attend a gathering at his house in Kotobuki-cho. When I got there, I discovered much to my discomfort that all the other guests were rather proper-looking, grown-up men and women. I sat down on the very edge of the group, trying to make myself inconspicuous. I continued to feel out of place, and went home having said hardly a word to anyone. That one experience of a haiku party was enough for me, and I never went to another.

For a paper concerned with commercial affairs, the *Trade News* was surprisingly liberal in the space it gave to more frivolous matters. Every day, for instance, they would print an engraved illustration of some scene done by Ogawa Usen; and they would often serialize a novel by someone like Maeda Shozan, whose *Ill-Fated Aristocrats*, if I remember correctly, was well received. I myself was gradually acquiring half-baked opinions, which I was only too ready to express, about Tolstoy and Maupassant, and about Akinari[13] and Saikaku in the field of Edo literature. No longer satisfied by now with the popular fiction of writers like Shozan, and having waded through the more realistic Shimei and Doppo without fully understanding them, I was soon infatuated, as apparently everyone is at some time, with Kyoka.[14]

It never occurred to me either then or later to want to become an expert on literature. I just happened to like reading fiction. In my choice of what to read, therefore, I was quite undiscriminating. If I took a fancy to one of Oshikawa Shunro's adventure novels, I couldn't rest until I had plowed through every other novel he had written.

Snug in my own small, private world of books, I was never bored, and seem to have spent much of the summer after being dismissed from the seal shop in a state of self-centered bliss. Then, one day while Mother was out, I noticed amongst the mail a gray envelope

13. Ueda Akinari (1734–1809), distinguished scholar and writer of fiction, best known for his novel *Ugetsu Monogatari*.
14. Izumi Kyoka (1873–1939), whose ornately written, fantastic fiction had little in common with the naturalism then coming into vogue.

marked with a censor's stamp. It was addressed to Mother, and on the back was printed the place of origin: Yokohama Negishi Prison.

It was almost certainly from Father. By then, I was vaguely aware of what had happened to him. Many times, early in the morning, Mother would tie up a few carefully chosen things in a small wrapping cloth and with my baby sister Chiyo on her back go out for the better part of the day. Ever since the first time I asked her where Father was, I had been silent, and she on her part had said nothing more about him. Thus while knowing that Mother was hiding something from me, I had no precise idea of where he was until I saw the letter from the prison. But my recollection of the time when I finally found out contains no hint of any overwhelming feelings of oppression or sorrow. I ask myself why this was, and the answer is that, whether through respect or fidelity, the fact of his finding himself destitute, or of his having been sent to prison, would never make any difference; to me, his son, he was quite simply the father I had always known.

I suspect that the way I felt would have been shared by other children of the Meiji period too. Our education certainly encouraged us to feel this way, as did the entire social system. Around that time, awareness of the family as the central reality had reached a peak throughout the nation, and no matter how lowly placed or poor one's father was, one believed him to be the best and truest person in the world. That, at least, was how I felt. So even when I found that Father was in Negishi Prison, I couldn't think of him in conjunction with crime. If anything it made him—a former object of fear—somehow dearer to me, and when in my limited child's fashion I imagined Father lonely in his cell, I shed a tear or two.

Summer was nearing its end. After sending the three children off to school, Mother quickly combed her hair and tied it in a tight knot at the back, wrapped a couple of forbidding-looking books, together with tissue paper and the like, in a cloth, settled Chiyo on her back, then reaching for her Western-style umbrella said to me, "You look after the house while we're gone, Hide-chan."

Until then I hadn't said a word about Father to her, but knowing where she was going I suddenly felt a terrible longing for him. "I'm coming with you," I said and, stepping into my clogs, rushed outside ahead of her. She must have felt quite helpless. She followed me out muttering to herself, closed the door after her, then saying no more took me along. There were no streetcars yet, and we were in no position to hire rickshaws. Carrying my baby sister on her back and leading my four-year-old sister Hama-chan by the hand, Mother walked without flagging all the way to Negishi under the scorching sun. To walk from where we lived to Negishi would be no problem at all nowadays. But we had to make our way along rivers and streams and meandering country lanes, so that by the time we could see the red brick wall of the prison, our legs felt like lead. A bridge led to the gate of the prison on the other side of the river. Lined up along the river on this side were scriveners' and prison caterers' establishments with open fronts. Mother went into one of these, and I could see her suckling my baby sister as she talked to someone inside. When her business was done, she came out and said to me, "Wait for me here. They won't let children in here." Leaving me behind, she crossed the bridge and disappeared beyond the brick-framed iron gate. I walked about, watching the anglers who stood or squatted in a row by the river, or finding other ways—some mischievous—of whiling away the time. It was a long wait, but luckily it wasn't boring.

Finally Mother reappeared, and in silence we started on our return journey under the sun. We must have been somewhere in Sueyoshi-cho when in desperation I blurted out, "I'm awfully hungry." We went into a small soba restaurant and Mother ordered a bowl each for the three of us. We had just finished eating when she said out of the blue, wiping the sweat off her face with a handkerchief, "Hide-chan, things are going to be hard for us, and you'll have to be strong. We're in a very bad way." That day, even I could feel deep inside me something of the reality of that "in a very bad way."

139

Tears filled her eyes as though summoned up by my gaze. She then gave her face one quick wipe and pulled her cloth coin pouch out of her obi, leaving the exact amount of copper coins on the edge of the tray.

Housewives in those days were not in the habit of carrying with them fancy purses shaped to hold paper money, the reason being that for most purposes silver and copper coins sufficed. Five-rin (half-sen) coins were still in use then. So these pouches made of woven material were, it seems, an indispensable possession. From that day on, it was in a different frame of mind that I closely observed Mother's cloth pouch as she brought it out in the kitchen with wet hands and groped for coins. If I caught a glimpse of silver inside I would sigh with relief, and if I saw only one-sen or two-sen coins I'd immediately start worrying about the rice for the next day or the rent due soon. I stopped trying to wheedle money out of her in order to buy magazines or pay the postage for things I was sending to them.

Without any prompting from Mother, and despite my immaturity, I'd slowly come to realize that our present condition could not be allowed to continue. I once asked her in trepidation, "When is Father coming back?" "Pretty soon," she answered noncommittally, her face showing that she was still reluctant to talk about him. By then I had begun to peruse the "jobs available" column in the newspaper every morning. And when I saw that there was an opening for a "boy worker" at the Nanchusha Printing Works in Minami Naka-dori, I immediately went and got the job.

I was to start the next day. Regular working hours were from seven to five, the wage being fourteen sen per day. For overtime, I would get two sen an hour. The daily wage, then, was about the same as the price of one *sho* of rice. When I told Mother about my new job that evening she gazed at me for a while, then suddenly her face crumpled and she burst into tears. She took me in her arms and went on crying. She had borne several children, the youngest that year, and her breasts were always full and damp with milk. Pressed hard against them, I felt like a baby again, and I found myself crying with her. In retrospect it was a rather silly scene. In fact, when one looks back far into the past, it seems to be full of embarrassments of this kind.

Every morning I walked resolutely to the printing works. At first I was put into the type distribution department, where I was made to carry compositors' frames and join the women workers in rushing about with oil brushes; later, I was moved to the rule mark department as a servant boy. Minami Naka-dori was lined with raw silk exchanges, rice brokerages and the like, and the printing works stood in their midst, so that its business consisted almost entirely of printing market quotations and materials dealing with commerce in general. Ours may have been the only printing works thereabouts that had a rule mark department, whose main job was to print the light indigo and red lines on ledger sheets. The other jobs done there included bookbinding and page-folding.

The department was situated on the second floor of the warehouse of the main works. As you went up the stairs, the smell of glue wrapped itself around your face. The floor of the workplace was laid with tatami, its original color invisible by now under the red and indigo stains. There were three women workers, none of them very young any longer, and three males: a skilled worker whom we called Jiro-san and who had his hair cut short and square and seemed to fancy himself a ladies' man; the foreman, who seemed to be about forty; and myself. That was the entire department.

Work started at seven for the others, but I was told to be there at half past six. I was to collect pieces of live charcoal from the caretaker's room downstairs, put them under the glue pot and the kettle, and have things ready for morning tea. I never resented these chores, but there were things I *did* mind. During the afternoon break, the others would sit in a circle and draw lots for a pool of money, and while they played I would be sent out to get snacks for them. As they munched the crackers or cakes I'd brought back, the five grown-ups would tell smutty stories which seemed to amuse them no end.

I by no means found the stories unpleasant; in fact, some were quite entertaining. Nevertheless, the breaks were painful times for me. Having no money, I couldn't take part in their game. But I felt it would look funny to go outside while the others were having a good time, and funnier still to sit there twiddling my thumbs and looking the other way. So I sat in the corner pretending to read market reports and other printed matter that held no interest for me whatsoever. From time to time one of them, as if suddenly remembering that I was there, would call out, "Hey, come over here," and throw me a cake or a cracker as I approached. To be called like that and have to eat the cake or cracker while they watched was painful. I was oversensitive, of course, but it made me feel like a dog.

I had to stay on for half an hour after the others had left in order to clean up, make sure the fires were out, and lock up. Of the three women, one was the wife of the foreman, and another was apparently the wife of a typesetter, but the third was an unmarried woman close to thirty whom we called Osei-chan. She had a chubby face, and was pretty in a dim-witted sort of way. Even during working hours she was forever worrying about her hair and makeup. She and Jiro-san would sometimes stay on after working hours even though there was nothing left for them to do. They would chase me away without offering any explanation: "Go downstairs for a while," they would say, or "Stay away for twenty minutes."

Each time, I wished that they would wait until I'd finished my chores and gone, but I suppose they didn't want to be seen leaving the premises too late. So I did as I was told, making myself scarce for the required length of time. Quite often when I returned, though, they would still be there, rustling and whispering. The shutter by the ruled line machine would be already closed, and there on the ink-stained tatami, in a dark corner that smelled of glue, they would be doing what men and women do during such assignations. Even if they heard my footsteps on the stairs, they never bothered to get up

142

but remained exactly as they were, their bodies together forming a strange shape, like something lying at the bottom of a deep ravine. I would put my head out of the window by the top of the stairs and gaze out over the silence that had fallen on the hitherto busy street, toward the rooftops and Iseyama standing behind them against the evening sky. I would think of Mother at home, and hear in my imagination the familiar sounds of water being poured out in the kitchen and the mosquitoes buzzing. Then Jiro-san with his square haircut and Osei-chan would go past behind me in a cheerful mood and down the stairs. I would catch a whiff of her hair oil, and of something else, a combination of scents that seemed for a moment to pervade my whole being.

I have forgotten his name, but a nice old man with a pock-marked face inhabited the caretaker's room. He slept there, and showed no sign of resenting the work he was doing. In the evening around the time the sooty electric lights were being turned on, when I went to his room to return the fire pan with the charcoal cinders and the kettle, he would often give me a kind of lunch box of red rice with strips of dried cuttlefish and egg roll. "You have it," he'd say, explaining that he had got it from some shop celebrating its tenth anniversary. I didn't feel the slightest embarrassment in accepting whatever this old caretaker offered me. If I left half of the food uneaten, saying I wanted to take the rest home to my younger brother, he would say gently, "That's a nice idea, yes, a nice idea." He was unfailingly kind to me.

Because of this, I took note of what the others said about him. I learned that he had been with the printing works longer than any other employee. He had come from the same hometown in Echigo as the owner. Some years before the time I knew him he had retired after several decades of continuous service, and having been given a commendation and a lump sum of money he was to have gone back to his hometown to spend his remaining years in happy retirement. But then, after he had already bought gifts to take back for people at home, he suddenly said that he'd decided to stay, and quietly continued to work and sleep in the caretaker's room. The others in the works had no idea at first why he had changed his mind, but they soon came to know the reason through rumors circulating among the local stockjobbers. What had apparently happened was that on receiving the large sum of money that was his reward for thirty or forty years of faithful service, he had immediately risked all of it in some speculation, together with the money he had carefully saved through all those years, and had lost overnight every penny he had. His co-workers would laugh when they talked about it: "What a fool," they'd say. And, listening to them, I too used to wonder in my childish way whether he was really the kind of man I thought he was. But no shadow of his loss lingered in the fine wrinkles on his face, nor did I ever hear him utter one bitter word. To this day I remember him simply as a warmhearted old man, and I can still recall his pockmarked face with a fair degree of clarity. Yet I have forgotten his name, for which I owe him an apology. True, I was at the printing works for only a brief period, and what I received from him was no more than the kindness, as it were, of a passerby. . . .

We were paid twice a month, on the fourteenth and the last day of the month. Even without a single day's work missed, and with added overtime pay, at a basic rate of fourteen sen a day the amount that was put in my envelope was very small.

Nevertheless, it was a uniquely exciting experience to hold in my hand for the first time money that I had earned on my own. At the Kawamura Seal Shop the understanding had been that during the early stage of my apprenticeship I wouldn't receive a sen of pocket money, and the printing works was the first place that actually paid me for the work I did. As I walked home at dusk on paydays with the money in my pocket, I felt a desperate urge to stop and buy something—fruit, toasted bean-jam cakes, anything—to take home for my little brother and sisters. I wanted to savor the value of the money I had earned. But I resisted the urge, for I felt at the same time that it would be a pity to spend a single sen of it before I'd shown it to Mother. Then, once I was home and Mother suggested having chopped beef or white rice for dinner that night, I would rush out to do the shopping. Sometimes I bought something extra— a side dish, perhaps, that Mother hadn't reckoned on. I would linger uncertainly among the local housewives in front of a boiled beans shop or a cheap tempura place, but I didn't feel shy on those occasions; in fact, I rather enjoyed myself.

I can't remember now just how many months I was at the printing works, but I'm sure it happened while I was still there. It was early autumn, and beginning to get cool. I walked home at the end of the day as usual, suspecting nothing. But in the entrance I saw on the earthen floor an unfamiliar pair of sandals; and as I stood there for a moment I realized with a shock that the whole atmosphere of the house had changed. Several days before, Mother had said to me almost in a whisper, "Father's coming home soon." There was a look of happiness and relief on her face such as I hadn't seen for months. Now, sensing Father's presence in the dimly lit and unusually quiet interior of the house, I stepped out of my clogs, half aware of how different even that trivial act felt. I heard Mother calling out, "Is that you, Hide-chan?" "I'm back," I said as I went to leave my empty lunch box in the kitchen. Though it was early autumn, it wasn't cold; yet that evening the sliding doors of the living room were pulled shut, as though to shun the outside world.

I was about to go in when the doors opened and Mother looked out. In a quiet, tearful voice touched with tension, she said to me, "Hide-chan, your father has come home." No sooner did I go in and say "Welcome back" than my arm went up to hide my face. My temples throbbed with pain and my ears were ringing, which is why, perhaps, I don't remember a word of what he said. For all I know, he may not actually have said anything at all. What I clearly retain is a picture of him in a dark pongee kimono with a stiff sash tied around it, his silk gauze haori folded and placed by the pillow, and his face smiling forlornly at me, like the face of a broken man.

He was probably tired, since his bedding was laid out for him. But he was sitting up on it, presumably not wanting to lie down until I had come home. There he sat, square and straight as always, greeting me with his eyes.

For all that, his appearance had changed terribly. His hair was cropped close to the scalp, and his moustache was gone. But still worse were his pallor and his sunken cheeks. Mother stroked my back, trying to comfort me. "There, there, it's all right," she said. "We were just saying that the main thing is to be together and be good to one another, and you must think that too. . . . So you had to work overtime tonight," she added. "You must be hungry." She went to Father and helped him change out of his clothes, then, once he was settled in bed, stood up and went into the kitchen.

My cheeks dry at last and in a somewhat calmer frame of mind, I was able to observe his face in sleep. He lay on his side, turned toward the darker part of the room. I sat behind the pillow, and as I looked down at him his hollow cheek seemed deeper in the light-and-shadow cast by the lamp. To escape from the feelings that seemed to constrict me to the point of breathlessness, I quickly got up and joined Mother in the kitchen. There, although she was busily preparing my dinner, I helped myself impatiently to whatever bits of food I could lay my hands on.

Father Returns

Thus after an absence of half a year Father, thoroughly changed in appearance, came home to a small rented house he had never seen and to a family that had undergone even greater physical changes. What I could not get over that evening, though, was the feeling that the man I was looking at was not at all the man I had known before.

I suppose that for someone who had led a life of dissipation for so long, the impact of prison life was more than usually severe. He seemed thoroughly broken in body as well as in spirit. Having once lain down in bed that evening, he stayed there for days. It was thought unwise to start suddenly giving him the now unfamiliar food he craved, so for a while he was fed rice gruel morning and night. Like a person made helpless by a serious illness, he allowed himself to be taken care of entirely by Mother.

But though he was a defeated man, a man society had seen fit to punish, and though he was jobless and behaved like an invalid, in the eyes of his children he was nevertheless a source of strength; and when he returned to us we felt that our little house was no longer an oarless boat buffeted on the waves.

I continued to walk to Nanchusha every morning, and when I came home in the evening I would sit down formally by his pillow, bow to him, and say, "Father, I'm home." Unless he was fast asleep he would invariably sit up and say, "Welcome back." Sometimes he even added a few words of sympathy, like "You must be tired." I had never known him to be like this before.

Perhaps because he was weaker physically, he had become oddly gentle. On the other hand, we heard no more boisterous jokes from him. Lying in bed all day, he slept and read with equal intensity. If I remember rightly, the books he had around him were mostly about divination or psychology. What caused such a sudden interest in something like divination, I have no idea.

Between him and Mother had arisen a show of mutual feeling we had never seen before. It was as though the winds of adversity had, paradoxically, encouraged the late blooming of a flower. Father's return meant of course an increase in our household expenses, and Mother's efforts to make ends meet became more desperate than ever. But equally serious was her insistence on not giving him any inkling of her desperation. Picking coins out of her nearly empty pouch, she would buy little pieces of chicken meat or white sashimi—food thought to be good for a convalescent—and put them on his breakfast or dinner tray. And Father, for his part, was obviously not unaware of her thoughtfulness. I remember how once, as he sat up and picked up his chopsticks, he said very quietly to her, "Thank you." The words seemed to come straight from his heart. In the dozen or so years after our family started going under, I heard him say "thank you" to Mother twice. The second time was two days before he died.

Though he never said anything outright to her, Father in those days seemed inwardly to be forever apologizing to Mother. During the time immediately following his return, he even seemed apologetic to us children, so much so that we felt hurt for him.

Whenever I see Kikuchi Kan's play *Father Returns*,[15] I see my

15. A well-known one-act play written in 1917 about a destitute man who returns to his wife and children after having left them for another woman twenty years before. His wife is prepared to take him back, but their eldest son, embittered by the memory of his father's betrayal, at first rejects him, then in the end forgives him.

own father on the stage, and am reminded of my family as we were at the time. True, he was by no means as cowed by his family as the returning father is in the play, nor was he as willing to reveal his own vulnerability; nevertheless, in their capacity for self-reproach and painful introspection, the two figures are not unalike.

People nowadays seem to be fairly unconcerned about going to prison. Even politicians have been known to boast of having been behind bars. But in Meiji society the very thought of someone being sent to prison invited immediate scorn. The mere fact of having worn prison clothes, even though for no more than a few months, was enough to damn you for life, unless you lived in the criminal world. It was not just the contempt and derision among people who knew. A term in prison, however short, was normally entered in your family register, and there the entry stayed, officially stigmatizing you and your family for life. In my vague way I must have known this, for after Father's imprisonment I would flinch at the thought of having to show the register to a prospective employer, even though Father had only that one black mark against him. On more than one occasion I received notification of employment only to decide not to accept it for fear of having to show the register.

Later, when I really needed to look at the document and asked Mother to show it to me, I discovered that I needn't have worried: I examined it closely, but found no mention of Father's having served a prison term. Even so, at the time of his release, when he couldn't have known that the dreaded entry would not be made, he must have felt despondent about the future of his many children.

What must have tormented him even more was the sense of his own dishonor, the conviction that he could not, ever again, show his face in the world he once knew. And this conviction, I think, naturally turned him in upon himself. One side of him was the Meiji man of samurai stock unable to escape from his own severely moralistic, unforgiving upbringing; the other side was the man who had once led the flamboyant life of a successful and respected merchant in an open port; on both sides, his pride had been destroyed, and it was his own sense of disgrace rather than fear of other people's opinion that drew him further and further away from the rest of the world.

Father had not long been out of his sickbed when one day he suddenly announced to Mother that he was going to set himself up as a fortune-teller, and that she was to go to a cabinetmaker and get a signboard made.

Perhaps Mother still retained some semblance of a sense of respectability, or perhaps she felt that it bordered on sacrilege for someone who had sunk as low as Father to presume to tell other people's fortunes; either way, for some days she resisted the idea. "Really," she said tactfully, "there's no need for you to try so hard to help us."

But then one evening on returning from the printing works I saw the sign hanging beside the front door. It was a most peculiar sight. Going indoors, I found Father seated at a desk in the room where, until a week or so before, his sickbed had been. Lying on the desk were divining blocks and sticks, and piled up beside him were books on divination. That evening, too, he sat intently reading some Chinese book or other. When I sat down to dinner in the next room I whispered to Mother as she served me, "Has he had any customers?" She merely smiled and shook her head.

Father seemed at last to have recovered. But once he felt he regained his health he started drinking again. At the time of his return he had said to Mother: "Smoking is something I simply can't stop. But this is a good time for me to stop drinking, and I want you to know that I've made up my mind never to drink again." Mother was very moved, and was almost in tears as she repeated to us what he'd told her. But as things turned out, his resolve was short-lived, and we were soon subject to the usual drunkard's demands: "Oiku, have someone go out and get some more saké," or "Oiku, heat up another small bottle." Just as every night we watched with dismay our solitary lamp eating up the oil that we could ill afford, so we would watch Mother, who never could say no to Father, standing disconsolately in a dark corner of the kitchen and getting out of her pouch the coins she'd kept for tomorrow's rice. I was then sent out armed with the money and an empty bottle, sometimes late at night, to fetch the saké. As I walked home hugging the filled bottle and feeling the chilly wind of late autumn, I would cast a sidelong glance at the warm smoke coming out of the baked potato shop. At home, Mother would go on with her sewing work while we children sat with empty stomachs watching Father drink cup after cup. The impression he gave was of someone bursting with resentments, and I could barely contain the anger welling up inside me at his inconsistency and lack of concern for the rest of us. It was when he started drinking again and made Mother suffer more than ever that I began to develop an unmistakable hostility toward him.

By then we had sold and pawned everything we could in order to eat, so that when Father took to the bottle, Mother had to give up even the bare essentials in the way of clothing that she had kept for herself against the coming winter. Not only were we behind with the rent, but we owed money to all kinds of stores in the neighborhood, including, of course, the saké and the rice shops. Almost incredibly, there were even times when Mother was unable to put any rice in the lunch box I took with me to work.

When this happened Mother herself, of course, would go without breakfast. As I left, she would apologetically put in my hand a two-sen coin with which I bought myself a baked potato on the way, eating half of it as I walked and keeping the rest for lunch. During the lunch break I found the hunger itself easier to bear than the embarrassment of having to hang about lunchless in front of my coworkers.

I used to walk home in the dark wondering how the family had fared that day, and if I saw lamplight in the house as I approached would wonder how Mother, who that morning had only had a few copper coins, had managed to buy lamp oil for the evening; I would wonder, too, if there had been any money left to buy food for my brother and sisters. Either way, I was sure to see the telltale signs of drinking on Father's face. Hiding my resentment, I would give him a barely adequate bow. He might say something friendly to me, but by then I had lost my capacity to respond in kind. Sometimes, sensing my insubordination, he flew into a rage. "How dare you look at me like that! So you've let the miserable pittance you earn go to your head, have you? What's so special about working, anyway? Everybody works! If you don't like what you're doing, chuck it!"

When winter came Mother, made desperate by our poverty, decided finally to send her eldest daughter Kino, then eleven years old, to serve as a nursemaid with a family who owned a Western-style restaurant near Yokohama Park. At the urging of the agent who arranged this, she also decided to send out her second daughter Kae, only eight years old, to work as a servant girl at a sweet-bean soup restaurant called Yoshino-ya in Isezaki-cho. No further reduction could be made in the number of children who had to be fed, for only Sosuke who had just entered primary school, Hamako who was three, and a nursing infant were left.

Mother may have received advances on her two daughters' wages, as she soon began making winter clothes for the baby. But whatever money she acquired was not enough to pay off what we owed in rent, and we were driven out of our house. The house we moved into was also in Nishi-Tobe, and it was tiny.

It stood in a recently cleared, hilly area to the west of the slum on Tobezaka. There weren't many houses around as yet, and you saw few people walking about. It obviously wasn't the sort of neighborhood where a fortune-teller could expect to get any customers; nevertheless, Father put up his sign and sat at his desk as if to tell us that he too was working. And if there was the slightest evidence that Mother had a little money to spare, he would want his saké from early morning on. For a while immediately after his discharge from prison he'd had little resistance to alcohol, but as his system became more and more accustomed to it he regained his old capacity, which was almost limitless. There were days now when he started drinking the minute he got out of bed, kept at it all day without a bite to eat, then finally tottered back to bed.

Inevitably, he returned to his old crazed self. Any little gesture or comment on Mother's part would be cause enough, in his groggy, distorted mind, for behavior that made her cry for hours. While they were living in a large house with servants about and visitors dropping in, his drunken rages were kept under some measure of control, and Mother had some protection. But in a cramped rented house there was nowhere she could escape to; nor could Father jump into a rickshaw and rush off to some teahouse for a change of scene; so that when this drama was played out between them, it continued without intermission until both were completely exhausted.

Quite often Father would suddenly wake up from a fuddled sleep in the middle of the night and sit up in bed with arms folded; sometimes he would simply sit there saying nothing, seemingly sunk in thought; at other times he would gaze at the ceiling and talk to himself, or wake up Mother, whose nights were already all too short, and tell her: "Oiku, I'm not going to end up like this, understand? I'll show them! I'll be someone to reckon with again, you'll see. And why did you talk to me the way you did today? So you think I'm a fool, eh? Well, I'm *not* a fool, and I won't have you treating me like one!"

He became more warped and resentful toward Mother as his drinking increased. Sometimes he behaved in the same way toward me. "Don't you dare treat me like a fool!" he would snarl, or "Don't be so damned pleased with yourself just because you've got a job!" And I can't say that he was entirely wrong in detecting on occasion a certain sullenness and contempt in my manner. Mother, though, was not the sort of person who knew how to feel as I sometimes did. No matter how bad things got, it never seemed to cross her mind that she might leave her husband and children and find a way of living on her own. I myself found it harder and harder to hear Father showering abuse on her, to watch her sobbing in despair. At times I felt close to losing my own sanity and attacking him. I was too young then to understand a drunkard's state of mind, to separate Father the person from the violent alcoholic. I could only join Mother in a corner of the room to cry with her in sheer misery, believing that the man I saw in front of me was all that Father was. Time and again I would tell her I wanted to go away and live by myself somewhere, and more than once I actually fled out of the kitchen door, only to be stopped by her saying, "Hide-chan, what am I going to do without you?" But I never did learn not to want to fight him for her sake. Having openly shown defiance, I would again start to leave, then again return in response to Mother's pleading and apologize unwillingly to Father. I don't know how many times this scene was repeated.

The year's end was approaching. The lamp had not yet been lit inside the house when I returned from Nanchusha. The place seemed frozen into silence, and all I could hear as I stood in the entrance was Mrs. Kojima speaking in a hushed voice and my three-year-old sister Hamako sniveling. I rushed in and asked Mother in alarm, "Is something the matter?" "Father coughed up some blood," she answered, then added uncertainly: "The doctor's just been, he said there wasn't too much to worry about. . . ."

But as I listened to her talking to Mrs. Kojima, it became apparent that this was the third or fourth time it had happened. Two episodes had occurred while he was living it up in places like Tonosawa and Omori, and he'd had to stay where he was till he recovered. Mother of course had not been with him, and she knew nothing about it until later when she received a warning from the family doctor.

In retrospect it would seem that he had already been suffering from stomach ulcers in the days when he was entertaining his foreign acquaintances and doing the rounds of the pleasure quarters. But this last attack of heavy bleeding seemed at last to have made an impression on him, and he stopped drinking altogether. Rather, I should say that he lost his will to drink, and took to his bed again.

He returned to his former state of catlike immobility. But his mind remained as twisted as ever, and he continued behaving tyrannically toward Mother. Actually, I believe now that it wasn't really her he was railing at but the world outside, which since his discharge from prison he seemed to fear and resent almost abjectly. Not only did he never seek out former acquaintances, but if one of them came to visit him for old times' sake, he would so hate the thought of seeing and being seen that he'd tell Mother not to allow him into the house. "He's been ill for some time," she would be forced to tell the visitor at the door, "and he can't see anyone."

Yet in spite of this total withdrawal from society, Father still talked like a man with large ambitions. "I'll set up my own business, you'll see," he would say. "I won't die before I've made a comeback." Beneath the bravado lay a misguided conviction that others had been responsible for his downfall and suffering. Toward Mr. Takase in particular, his opponent in the trial, he seems to have harbored a deep grudge to his dying day. But Mother for her part refused absolutely to say anything suggesting that she held Mr. Takase responsible for our desperate condition. Once, when Father was being more than usually excessive in his abuse of the man, she impulsively came to his defense: "But why shouldn't he have been angry when you hit him like that? He deserves our thanks for all the kind things he did, and I don't think he did anything we could blame him for." Losing all control, Father jumped up and knocked her to the floor. Then he kicked her. Those of us who witnessed the scene would never forget it. Gasping for breath, the veins on his forehead swollen and his body shaking, Father himself collapsed in a heap. We rushed to either side of Mother, who lay still and seemed not even to be breathing, and dragging her up escaped with her into the kitchen. Still crying, we ladled cold water out of the bucket and brought it to her blood-covered lips.

As I have said, I feel now that in being so violent toward her,

Father was in fact giving vent to his rage against the outside world. But such speculation was beyond me at the time, and I was at a complete loss as to why he behaved in that way, or why she should still want to stay with him. Kinship, though, is a strange thing: even as we lived through such hellish scenes there were times when, lying under our thin bedclothes with our bodies touching, we would listen together to the distant sound of the wind in the leafless branches and feel that our house was the best and warmest place of all. And I never could bring myself to think seriously of leaving Mother. Had it been only Father, I suppose I might have been able to consider taking wing and leaving him to his own devices. But in her case, it was out of the question; indeed, I felt that I would and could do anything so long as she was with me. Whatever it took to bring a smile to her face, I was ready to do; and I found comfort in the thought that that alone made my life worth living.

By the riverbank as you crossed Hanasaki bridge from Iwakame-Yokocho toward Takashima-cho there was a wholesale supply shop with a large sign outside saying: "Peddlers of toiletries wanted. Merchandise lent to peddler by the shop. Earn one yen clear or more daily, depending on ability."

Every day I had seen the sign on my way to and from Nanchusha. It intrigued me, so one day I braced myself to go in and timidly asked a man who looked like either the owner or the senior clerk, "Do you think I could do it?" The man was unexpectedly helpful. The shop, he said, would lend me the merchandise and the necessary peddler's equipment, so long as I put down a deposit; normally, this would be fifteen yen, but in my case he'd make it ten. At the end of the day the money I brought back would be checked against the sales recorded in my notebook and the articles remaining, and I would be paid a percentage of my sales. He asked me where I was working. I told him, and said that my daily wage was fourteen sen. In that case, he said, I should by all means take up peddling. No matter how inexperienced, I was bound to make more than that in a single morning's work. If I didn't mind rain, I would find that business was even better on rainy days. Greatly encouraged by his enthusiasm and feeling as though I'd been saved by divine intervention, I went home and immediately told Mother about the new opportunity, asking if she could find the deposit money.

She looked at me in consternation. She was hardly in a position to hand me the money then and there; nor could she, offhand, think of any way of borrowing such a sum. After much thought, she finally decided that we would go to Mrs. Kojima and see if she could lend it to us.

Mrs. Kojima lived near us in a house belonging to the National Revenue Service. Her husband was a section chief in the Yokohama office of the service. They had no children and lived by themselves. She and Mother had first met when she brought over some sewing she wanted done, and they soon became friendly. They often met and talked about their respective circumstances, and Mrs. Kojima came to sympathize deeply with Mother. She was a frequent visitor at our house and before leaving would often look in on Father, lying grimly on his sickbed, and try to cheer him up. Much as he hated people, he would actually smile when she talked to him. Perhaps because she had only recently come to Yokohama from the provinces and didn't know many people, she was friendly and affectionate toward us. Unlike the typical wife of a bureaucrat, she put on no airs but was cheerful and open in her manner. At thirty or thereabouts, dark-complexioned and on the skinny side, she was hardly a beauty, and she spoke with a marked provincial accent which she made no attempt to modify. She had charm, though, and it was strange to see Father, whom we treated with such caution, good-humoredly accept any amount of teasing from her. Indeed, he became a totally different person in her presence and would laugh out loud at her jokes, even telling some himself.

Her husband, Kojima Ichitaro, a bureaucrat through and through, couldn't have been more different. When we went to Mrs. Kojima to ask for a loan, she said: "It's no use talking to my husband about this. He knows nothing about the world and wouldn't begin to understand your problem. I'll simply take out what you need from my own post office savings." The very next day, she appeared with the money. It was an act of true kindness, and perhaps because I was so moved by it I still remember very clearly her bony fingers, and even the gold ring with small chrysanthemums engraved on it, as she put the ten-yen note down in front of us. I remember, too, her scolding me: "Pull yourself together, Hide-chan, this really isn't the time to be sniveling."

I forgot to say that it was already some days past the New Year when all this happened. Thus it was early one morning sometime in the first half of January when I went to the shop and sat down on a bench just inside. I must have arrived too early, for there were sounds of people having breakfast somewhere at the back.

I sat waiting, frightened by the prospect of doing something I'd never done before, my mind full of forebodings. Eventually half a dozen energetic-looking men appeared and, without giving me so much as a glance, proceeded to put on their footgear, strap their peddlers' chests on their backs, and march out one after the other. I realized then that there were peddlers who slept and ate there. Soon afterward, other fellows started coming in and, picking up and strapping on their backs the chests they'd left there at the end of the previous day, marched out like the others. I noticed uneasily that not one of them was a boy like me, that they all were sturdy grown men.

So I had to wait until all the peddlers had left. Finally, the owner of the shop appeared and showed me the chest and merchandise I was to carry.

The straps you put around your shoulders were flat and fairly wide and made of tough, woven material. The chest was so designed as to fit against your back. The upper part consisted of layers of fitted boxes and the lower part of shallow drawers. The owner filled each of these with various articles of toiletry, then gave me a notebook in which were listed all the items and the price of each.

Your sales were confirmed, and you received your percentage, when you returned to the shop in the evening. Each peddler's supply would then be replenished, ready for the next day.

The merchandise included soap of various kinds, hair oil, stick pomade, cheap perfume, plain or lacquered wooden combs, pomade in jars, and switches of hair; and for young girls there were several kinds of brightly colored hair ornaments like ribbons, decorative combs, and pins. The drawers and fitted boxes were so ingeniously packed that when you spread them out, the prospective customer felt he was seeing a representative sampling of the entire stock of a cosmetics shop. "So go and give it a try," said the owner. "Don't give up as soon as someone says 'no thank you.' That's no way to do business. What makes a good salesman is charm and push. Our business is with women, so you've got to understand them. I know it won't be easy for you. But look how well those kids from the orphanages manage to sell things. Just tell yourself you're in the same game with them, and don't let them beat you." He picked up the chest. "Don't worry, it's not that heavy. Turn around and I'll show you how to put it on." Despite his assurance that it wasn't heavy, when I stood up with it strapped on my back my shoulders hurt a lot. And with the pain came a sudden sense of the hardship of it all, and I could have wept. I don't know what I said to the owner as I went out. I felt as if everybody on the street was staring at me, and I had no idea in what direction I should go. I just walked, and it didn't seem that it was my legs that moved me forward. In short, I was in a daze. Yet I was sufficiently myself to hurry through streets lined with houses where lots of people were about, and to let my legs take me to remote and deserted places.

The Incompetent Peddler

I suppose we were still in what you might call the age of itinerant vendors at that time. Not dominated yet by department stores with their delivery services or by strings of small retail shops, all kinds of consumer demands were met by peddlers selling clothing materials, fancy imported goods, medicines, hardware, stationery, even cooked beans. So though the idea of selling toiletries door-to-door might seem a little strange nowadays, it was a perfectly respectable occupation for an able-bodied man back then.

But, no matter how much I tried, I couldn't get used to it. I might summon enough courage to walk up to, even slide open, the front door of some silent house, but I just couldn't bring myself next to say out loud, "I'm selling toiletries. Is there anything you need?" It must have taken me at least three weeks to get it out more or less audibly. And if someone came out to the front hall and said bluntly, "Nothing at all," I would rush outside, my face flushed with embarrassment, and hurry blindly past the next half-dozen houses. Even when, occasionally, the woman of the house asked, "What sort of things have you got?" I would get so tongue-tied and take so long to bring out my wares that she'd say, "Next time, then," and send me away.

Even I came to realize that for a peddler I was oddly bashful. Boys too, in their own way, have a fear of indignity. It was an age of clear-cut notions of propriety; the boys of those days in particular were like innocent girls in their sentimental regard for honor and appearances, and I was constantly aware of how shabby I must appear in other people's eyes. (Or was I, perhaps, not so much typical of the times as simply oversensitive?)

Feeling as I did, I was careful to avoid residential neighborhoods close to the center of the city where I might encounter former school friends and people who had known my parents, and deliberately chose what were then remote parts of Yokohama such as Hiranuma, Hodogaya, and Kanagawa. There, I would tentatively announce myself over fences and through the doors of widely separated dwellings; and that was about the extent of my peddling activity.

My sales record of course was hardly likely ever to improve. It was a miracle if a day's sales amounted to two or three yen, which, after the shop had deducted eighty percent, still left me with about four times more than I'd made at Nanchusha. But it was only once in a blue moon that I took home as much as that; usually, after trudging through thawing mud the entire day, I ended up with gross sales of a mere thirty or forty sen.

I discovered, too, the inaccuracy of the owner's claim that since the business was directed at women, rainy days were in fact more profitable. Renting a peddler's waterproof cape from him for a few sen, I would wander about until dark in the driving rain, knee-deep in the mud of roads in newly developed neighborhoods, only to find that I sold no more than I did on fine days. There were times when, on returning to the shop, I was charged for mud-soiled articles and had to go home with nothing in my pocket. All in all, it was very hard work that paid very little. Night after night for months on end I went home feeling wretched at having earned such a paltry sum. It was always past seven and dark when I got back. What I looked forward to most was going to bed with a book or two and, my exhausted body at rest at last, reading until the oil lamp gave out with a mournful sigh. I remember that winter of my fourteenth year as a time of constant hunger and embarrassment. The New Year seems to have passed without leaving any mark. In a sense, I suppose, I went through those months in a kind of trance.

Writing about this makes me ask myself what I remember of the Russo-Japanese War. My fourteenth year was the thirty-ninth year of Meiji [1906], so the fighting ended in September and the treaty was signed in October of the preceding year. I read that in October a naval review took place outside Yokohama harbor to celebrate the victory. The entire city must have been decorated with flags, triumphal arches and the like, the night sky red with the reflected light of lantern processions, the citizenry in a state of wild excitement. Yet I can't recall such scenes with any certainty of detail or sense of reality. I do have a very vague recollection of long processions of jubilant people with small paper flags winding snakelike through the streets, but I can't find myself in any particular place or time either watching them as a spectator or mingling with them.

Earlier events in the war such as the Battle of Mukden and the fall of Port Arthur took place while I was working at the Kawamura Seal Shop. On the occasion of such victories I remember seeing through the glass of the front door young men with rakishly tied headbands and small jangling bells around their waists rushing past selling extras. That was the extent of my awareness of the war. As the fireworks burst in the sky over Yokohama, its harbor ablaze with lights and filled with cheering crowds, I myself, I imagine, was bent over my apprentice's desk thinking of home.

I do remember, however, that in the early phase of the war I used to walk alongside the neighborhood brass band whenever it followed the funeral procession of a local man killed in action, and mingle with the people seeing off someone who had been called up. Apart from that, though, I am not aware of having been affected at all by the wartime atmosphere or by occasions of national sorrow or rejoicing. In this, my experience of history was, perhaps, vastly different from that of many others of my generation. Either way, the lack of response to the war in my case was due to my own personal circumstances. The thirty-seventh and thirty-eighth years of Meiji

[1904–5], those years of critical importance to the nation, were a very special time for me personally; so preoccupied was I with my immediate situation that I had little capacity left to respond to anything else, be it the Rising Sun flags, or fireworks, or marching bands. So much happened in my life during those two years: the sudden impoverishment of our family, the disappearance of my half-brother, Father's imprisonment, my own job-hunting, the departure of my little sisters, Father's internal hemorrhages, and Mother's endless trial by poverty. No doubt as a boy I had only a limited sense of Japan's nationhood; more important, though, was that the day-to-day survival of my family inevitably concerned me more than the fate of my country. This is the only way I can explain why I have so little recollection of external events at the time.

Despite a feeling of guilt toward Mrs. Kojima, I reached a point where I wanted to give up peddling. And once that point was reached, the job became all the more difficult to bear. Though I came across occasional housewives who said kind, encouraging things, the brusque rejection was far more common. In time I learned not to mind so much being treated rudely by adults, but when children of my own age teased me, or when I thought groups of middle school students were making fun of me as they passed, I felt like throwing my peddler's chest into the nearest river.

But Father was still on his sickbed and Mother's life was as hard as ever. And then, to make matters worse, I returned home one night to find a strange little child of about two wailing in Mother's arms and being fed some kind of gruel with a spoon.

It seemed unable to sit up, and its arms and legs were terribly thin. A narrow head seemed to perch precariously on a pile of ribs, and the crying creased its face like a little old lady's. "Whose child is it?" I asked Mother, but neither she nor Father on his bed would answer.

Later that night Mother told me that the baby, a girl, was my half-brother Masahiro's. I have written earlier about his marriage to his mistress Oyae and how they lived with us in our house in Shimizu-cho; how Oyae went back to her family after barely six months; and how Masahiro later disappeared. The marriage was annulled, and it was our understanding that the relationship with Oyae and her family had thereby ended.

It transpired, however, that there was something very wrong with the child she gave birth to after returning to her family. Whether because it was prematurely born or because it suffered from some debilitating inherited disease, at the age of two it could still neither sit up nor walk, nor utter normal sounds.

Oyae's father, the unsavory stockjobber named Yamada, had shown what kind of man he was by the way he badgered Father, at great cost to Father materially and mentally, prior to Oyae's and Masahiro's marriage. He was hardly the type to want to bring up a retarded and deformed grandchild; besides, a child like that would harm Oyae's chances of remarriage. So he started threatening Father again, in writing and through intermediaries, claiming that since the baby was clearly Masahiro's, it was Father's responsibility to take care of it. Obviously, parents whom poverty had already forced to put their own children into service could hardly be expected to take in yet another child, especially one so helpless. It was Mother who repeatedly had to do the declining, as Father was in no condition to deal with Yamada. Then, on the day on which I saw it for the first time, a man had brought the baby to our house in a rickshaw, saying he'd been sent by Yamada. He had dumped it on the floor by the entrance and left immediately. All this Mother explained to me that evening.

Mother was in a dire predicament. She had her own baby to nurse, and saddled now with this feeble, retarded kid she would have no time to sew for extra money or work in the kitchen. If the little thing had been her real grandchild, she might have found it easier to accept the responsibility thrust on her. But this was the discarded child of her stepson and a woman who had stayed with us for only a short while.

All that night she was kept busy trying to pacify the squealing baby and keep it clean. Taking care of it was henceforth to prove a terrible ordeal for her. There was so much to do on top of her other chores—making special food that it could eat, constantly changing and washing its soiled clothes—that it seems incredible that she managed to get through the day. The trouble the child caused her beggars description, and a household already in despair was made even more desperate by its presence.

"Beggars description" may sound like an exaggeration. But to begin with, the baby had an abnormally large belly that stuck out like a balloon, and no matter how much or often it was fed it would cry for more. And as is often the case with retarded children, it had no control over its bowels, a problem that was itself enough to keep Mother frantically busy.

If taking care of such a child under conditions of extreme poverty had been the only thing she had to contend with, she would probably have said cheerfully that the work was worth it and that she could go on coping. But matters were made much worse by Father. Unable to bear the kid's persistent wailing, he would get up from his sickbed and angrily shake or slap it, so that the house was filled with its feeble cries.

Since the child could not be left lying about unconfined, it was put inside a straw rice-tub cover and spoon-fed as it lay there. It was rarely in a good mood and constantly cried for food. To Father this must have sounded like a voice relentlessly accusing him, day and night—like the devil himself come to taunt him, in the guise of this misshapen child, for his past misdeeds. He must have been tormented by anger too—anger for which there was no proper outlet—at his son Masahiro for deserting him, then leaving him this monstrous memento into the bargain. Mother and I could at least understand such anger.

Yet after he had smacked or yelled at it he would be overcome with self-loathing and in shame bury his face in his pillow until his breathing was steady. The ulcers that had been more or less under control since he last coughed up blood were rearoused by the baby's arrival; and, possibly due to nervous exhaustion, his face acquired, in addition to its sickly pallor, a look almost of madness.

Recalling all that happened around then, I can't help feeling that Mother was really a very remarkable person. I say this without overdoing it, and not simply because I'm her son. She took care of the baby with the same love and tenderness she gave us—so much so, in fact, that we were sometimes resentful. And when Father lost his temper with it she did her best to protect it.

To be honest, we children too were apt to blame the baby for our half-brother's irresponsibility, and to hate it for the trouble it caused. But in Mother there was no such meanness. No wonder the neighbors believed the thing was hers.

A year or two later, the child died of some illness, but we were still too poor to give it a proper funeral. I remember Mother going to the local fruit shop and bringing back an empty wooden box. She washed the little body with warm water, then put some makeup on its face, saying, "She's a little girl, you see." And as she put it in the box she murmured, as though to herself, "What an unfortunate child you were! Next time you're born, make sure you have nicer parents!"

With the makeshift coffin done up in a wrapping cloth, I got a rickshaw and went to Renkoji, our family temple, for the funeral service that Father had requested by letter. I was the only person there apart from the priests, and I still have a vague recollection of sitting there feeling shy and out of place. We couldn't pay anything toward the service, but because of our long association with the temple the chief priest and his assistants were understanding, and chanted the sutras without hurrying through them.

My half-brother remained ignorant of the entire episode involving us and his child right up to his death around the age of fifty. On his one visit to me, thirty years years after he left us, there was no mention of his former wife. Perhaps he had completely forgotten about her, because he didn't even ask what had become of her after he went away.

To pick up the main thread of my narrative again: I stopped being a peddler not long afterward, impelled perhaps by the events I shall now describe.

I had in fact been miserable in the job for quite a while, but the unexpected arrival of Masahiro's child made it all the more necessary to go on however much I hated it.

With this attitude, I could hardly expect to get better at the work. One evening, the owner of the business said to me, "Exactly where do you go to do your peddling?" "Hiranuma," I answered, "then Hodogaya, Aoki-cho, and thereabouts." "But that makes no sense! They're all new neighborhoods, mostly fields and hilly roads still. Look—" he said, "I hear that your family was well-off once. Why don't you try going to some of the houses you used to know?" I said nothing. "There must be families your father and mother knew well," he continued. "Start with those, and stick to the respectable residential areas. And don't let barking dogs and unfriendly maids scare you off. If you do, you'll never make a living out of it."

I suppose he was trying to be helpful, but he certainly treated me like a fool. After all, to go and throw myself on the goodwill of people we'd once known was hardly a new idea to me. But Mother had said I shouldn't, and, besides, I had a certain pride—not more than was good for me, but pride nevertheless. On the other hand, what the owner said did make me feel a little more comfortable with the idea and a little more hopeful, and I began to wonder if it wasn't foolish to avoid our old acquaintances. There was also a lurking desire, perhaps, to sell a great deal and impress my employer.

Some days later, then, I decided to change my territory and go to the Bluff, where I walked about, stopping at a number of houses belonging to people Father had known well. Hot with embarrassment, I would say to whoever appeared, "I'm selling things these days, and I was wondering . . ." At the Miura house—Mr. Miura worked for a foreign trading company—I managed to sell a cake of "Racing Horse" soap. Next I went to Mrs. Togashi's house, but she wasn't at home. After that—I can't remember if it was on the same day or the next—I ventured through the imposing gate of the Furukawas' newly built residence on Ushijimazaka.

In the early days of Father's employment at the Yokohama Pier Company Mr. Furukawa had a hut on the waterfront where he took on casual laborers as a subcontractor. Father came to trust and like him, and—he never did anything by half measures—finally made him sole supplier of labor to the company, entrusting him with loading and unloading goods on the pier, work on ships afloat, obtaining and loading coal, and so on. Thanks to this patronage Mr. Furukawa had made a lot of money, and now, having withdrawn completely from harbor work, lived in comfortable retirement in a splendid mansion on the Bluff with a sweeping view of all of Yokohama.

The front hall was so grand that it seemed inappropriate to spread my wares out there. First, a maid appeared from inside the house and looking dubiously at me went back. Then, after a while, Mrs. Furukawa appeared. She stared down at me from the raised floor of the hallway and said with affected incredulity, "Why, if it isn't Mr. Yoshikawa's son!" I don't remember what I replied, but it can't have been anything very coherent. It's one thing when strangers make a fool of you and quite another when someone you know does it. There was a long, hard moment as I tried to get a grip on myself, my ears ringing and my mouth very dry.

The squat figure of Mrs. Furukawa disappeared from the hall. I stood in the entrance looking blankly at my wares lying on the raised floor in front of me. They were a pitiful sight.

Mrs. Furukawa came out again, this time with her husband. His arms were tucked casually inside his loose-fitting padded kimono, and the crepe sash was tied in front with its ends left dangling. They were followed by a girl of about my age dressed in a long-sleeved kimono and an older, pretty woman. "Who is this boy?" they asked.

Then they looked at the drawers and boxes I'd laid out and said, "My, what a lot of things he's got," and started giggling.

Without giving my wares a glance Mr. Furukawa looked me up and down: "When did you start doing this?" In the old days he and his wife would come to our house on festival days bringing inordinately expensive gifts with them. He was a good drinker, and he and Father would drink and chat merrily for hours. Once he dropped in and, saying "Hide-chan, I've ordered a custom-made suit for you," took me with him in a rickshaw for a fitting with a tailor in Chinatown. Since that was the sort of man he was, I felt all the more self-conscious in his presence now. And it was painful to be stared at by the pretty creatures—were they his daughters?—standing beside him. I wished I had never come.

His complexion was the same grayish color as before, and his lips and the skin around his eyes were dark. He was also fat, in a very soft sort of way. Like a man who had got hold of a dog just to tease it, he needled me with questions like, "Is it profitable work?" and "What do you make in a day?" Yet he showed no interest in buying anything from me.

Then he started talking about Father. "He's only paying for his past sins, you know," he said. "His problem was that he had too high an opinion of himself. Of course, while the going was good he could do anything he liked, so at least he's got that to look back on, but he must know he has only himself to blame for the way he is now. And look at what he's done to you—I'd be surprised if he can get to sleep at night."

If he had stopped there, I might have been able to accept it more or less as a kind of sermon. But he went much further. Sneering with contempt, he made one insulting remark after another about Father, until even Mrs. Furukawa, seeing my tears, tugged at her husband's sleeve and said, "That's enough, now."

Half blindly, I began putting my things away in the chest. Somehow, I don't remember how, I managed to hoist it on my back as they looked on. But I do remember his wife in some agitation putting something wrapped in a piece of paper in my hand. Presumably it was money. I don't know where or when, but I must have thrown it away.

Without a backward glance, I ran down the stone steps outside the gate and kept going. When at last my tears had dried up and I looked around me, I found that I was in some back street and the lights had come on.

Boy Thief

That was my last day as a peddler. I was tired of rich acquaintances' front gates. And I detested the thought of ever again having to plead for favors across a stranger's fence.

Obviously, it was my experience at the Furukawa house that made me decide to quit, but I never mentioned it to my parents, so they probably found my decision, and the sudden change in my mood and behavior, hard to understand. Like any boy whose father has been too strict, I was unable to speak openly about my feelings, but I became sullen and quiet. Father was irritated by my inactivity and unfriendliness and became persuaded, I think, that I was going to the dogs.

After about a week I received a note from the wholesale supply shop saying that I was to come and collect my deposit money. When I went, I was given six yen instead of the ten I had put down. The explanation was that I was being charged for damage to the chest, use of the premises, rain gear, etc. I thought it very unfair, but there was nothing I could do about it. I suppose adult peddlers under the same circumstances would have been given the same treatment and would have had no recourse either. I took the six yen home, then went to Mrs. Kojima's with Mother to return it.

When Mother apologized for not returning the whole sum and

said that we would pay back the rest in due course, Mrs. Kojima replied in her direct and simple way, "It's perfectly all right. We all need help at one time or another." Then she turned to me and said, "But what do you think of doing now, Hide-san?"

The reply I gave, in all seriousness, was self-indulgent and impracticable: "I'm ready to do anything if I can go to middle school." Upset by what I said, Mother looked away. But Mrs. Kojima looked me straight in the eyes and said sympathetically: "I understand very well how you feel, indeed I do. But think, Hide-san—who's going to help your mother if you don't have a steady job? Have you considered going to night school? That way you could work during the day and go to classes at night. I'll see if something of the sort can be arranged."

I had become touchy and suspicious with most people, but with her I was much more trusting, and again I disgraced myself by shedding tears of gratitude.

It seems that Mrs. Kojima later talked about me to her husband, hoping that he would know of some suitable job or night school. But his world was that of the National Revenue Service, and he was apparently of little help. Mother, moreover, not wanting to impose any further, kept away from them. Or perhaps it was that after I quit my job, she was concerned even more exclusively with the immediate problems of day-to-day survival. Father remained on his sickbed, his bullying ways showing no signs of abating; and taking care of Masahiro's child was appallingly hard work. I wonder how Mother managed to get by, even at our minimal level. There were nights when we couldn't afford oil for the lamp, and for dinner made do with sweet potato porridge. Immature as I was, I felt the sharp reality of extreme poverty.

Father was so fond of tobacco that when he ran out he'd go almost crazy and start crying out from his bed: "My tobacco's all gone! Don't tell me there isn't enough money for just a little smoke!" The look of helplessness on Mother's face when this happened was almost more than I could bear.

Sometimes she had to pawn her one and only kimono and go about the house wrapped in the shop curtain that had once hung outside Midori-ya. That meant of course that she couldn't step outside the house all day. "You know," she once said to me, momentarily forgetting herself, "I get frightened when dawn comes and I have to face another day."

Frustrated at being bedridden, Father constantly took it out on me. Lacking the go, or the ability, to find a job, I spent much of the time reading. He found this unforgivable, and often complained about my fecklessness. When he was really angry he would shout: "You good-for-nothing!"

I began to leave the house with no particular aim in mind and stay out till late at night. For pocket money, I took books and sold them at a secondhand bookshop. I would spend hours in a cheap seat at one of the theaters, then go home and pretend I had spent all the time looking for a job. When I had no money to go to a theater I would sit on a bench in Yokohama Park eating salted beans or something. There were lots of young layabouts of roughly my own age, as well as tramps, in the park. I felt rather comfortable there; the boys would come and speak to me, sometimes inviting me to join them in some venture or other. Being a coward, I used to make excuses if what they had in mind sounded risky, and follow them if it was only mildly unlawful. The escapades I took part in usually involved lifting food from shops in the back streets of Chinatown, from stalls in the grounds of the Yakushi shrine in Moto-machi on festival days, or from warehouses for sugar-carrying carts. We would divide up the spoils in the park and eat our share behind the trees.

Periodically, the police raided our hangout in the park, and for days after each raid we were careful not to be seen there. At such times I wandered about aimlessly in Isezaki-cho with not a penny in my pocket, for I had no more books to sell. More than once I fetched my eight-year-old sister Kae out of the bean soup place where she worked, and took away what little money the poor girl had saved from tips, telling her Mother was in a fix. Then I squandered it on snacks and cheap theater tickets.

In Knut Hamsun's *Hunger*, which I read around that time, there is a scene where the protagonist finds a bone with a bit of rotting meat on it lying on the ground; he picks it up and gnaws at it, then vomits. Like that character, I must have gone about with the gleam of hunger in my eyes.

Unable to stand being in the house, I would go out and wander. One night I slept on a bench, torn between a vision of Father shouting "You good-for-nothing!" which made me want to stay where I was, and the thought of Mother, which made me badly want to go home and be near her.

Then, one day, I was taken by some of my fellow loiterers in the park to where they were building No. 2 Pier. And at last I started working again.

In the middle of a stretch of reclaimed land stood the temporary office of a construction company. There we gathered every morning, and were assigned various kinds of work by the boss. Besides the male laborers, there were a lot of women wearing cotton gloves and gaiters—the *Yoitomake* women [so named after the work song they sang], whose singing, as they began pounding the great expanse of earth that was to be the foundation of the pier, signaled the start of our working day. We boys were made to go into town on errands, distribute lunches, and in the remaining time carry logs. At the end of the day we were given thirty sen.

I worked there for two or three months, from spring until summer.

Whenever we or Young Toshi the office boy went past, the *Yoitomake* women would break into a bawdy song, then with great amusement watch us hurry away. The lyrics—"Still a virgin, sonny?" or "Come over tonight, I'll give you a treat"—were sung to primitive tunes reminiscent of the Bon Festival dancing songs, with a touch of "Yoitomake" added, and some of the improvised words the woman who led the chorus came up with were extraordinarily crude. Though I blushed and ran away, I secretly rather enjoyed being the butt of their jokes, for among the women were quite a few who were young and pretty, wearing straw hats and bandannas.

Young Toshi, who had once been awarded a certificate of commendation by the police for "outstanding filial piety," was much admired not only by the boss but by everyone else on the site. Aware of his own distinction, he once took me aside to give me a detailed account of his life and show me a photograph of himself taken at the award ceremony. At a later date, he again took me aside and with a "Here, have a look at this," proudly produced a pornographic woodblock print. Until then I'd looked up to him as someone far superior to me; but that made me relax with him, and I grew to like him in a way.

Unfortunately, I was only a temporary employee, and it wasn't long before I was told abruptly, "There won't be any more work for you to do, so you needn't come tomorrow." What saddened me was not so much losing the job as not being able to hear the *Yoitomake* women singing any more.

It was in August or September that the Kojimas, who had been keeping me in mind for likely jobs, informed Mother of an opening for an office boy in the Revenue Office.

First, though, there is something else I feel I should write about.

Before starting in my new job, I must have hung about for a month or two, doing little apart from looking for work in a desultory way. The incident I am about to describe took place around the time of the Bon Festival [August 15], so it would be fairly safe to say that it happened during that idle period.

One evening, I saw Mother sitting dejectedly on the kitchen floor with the mosquitoes buzzing all around her. She had a lost, faraway look in her eyes, and I knew immediately what was the matter: we had nothing to eat that night. "Nothing to eat" in our case meant literally that—not even an eggplant or cabbage leaf left in the pickle tub. Perhaps I made some pointless remark in an attempt to comfort her before leaving the house, or perhaps I walked out quickly without saying a word; either way, soon afterward I found myself standing in the dark above the terraced slope of a potato field not far from where we lived. There was a pond at the bottom, and the rows of potatoes went to the very edge of it. The stars above me were like the eyes of the gods, or of other human beings, watching me. The turmoil inside me was frightening: I was about to commit a crime in full knowledge of how wrong it was.

Because of the way I felt, my memory of the incident has remained extremely clear. On top of the thinly wooded hill on the other side of the pond stood the main building of the Kanagawa Prefectural Middle School. This was the school I had wanted to go to. The white wall of the building so clearly visible in the distance was oddly unnerving. I had an eerie feeling that my former school friends were peering at me through its windows. A moment later, nevertheless, I was down among the potato leaves madly digging in the warm black soil with my fingernails. Potato after potato tumbled out of the hole as I dug deeper and deeper. The soil got warmer further down, a living, almost human warmth. I had soon collected enough potatoes to fill my wrapping cloth. Hugging the bundle I ran up the field, out of the night dew that covered it. I ran and ran, apologizing as I went—to whom, I didn't know—and so filled with fear that I couldn't even find the shortest way home.

That night, sitting around the table, we ate the potatoes boiled in salted water and steaming hot. Father of course had no idea what I had done. As for Mother, I wonder, considering that I don't remember her being angry with me, whether she wasn't—against all that she believed—giving me her tacit approval. If so, then we as a family were getting very near the danger level.

That summer I did the same thing two or three times. I must, there's no denying it, have had a streak of thievery in me. In my elementary school days I'd stolen coins from Mother and from the Midori-ya cash box. Nor is that all: I once stole a book from a secondhand shop on Nogezaka. I was browsing in the front part of the place as was my habit, when suddenly I was overcome with a desire for one of the books. I looked around and saw that the owner wasn't there; probably he'd gone into a back room to have his breakfast. I dashed out of the shop with the book and started running up the street. But as I ran I thought I sensed the owner's angry face close behind me. To my left was the high stone wall buttressing the side of Iseyama. In fear and remorse I threw the book into the stream that flowed along the bottom of the wall, and went on running. Some days later when it got dark I went back to the spot for a furtive look, and found the thing still lying there in the clear water. For several months afterward I kept away from Nogezaka in broad daylight.

To some extent, I suppose, it depends on the individual's circumstances, but I suspect that all boys have a touch of the thief in them.

The stealing I did with my fellow delinquents from the park may sound like plain dishonesty, but I think it was done more for the fun of it than for material gain. It was the sport of little daredevils motivated by a combination of thrill-seeking and the group psychology. Left unchecked, of course, we might in time have become capable of real evil; but even conventional children aren't entirely free from similar inclinations. The tendency to steal exists side by side with the desire to play, and the two together lead to actual acts of pilfering. Nor is the tendency necessarily absent in older and wiser people.

I have no intention, however, of trying to justify my own past. The unpleasant memory will stay with me for the rest of my life—a crack in my morality that I am afraid to examine too closely. The things I did in the potato field and the secondhand bookshop are like old wounds that have never quite healed.

What is much more frightening, though, is that Mother, knowing how I had got the potatoes, did not protest.

It was at this critical point in our lives, then, that Mr. and Mrs.

Kojima put me up for the job in the Revenue Office. In a sense, the gods had intervened on our behalf. I was immediately given a test, quickly followed by an imposing notice of appointment. The salary was to be seven yen a month.

The Revenue Office was on the main street of Tobe by the turning into Iwakame-Yokocho. Sharing the same grounds with this Western-style brick building was the Yokohama branch of the government Tobacco Monopoly, a shoddy structure that was half factory.

The factory lay across the lawn on one side of the path as you went in through the main gate. Through the row of windows you could see women workers in their white uniforms. They had the same look of purity as nurses, and we office boys basked in the privilege of their attention as we went past on errands. We soon came to exchange special looks and smiles with some of them, and watched out for them leaving at the end of the day carrying their empty lunch boxes. It was somehow sobering, however, to see that while in their uniforms they had an air of distinction, in their not very clean muslin kimonos with obis tied in puffed bows they looked much like any daughters of poor parents.

I and another office boy by the name of Honma, my senior, occupied shabby chairs in a corner of a downstairs room assigned to subordinate officials. Honma, who knew half the women in the tobacco factory by name, told me all about going with one of them to the beach at Honmoku one Sunday. I listened with envy, thinking that in time I, too, might be so fortunate. "One of these days I'll introduce you to someone you fancy," he said, and I nodded solemnly, almost breathless with anticipation.

The clock on the wall facing us gave a weary tick-tock, tick-tock, and the sounds of pens scratching, tobacco being knocked out of pipes, throats being cleared, and fingers clicking abacuses made the silence hanging over us seem even heavier. The clerks sat with humped backs like sleeping cats, some of them wearing kimonos and hakamas, others grubby suits and stiff collars. (That was the period when the word *haikara*, meaning "stylish," "in fashion," from the English "high collar," was in vogue.) From time to time, one of them would call out "Boy!" in a special tone of voice and give one of us some papers to deliver to another room in the building. On Wednesdays, when an administrative officer who had been put in charge of the Yokohama branch came down from headquarters in Tokyo, I often had occasion to go to his office.

He was an elegant young man with gold-rimmed spectacles who sat at a grand desk in a large room. Before being sent to him for the first time, I was given lessons in the proper etiquette for the occasion by our gentle, aging supervisor. The tray with the Kutani-ware teacup on it was to be held at eye level with the head bowed, and there were special ways of opening the door, approaching the desk, and withdrawing with a final bow. The instructions were extremely thorough. This must be a man of great importance, I thought, and my hands holding the tray would shake as I approached his desk.

Ending at five, the work also began later in the morning than any other I had done, and there was time for reading; not to mention the pleasure of exchanging glances with the angels in white. I walked to work with an unprecedented lightness of heart.

Sometime in the autumn, Mrs. Kojima, who had been urging me to go to night school and bringing me various school prospectuses, suddenly stopped coming to our house. Mother said nothing, but I was sure something had happened. For one thing, Father in his more emotional moments started muttering ominously: "I don't like women who don't behave like women—doing us a small favor or two doesn't give her the right to poke her nose into our affairs— what's all this talk about Hide's schooling and how to arrange it, anyway?—does she think I haven't thought about it?—natter, natter, natter until you're so fed up you give in." Had he and Mrs. Kojima got into an argument over me? If that was the case, I thought, I would give up the idea of going to night school.

So I questioned Mother directly and she told me the full story. It wasn't just a disagreement about my schooling. Tempted by Mrs. Kojima's generous nature, Father had asked her for money, and in her typical friendly way she had said she would try to find it. But when she went home and talked to her husband about it, he not only refused to let her do anything, but was so upset that he insisted she stop associating with us. "She was put in an awful position," Mother commented sadly. "I feel sorry for her. I don't want to say anything against your father, but really . . . it wasn't as though the Kojimas hadn't done enough for us already. . . ."

Shortly after that Mr. Kojima was transferred to a neighboring prefecture. We received no notice from them of their new address. "We didn't do anything to repay them for all their kindness," was Mother's reaction, but Father wasn't the sort even to hint at any such feelings about them. Inwardly he might have felt some remorse, but all he showed from his sickbed was contempt. "What did they do for us anyway?" he once said. "All I know is, they made damn sure he got a job that paid only seven yen!" "All right, then," I said, "I'll quit." "Quit?" he demanded, his temper rising visibly. "And where are you going to find another job?" In a rebellious mood, I searched for the most hurtful way of striking back at him, of really upsetting him. "Why should that matter?" I sneered. "What you want is for me to quit the job I've got now, right? After all, what good is a lousy seven yen? That's right, isn't it, Father?" "You little bastard!" he shouted. "How dare you talk to me like that!"

His face went dark red, and before he could shout at me again he succumbed to a violent fit of coughing. By now he was suffering from asthma with complications, in addition to ulcers, and whenever he started coughing like that Mother would sit by him and rub his back for hours to ease the pain. So if she heard me answering Father back, she would rush in from wherever she happened to be and firmly tell me off. I never minded that, nor having to defer to her. But I couldn't bring myself to apologize to Father, even to offer a token apology, despite all his angry demands.

Yet there were other times when for Mother's sake I had to bow to him and say I was sorry, whereupon I would burst out crying and not be able to stop. These fits of weeping frightened me, for they reminded me of Mother's two brothers who went mad. More than once, in fact, I ran headlong out of the house, unable to control myself, and stayed away all night, leaving Mother to worry about where I had gone. In time, I lost my boyish lightheartedness and became more and more prone to hiding in corners till I had cried myself out. Father took umbrage with increasing frequency, and kept calling me a good-for-nothing or a freak. The older I became, the more sullenly I behaved toward him, until I did nothing but show hostility with full intent to cause him pain.

It was December, close to the end of the year. One day Mother, presumably at the end of her tether, wrote a long letter and putting it in an envelope said to me, "Hide-chan, can you go to Tokyo by yourself on an errand for me?"

Shotoen was being opened up as a public garden in Shibuya, and Mother's younger brother Yamagami Saburo was working there as chief civil engineer. I was to go to see him, without telling Father. So with just enough money for the train fare I went to Tokyo and found Uncle Saburo in his office in Shotoen.

He had once stayed with us for a long time, so I remembered his face well. He'd had the nickname of Nonkiya-san [Happy-go-lucky] in those days. A slightly plump, pleasant-looking man, he always wore a big smile on his face. Later, as I have mentioned, he had a nervous breakdown and required professional care for quite a while. On recovering he was given the job at Shotoen by a family with whom he'd had some prior association.

Having read Mother's letter he said, "Really, she can't expect to go on like this forever!" He put a one-yen note in an envelope and handing it to me left for the work site. There was nothing for me to do but go home. The trouble was, Mother had given me just enough money for my single fare, so if I were to return by train again, I would have to open the envelope and break into the one yen. This I couldn't bring myself to do; I wanted to be able to give Mother the envelope with the money in it intact. So I walked back to Yokohama [a distance of about twenty miles], constantly stopping to ask the way. It was in the early hours of the morning, close to daybreak, when I got home, my legs stiff and aching and my stomach hollow with hunger.

The one yen of course disappeared like a drop of water on a hot stone. At the end of the year my two little sisters Kae and Kino came home very briefly, bringing their meager savings to give to Mother. If Uncle Saburo had been "happy-go-lucky," then Kino, the eldest girl, was another, died-in-the-wool example of the same quality. Typically impervious to the poverty all around her in her own home, she talked with high-pitched gaiety about being taken to the theater, her master's luxurious style of living, and so on, before departing apparently without a care in her head. Kae by nature was the very opposite. Every time she came to visit, she asked if she could stay; if they let her, she wouldn't mind selling soybeans on the streets, she said. Father liked Kino the better.

I had decided by then that I really wanted to leave home.

I went to various employment agencies, and was finally told that there was an opening for an apprentice boy in a shop called Tsuzuki's in Hinode-cho. This was one day close to the year's end. I asked through the agency if I could be given an advance on my wages, and at an interview in the shop on New Year's Eve both my employment and the advance were confirmed. I went home that night armed with the money and some pickled vegetables that the old lady at the agency had given me. I presented Mother with these and told her that I was to start my new job as a live-in apprentice on January 5. Instead of showing pleasure at the sight of the money, she looked at me forlornly and said, "So you'll be going away." I could see the tears welling in her eyes. She was pregnant again, and the thought of not having me there must have been hard to bear.

My decision to leave had been prompted partly out of resentment and vindictiveness toward Father, and now, seeing Mother's unexpected reaction to my good tidings, I regretted it immediately. She was, of course, pleased that I had thought to get the advance for her sake; possibly she really wanted to show pleasure but couldn't suppress the sorrow that came with it. I took my younger brother with me to the year-end market on the main street of Tobe, and went around the various stalls buying things such as a large slab of rice cake and New Year decorations.

A Budding Poet

Tsuzuki's dealt in foodstuffs, foreign liquors, and sundry goods. It was one of the more prominent shops in Hinode-cho, but it wasn't much occupied with the retail business it got there, its main activity being to lay in stock for sending to its branch in Yokosuka. The signboard outside said "By Appointment Suppliers of Sundry Goods to the Navy." The shop also served as Mr. and Mrs. Tsuzuki's home.

On my first day as an apprentice I was given a new first name. "We'll call you Hidekichi,"[16] the master said to me, and from then on I was Hidekichi to him and his wife, and Hide-don to those who worked in the shop or the living quarters.

The master, Mr. Tsuzuki, was short but carried himself like the rich merchant that he was, and apart from a regrettable weakness for gold—gold teeth, gold chains, gold-rimmed spectacles—was a highly presentable man of about forty. He always had an expensive cigar in his mouth. With his pretty, elaborately coiffured young Goshin-san (an abbreviation of Goshinzo-san, the polite way of addressing a merchant's wife) he spent alternate weeks in Yokohama and Yokosuka.

I learned soon enough from my fellow employees that Goshin-

16. The name Hidetsugu was a little too fancy for an apprentice. Hidekichi has a more plebeian ring to it, and was therefore more appropriate.

san had been a star courtesan in an establishment called Shinpuro in the pleasure district of Magane-cho. However, there was absolutely nothing in her appearance or manner to suggest such a past. A fine figure of a woman, she also seemed to be educated, and always maintained an air of propriety. When she and her husband were together, it was she who looked the more distinguished. We employees would often stand outside the shop to greet or see off the handsome couple as they came and went in their two rickshaws; at times like these she made such a striking impression that passersby would stop and stare. It was also true, however, that we employees, including the household servants, were more apt to tremble in her presence than in the master's. We understood implicitly that to incur her displeasure was fatal. Even a novice like me quickly learned to be worldly-wise where she was concerned, and to hear her call "Hidekichi!" was to be immediately on the alert.

Having already worked once as a live-in apprentice, in the Kawamura Seal Shop, I was not quite so naive this time, and however much I was harassed by the aging senior clerk, who lived out, or the young live-in shop assistants, or those fellow apprentices who were senior to me, I did their bidding cheerfully enough. Yet all the while I kept thinking of home, wretched place though it was. Perhaps it was my nature—perhaps I was too attached to Mother—but I couldn't stop wondering how they were managing since I left.

Then one evening, less than a month after I started working in the shop, I saw my eight-year-old brother Sosuke wandering up and down outside. With a sudden foreboding, I rushed out and asked, "Why are you here? Did something happen at home?" Tearfully, he explained. The gist of his story was that they hadn't eaten anything for two days. I was wondering in despair what I could do when I remembered that I had a five-sen piece on me. One of my nightly chores at that time was to go to the room of the master's old mother, around nine or ten o'clock, to give her a massage. I'd had some practice massaging Father's legs at home, thanks to which I was, in her judgment, "the best of the lot." After a few sessions she gave me the five sen as a present. This, then, I gave to Sosuke. But no matter how cheap things were in those days, it seemed unlikely that any family could have warded off starvation with a five-sen coin.

That night at dinner I could hardly swallow my food, saddened by the thought that I was the only one in the family to eat a proper meal. Later, I went up to Hirai-san, the senior clerk, as he was preparing to go home. "Could I have just this evening off?" I asked. "My mother has been taken ill suddenly." Hirai-san frowned and said, "As you know, the master isn't here." In the end, though, he went away to consult the old lady, and it was decided I could go. "Mind, you're to be back by eleven o'clock," he said. "Eleven o'clock, right?"

Taking advantage of Hirai-san's generous mood, I went and helped myself to two tins of beef from the shelves in the shop. "I'll pay for these out of my wages," I told him. And almost at a run I made for home.

On the way, I did something eccentric that later seemed rather funny to Mother and me. Believing that my family was on the verge of death from starvation, I stopped at a soba shop and asked for several bowls of hot noodles to be delivered to the house. To my boyish way of thinking—and I thought very hard about it—the crucial thing was to get them something they could eat immediately.

As it turned out, the soba may well have saved my sick father and my small siblings. When I got home, even Mother was lying on the floor, too weak to get up. They hadn't had a bite to eat for two days, she said. The shutters had been left closed all day, and the room looked like a little graveyard.

In those days when welfare systems were unknown, it was quite possible for a whole family to starve to death without their neighbors realizing. It is also true that my parents were the kind of people who, finding themselves in that dire condition, were incapable of devising any way to save themselves. They were definitely on their last legs when, soon after me, the cheery delivery man arrived with his bowls of hot soba, which they promptly gobbled down.

We then opened one can of sliced beef—diluting the leftover juice in it with hot water and drinking that, too—and I returned to the shop feeling that the latest crisis, at least, had been averted. Which was all very well, but Mother later told me with amusement that a man from the soba shop came to their front door several days running demanding payment for the large quantities of noodles I'd ordered so impulsively. It was very embarrassing, she said. I'd been so frantic at the time that I never stopped to think how we'd pay for it all.

About a month and a half after that I was transferred to the Yokosuka branch of Tsuzuki's.

As I wouldn't be seeing my family again for some time, the master gave me a half-day off to visit them. This visit is more clearly etched in my memory than the one I have just described, the reason being that when I got home I found to my surprise that I had one more younger brother. Mother was lying in confinement with the newborn baby beside her. This was Susumu, my parents' third son.

I sat by her pillow and gazed at the new arrival. He seemed awfully small and wizened. His face was bright red, with sparse hair framing it like the beard on an ear of corn.

When I told Mother about my transfer she didn't seem too downcast; maybe she didn't want me to feel bad about going, or maybe family circumstances had improved for some reason. Father, too, was in a good mood that day, so I left for Yokosuka with a light heart.

The Yokosuka branch of the shop was located on a main street in the Wakamatsu-cho area not far from the bottom of the hill. Directly opposite it was a restaurant with a light blue shop curtain above the entrance saying "Wakamatsu Tempura." A young woman, dressed like a waiting girl in a kabuki play with a long wadded ribbon in her hair and a sash of spotted cloth, was often to be seen standing under the curtain, flirting with naval officers and other customers.

Non-commissioned officers, paymasters, and the like were always coming into our shop to place orders or discuss business. Sometimes they would stay on for a beer and to be regaled with jokes by a waggish young assistant named Wahei-don. The shop here was livelier than the main establishment, and since the older men used to go out in search of entertainment after the place was closed, I had some free time in the evenings.

I suspect that it was now that I began to recover my boyish cheerfulness. Now that I was so far from home, I more or less stopped pining for it. And the people around me—the congenial, interesting old caretaker, the maid, the young shop assistants and the customers, all of whom were from the navy—left me little time for adolescent melancholy. I often accompanied Ito-san—the senior clerk, nicknamed the Moustache—and Wahei-don when they went out to warships moored offshore to take orders. We would be taken to the ship on a launch, and there I would be given something to eat in the canteen, or would sit and listen to all the frivolous talk. If I was with Wahei-don, the NCO placing the orders might say, "Milady from Shinpuro hasn't been coming to the Yokosuka shop lately, has she?" And Wahei-don would tell him, with appropriate jokes thrown in, about the long-standing romance between her and the master and about what went on privately between them in the dark, this with such vividness that one could imagine him actually peeping into their room. For this reason Wahei-don was better received in the canteens than Ito-san the Moustache.

One day, I got a wonderful surprise. A rather large wooden box was delivered to me, and on opening it I found it packed with hundreds of old haiku magazines. The sender, named on the box, was the Kinko-do Secondhand Bookshop on Noge-dori in Yokohama.

A letter from Mother arrived at the same time. "A Mr. Okuda whom Father once helped," she wrote, "recently learned about the reverses he had suffered, and has been extremely kind to us. He also repaid Father an old loan that we had forgotten about, which has suddenly made things much easier for us. Perhaps because of this sudden good fortune, Father is much better and is up and about. So there is no need for you to worry about us any more." The magazines, she explained, had been bought by Father himself when he went out for a walk, and he had asked Kinko-do to pack and send them.

I took some of them with me to bed that night. I was so happy and excited that I had trouble getting to sleep. The box, as I remember, contained back issues of all or nearly all the leading haiku magazines—*Hototogisu*, *Uzue*, *Shusei*, and *Nihon Haidan*—so Father hadn't forgotten my interest in this sort of thing. It made me feel that perhaps it was the stress of illness and poverty that had made him call me a "good-for-nothing" so often; that since my departure he might be thinking of his far-off son with love. The thought touched me deeply, and on nights when I'd taken copies of *Hototogisu* to bed and read until I could stay awake no longer, the dreams that followed were those of a calm and comforted boy.

Wahei-don was a popular young man, but his clowning around sometimes got out of hand. One night after the store was shut up the assistants got very drunk, the master and his wife being away. I heard Wahei-don calling me, so I went into the room where they all were, only to be pushed down on a futon and rolled up in it. They next got hold of Oyumi-san the maid and, unrolling the futon, forced her to lie beside me, then rolled it up tight again. I heard Wahei-don shouting, "Come on, give me a hand!" and felt the rolled futon being tied in the middle with a kimono sash or something.

Both Oyumi-san and I resisted, of course, but we were no match for them, and were tied together so firmly that Oyumi-san had to put her arms around me. Not knowing where to put mine I lay rigid with eyes closed, my face hot with embarrassment.

Having treated his drinking companions to this amusing spectacle, he proceeded to entertain them further, as he drank, with a string of snide remarks directed at Oyumi-san, which he accompanied with maniacal cackles. Apparently he resented her friendliness toward me, Hide-don, and many of his comments were frankly obscene. When Ito-san finally came and freed us, the girl was crying. I myself ran away and hid in a dark corner of the shop.

Another incident involving Wahei-don occurred sometime in late spring. The caretaker who normally did such tasks being in bed with a cold, Wahei-don and I were given the job of delivering some white saké to a retail shop in Uraga which supplied provisions to the shipyard there. We loaded a cart with cases each containing four dozen bottles and, with Wahei-don pulling and myself pushing, proceeded along the Uraga Highway. As we started the climb toward the pass, he decided we should stop for a rest, so we sat down at the side of the road, and for a while nothing out of the ordinary happened. But then he turned to me and said, "Look here—no tale-telling when we get back to the shop, you understand? I'll say it got broken on the way." With this warning he got up and pried open one of the cases. He finished one bottle in no time at all, then gulped down most of a second, and let me have what was left.

My own head was soon spinning, which was bad enough, but Wahei-don by then was thoroughly plastered. On our way down on the other side of the pass, he almost fell over a number of times, and kept crashing the cart against the banks that rose sheer on either side. Many bottles got broken in the process, leaving a trail of spilled saké behind us. All I could do was follow the cart, wondering what was going to happen. I never felt more helpless, but I never enjoyed myself more, either.

The hardest job I had to do while working in Yokosuka was delivering things like beer and cider to the warships. Whether the seamen gave you a hand or not depended on the ship; if they didn't, the senior clerk and I would have to climb up the long rope ladder carrying whatever we were delivering. I was often obliged to carry a case containing four dozen bottles of Battleship Cider. Poising the case on my shoulder with one hand, I would hold on to the ladder with the other as I slowly pulled myself up rung by rung. I have never forgotten the time I lost my balance as I was climbing up the side of the battleship *Niitaka* and fell headlong into the sea, still clutching the case. When I regained consciousness I was in the ship's canteen, surrounded by laughing sailors who had rescued me.

After that they always teased me when I went on board. They were kind to me, though, and the *Niitaka* became my favorite ship. I looked forward to visiting its canteen, since it was well stocked with all kinds of candy, of which I was regularly given some.

Once, I was sent to the ship alone on some sort of errand, and found them getting ready to sail. My business finished, I was walking about on the deserted middle deck when I began to imagine myself hiding in the bilge or coal bunker and sailing off to some foreign land. The temptation to act out my fantasy had just become irresistible when I was discovered and hauled up to the upper deck. They were about to pull up the rope ladder, and as they led me to it they gave me a thorough dressing down.

Another notable event occurred that autumn. The local newspaper had invited entries for a haiku contest in celebration of some anniversary or other, and I had surreptitiously submitted one. It won, and I was given a modest cash prize. No one in the shop knew about any of this.

From then on I continued to send them the odd haiku or two, till one day a professional haiku man who did the judging came to the shop with a man from the newspaper. Since the journalist's card had the name of the paper on it, one of our assistants took it straight to the master and his wife, who were down from Yokohama for their weekly stay. When I learned that in fact it was me the visitors had come to see, I almost had a fit. That night, Goshin-san called me in and in her haughtiest manner said, "Please remember that this is a *shop*." From that time on, whenever the master and his wife were there I was careful not to go to bed with my haiku magazines. And I stopped sending poems to the newspaper altogether. The vague feeling of having been taught a lesson by this still lingers with me. I imagine that my fellow employees didn't look particularly kindly on my furtive haiku writing, either.

One day that winter I had a chance encounter with Mrs. Kojima on a street in Yokosuka. There had been some snow, and I fancy sleet was falling. It was a cold day, at any rate, and muddy. I was pulling a cart loaded with empty barrels—probably of the kind used on warships for keeping pickles in—on my way to the harbor. The barrels were quite light, but there were an awful lot of them piled high on the cart.

The encounter took place on the busiest street in Yokosuka. Mrs. Kojima saw me before I saw her. She must have just come out of a shop or somewhere, but all I remember—and I remember it very clearly—is that she was suddenly beside me with her hand on the shaft, saying, "Surely it's Hide-san?" We must have stood and talked for a while, as I seem to remember being embarrassed by the curiosity of the passersby. I know both of us were crying. Just before saying goodbye, she realized she'd forgotten to give me her address, but I didn't take it in. In all likelihood I was too concerned about people staring at us and too confused by my own emotions to know exactly what I was doing. I made no attempt later on to find out where she lived.

She was not the only acquaintance in Yokosuka whom I didn't seek out. There must have been quite a few friends and distant relations connected with the Yokosuka shipyard—people like Baron Kondo and Vice Admiral Yamanouchi whom Mother knew through her earlier association with Kondo Makoto's academy—but she made no reference to them whatsoever in her letters. It was simply not in her nature to make use of old connections or ask for help from relatives, the one exception being the time she had sent me to her younger brother, Yamagami Saburo. So, quite naturally, the idea of "old connections" never occurred to me from the start, and I thought of our desperate struggle to row our leaking boat ashore as something we had to do alone.

Even so, there are times when one is given generous assistance by the most unlikely people. It would seem that the Mr. Okuda whom Mother had mentioned in her letter continued trying to instill hope in Father, and even provided him with some capital to set himself up again. "Your father now goes to work every day," Mother told me in one of her letters. But I later learned that this involved, not real work, but paying a daily visit to Naka-dori to dabble in the raw silk market. However, this is to anticipate.

Yokohama Scenes

Perhaps at the request of my parents, I was given permission to leave my job in Yokosuka and go home. They in the meantime had moved to Onoe-cho 2-chome in the Kannai section of Yokohama, and now lived in a fair-sized shop facing the main street. The signboard on the roof said in large characters "Nisshin-do" and, in smaller characters at the side, "Agents for Newspaper Advertisements Throughout Japan."

Mr. Okuda had apparently handed over the running of Nisshin-do to Father, together with the goodwill and liabilities that went with it. I remembered the Okudas from our Shimizu-cho days, but I knew nothing about the nature of Mr. Okuda's relationship with Father beyond the fact that he was a fairly successful Yokohama businessman who, hearing about Father's unhappy circumstances just as he himself was preparing to retire to his hometown, not only repaid his old debt, which was quite substantial, but left his own agency in Father's hands.

Whatever his reasons, there was no question that he gave Father the opportunity to reestablish himself. After the move to Onoe-cho Father became more active, my two little sisters who had been sent out to work were able to come home, and I became an assistant sitting at the accounts desk behind a lattice partition in Father's shop. That year and a half might be called a period of moderate well-being in our family's history.

The place where Nisshin-do stood doesn't look very different today. It's to your left as you cross Oe-bashi from the Sakuragi-cho Station side, where the Yokohama office of the *Asahi Newspaper* now is.

In those days, though, the neighborhood merged with the geisha house part of the Kannai pleasure quarter, and a number of geisha houses such as Konparu and Chiyomoto stood in the same row with Nisshin-do. Immediately behind our place was the garden of Kaneda, a restaurant serving chicken dishes. At the southern end of Oe-bashi bridge, Fukiro, the famous house of assignation, was still standing, though presumably under new management, to remind one of its former splendor. Thus during the day the sound of a samisen being softly plucked in practice would float past you, and as it got darker you heard the tinkling of the little bells on a geisha's clogs, and would see geisha going back to their houses from the public bathhouse, their hair swept up, cool and refreshed. Such sights and sounds gave the neighborhood an air of subtle eroticism, yet did not disturb the lives of the conventional households there. The two worlds lived in harmony with each other, giving the district its distinctive flavor.

Nisshin-do's main business was newspaper advertising, but there were also shelves with a display of cosmetics and a sign saying "Exclusive Wholesalers of Toilet Water." "Toilet water" of various kinds was getting very popular around that time, so Nisshin-do may have arranged for its own to be manufactured somewhere. The articles on display were wholesale samples, but geisha from the neighborhood would often drop in and ask for this or that. If no other customers were about, the shop assistants would exchange banter with them, then give them some of the samples free to show their appreciation. I was usually behind the lattice partition, immersed in a book or doing crude ink-wash sketches, but whenever the geisha appeared all my attention was focused on them, despite the outward indifference I affected.

Diagonally across the street from our shop was a Christian church with steel doors that were always closed except on Sundays, as well as the house of Wakizawa Kinjiro, one of the more success-ful Yokohama businessmen. A white-haired old gentleman, he often came in and made himself comfortable in one of the chairs. Noticing that I was always drawing something, he once looked in through the partition and said, "Tell me, what sort of career do you have in mind?" In all seriousness I replied, "I want to become an artist." "Then you should get proper training," he said. "Ask your father to send you to Tokyo to study with a proper teacher or at a decent art school." His comment left a deep impression, and I began dreaming of going to Tokyo and becoming a full-fledged artist. But I knew that, given Father's mood at the time, there was no chance of his agreeing, so I said nothing.

Father was hardly ever in the shop, spending most of the day hopping like a family doctor in a rickshaw from one place of busi-ness to the next. Admittedly, he had only recently recovered from his illness, but he'd never liked walking anyway. His absence from the shop was perhaps not such a serious matter in itself, for the busi-ness there could more or less be taken care of by experienced assis-tants. The real problem was that his time away from Nisshin-do was spent in all kinds of speculation, probably in the hope of acquir-ing sufficient capital to set himself up in the same sort of job as be-fore. No doubt, too, his frantic activity was motivated in part by a desire to face down his former business acquaintances.

Mother was not the sort of person to oppose lightly whatever he was doing. Yet it seemed that following his illness he became more reticent with her about his business affairs, so that she was left unin-formed about the speculation in raw silk and other things, things on which he wasted time that should have been spent on the shop he was fortunate enough to have been given. She must nevertheless have known something, for sometimes as she sat down to a meal with us she would make remarks like, "Whether he's sick or well, your father can be a very selfish, willful man!" Coming from her, this was complaint indeed.

She told me later that what with trying to keep up socially with former associates and dabbling in the raw silk market, Father within a year had spent all the money that had come into his possession; all that remained were the original liabilities attaching to the shop and newly acquired debts, so that keeping creditors at bay became the shop's main business.

The dunners who came so regularly to Nisshin-do held no fears for me myself; knowing nothing, all I did was repeat what I'd been told to say: "Sorry, no one is in today," or "Please come back on such and such a day." The staff of four shop assistants was reduced to one—a young man by the name of Mizuno—and even he was apt to disappear for a whole day to avoid the ordeal of having to face the dunners. We were soon in such straits that at the end of the month our electricity and water would be cut off until we managed to pay the bills. Yet in my own daily life there was no change at all. On the whole, I was freer to do what I liked during the year and a half I spent in Onoe-cho than at any time before or after. The shadowy area behind the lattice partition became my own small, private study, and the only intruders on my privacy were the creditors.

It was there that I wrote my first short story. The magazine *Students' Literary World* had just been launched, and my story was accepted for publication in its second issue. The title I gave the piece—"Ukinedori" [Bird in Floating Slumber]—now seems to me appallingly old-fashioned. It was, I think, thirty or forty manuscript pages long. The length prescribed by the magazine for stories was based on pages of twenty lines each containing twenty-four characters. I looked all over Yokohama for the right kind of paper, but there was not a shop in the city that stocked it. I remember drawing the lines myself, on plain paper, vertical and horizontal, then writing out the story with brush and black ink.

One thing I found fascinating at the time was seeing how the illustrations for serialized novels in newspapers were produced on woodblocks. I was often sent to the woodblock shop to fetch engravings of illustrations for our advertisements, and I used to stand and watch the men at work.

The shop, called Horishige, was in Masago-cho. Their work for the newspapers included the blocks for Ogawa Usen's illustrations of Yokohama scenes as well as the daily illustrations for serials. The job was divided up among several engravers, each picture having to be completed in time for either the next day's issue or the one after. In those days copper plates were often used for advertisements but not, it would seem, for such illustrations. The original image was drawn on a thin, high-quality Japanese paper called *ganpishi* which the engraver pasted directly onto his block of cherry wood, before carving out each line with a small chisel. To do this day after day seemed like very hard work to me, but to see the end result in the newspaper within a day or two gave me a gratifying sense of knowing something about the process of printing a serialized novel.

By now I can't pinpoint the year and month in which my time in Onoe-cho began and ended, but I have the impression that I spent the whole of my sixteenth year there. And, like any man's memories of his childhood at that stage, mine contain images of several girls of whom I was fond. Just off Kane-no-hashi—the Ginza of Yokohama at the time, you might call it—there was a dental clinic owned and run by a Mr. Sekikawa, who had a daughter I found particularly attractive. Another girl I liked was the daughter of the owner of a traditional footwear shop which stood on Oe-bashi-dori, just around the corner from Basha-michi. I wouldn't have been so daring as to call my feelings for them "love"; I was simply in that muddled emotional state where even the swaying branches of the willow trees lining the streets was enough to move me.

I also frequently attended the meetings of amateur literary circles such as the Shakespeare society, the *Tale of Genji* society, and haiku and tanka groups. There were monthly meetings of a haiku society sponsored by the *Yomiuri Newspaper* to which a well-known poet often came to officiate as judge. At these get-togethers you encountered people like Miyajima Yukari, who assumed all the airs of a "new" woman and may well have been a member of the *Seito-sha*

[Bluestocking Society]. There was a whole unfamiliar world in Yokohama, it seemed, where well-to-do people like her and other young men and women expressed their longing for another, less materialistic way of life.

Short though it was, I am grateful for the period of eighteen months I spent in Onoe-cho, exposed however distantly to that unconventional side of Yokohama culture, and able to indulge my penchant for reading books and drawing pictures.

As we came closer and closer to surrendering the shop as collateral and returning to life in the slums, we saw Mother sinking again into a state of permanent dejection. One day, a telegram arrived from her elder brother, Yamagami Kiyoshi, saying that their father, my grandfather from Sakura, was dying at my uncle's house in Tokyo; but—presumably because of our current situation—Father wouldn't give her permission to go to see him. I remember Mother crying in the back room and saying to me, "I've sunk so low I can't even go to see my father before he dies." Even allowing that people in those days didn't commute freely between Yokohama and Tokyo as they do now, I can't see that the trip would have been such a big undertaking. Perhaps Father was just being his perverse and arbitrary self. I can still hear Mother weeping that day, and wish I knew what made him refuse to let her go.

In the months prior to leaving Onoe-cho our water supply was constantly being cut off for failure to pay the rates. But even at such times my parents' way with money was oddly careless—a reflection, perhaps, of the "Hama spirit." On one occasion Mother handed me a hundred-yen note and sent me in haste to the water department to avert yet another stoppage. A hundred yen being a large sum of money in those days, I got a rickshaw to take me there. But when I reached the window where I was to pay, I couldn't find the envelope with the money in it. The rickshaw man and I searched frantically, but we never found it. I remember it as a very windy day. I don't think there was ever a time when Mother—who kept repeating "Oh dear, oh dear"—was more openly distressed with me, or when

I felt more panicky. The hundred yen, to say the least, wasn't money we could spare.

I still associate the old place-name "Nishi-Tobe" with hunger. It was there that we found ourselves again on moving from Onoe-cho. Rents and daily necessities were cheaper there, and one's neighbors were in the same predicament as oneself, so that being poor was easier to bear.

Immediately after we moved to Tobe, Father's health took a turn for the worse. His ulcers began troubling him again, and he coughed up blood for the umpteenth time. But Mother's comment —that whether in sickness or health he was always willful—remained true. He was a man ruled by, tormented by, emotion, incapable of saving himself by exercising moderation. Mother did everything she could to take care of him, but in the meantime we had to move twice. The first time was when he insisted that the way the house was situated was unlucky, so that he would die if we stayed there any longer; the second was when we couldn't pay the first two months' rent and the landlord threw us out.

Landlords in those days, unlike today, evicted tenants with uncommon ruthlessness. Those who dealt with poor tenants were especially bad—partly, I should imagine, because they were so accustomed to using the whip on defenseless people. They would press you so hard that unless you were unusually thick-skinned you'd have no choice but to leave, even if it meant sleeping without a roof over your head.

One rainy day, Mother and I together were looking for a house we could move into. Separately, we could have covered more ground, but we had only one umbrella between us. Mother was carrying my one-year-old brother on her back. With a torn Western-style umbrella she was trying to shelter both Susumu and me, and she herself was soon soaked to the skin.

Walking beside her trying to help hold up the umbrella, I kept thinking how unfortunate she was; I doubt if I ever felt it more keenly than I did that day. The fact that we were in practice homeless probably made me especially vulnerable; and I was exhausted by all the walking in the rain. At any rate, the history of her half-life churned over and over in my mind until I had lost whatever hopes for my own future I might have entertained, and I was overwhelmed by a desire to make her happy, if only for one brief period, in the years to come. I even told myself that it wouldn't matter if I had to give up reading books, give up any idea of becoming an artist. But it wasn't really me I was addressing, it was Mother. "You're not going to go on suffering like this," I was telling her. "You're going to be like other people, you'll see!" In essence, I suppose, what I was experiencing was that special, primitive, protective feeling one has toward one's own kin.

The place that we found eventually, that rainy day, was one of a line of tenement houses built halfway up a hill still covered with undergrowth. A communal well stood close by.

We discovered after we had moved in why this row of houses was called the "Guards' Tenements." In the old days, when Tobe Prison was in existence, the prison guards used to live there; I don't think anything more need be said.

A laborer called Tome-san and his wife lived two or three doors away from us. We presented them with the traditional gift of soba when we moved in, and we were soon on good terms. Tome-san kindly suggested that I get a job where he worked, and offered to take me there the next morning.

He duly arrived at the crack of dawn wearing straw sandals, gaiters, and a livery coat, looking for all the world like one of the dashing firefighters of old Edo. A large lunch box with a strap attached to it was slung over his shoulder. He gave me precise instructions about what I should wear, then showed me how to put on the new straw sandals he had bought for me. After tying the cords around my feet, he undid them again so that I could watch him do it one more time: "I'm not going to do this every morning," he said, "so watch closely, Hide-san."

He worked in Hodogaya. Where there are factories now, there were paddies, open land, and large puddles as far as the eye could see. But here and there huge chemical plants had already sprung up, and new brick buildings with tall chimneys were in the process of being built—for what purpose, I couldn't tell. It was at one of these that Tome-san worked.

My job was to carry water for mixing concrete. I had to balance on my shoulder a long pole with a large barrel on each end, go to a stream, fill the barrels with water, and take them back to the work site. I don't know how many such trips I made during the day, but at the end of it my shoulder was so painful I could barely touch it without flinching.

Every evening I went home with thirty-five sen in my pocket. I was overjoyed to get the money, but as the days passed the cement started eating into the soles of my feet, and I found myself limping. If I'd been properly shod, of course, I wouldn't have suffered so, but I was reluctant to buy a new pair of sandals several times a week, and, besides, on more days than not I was simply unable to afford them. I would set off in the morning knowing that my feet weren't adequately protected, and if on the way I found a pair of discarded sandals lying on the road, I would pick the better of the two and replace one of mine with it.

Given the way I hobbled about, it was only natural that my fellow workers should laugh at me. I must have exasperated some of them too, for on a couple of occasions I was beaten with a stick.

But Tome-san and his wife had got the job for me out of sheer kindness, so unless it rained I went to work every day. In due course, I took to going out in the evening as well, without a word to my parents, to earn some extra money as an itinerant masseur. As a substitute for the pipes that such masseurs played to announce their arrival, I tied together two of the toy pipes that came inside the bags of toasted barley you could buy in cheap candy shops. Thus equipped, I would go to some neighborhood where I knew no one and ply my trade. I kept this up for quite a while, then stopped for some reason or other. But so long as I was doing it Mother, and she alone, knew; for at the end of the evening I would give her the ten or fifteen sen I'd made.

Guilty, perhaps, about my doing all the earning for the family, Mother started coming with me to the construction site every morning and selling the workers sweet rice cakes from a large box she carried on her back. She stayed at the site all day, making the rounds of prospective customers, then walked back home with me. Since the place where she laid in her daily supply was by the river in Takashima-cho, we had to leave the house while the stars were still out, and had little time for sleep. Yet for all the hardship, I remember with some nostalgia those mornings and evenings when we walked together, tired out, in the darkness; and at the time, too, I honestly didn't think it an ordeal.

But in the end Mother's experiment as a sweet cake vendor proved a failure. As she and the workers got to know one another better, they started asking for credit, and once she'd let that happen they were reluctant to pay up. It had been all she could do to scrape together the money to get started in the business, and she of course had no reserve of cash. She lost whatever she had put into her little venture, and withdrew in defeat.

Wooden Clogs

The building project in Hodogaya was about to come to an end, Tome-san had found a job elsewhere, and I myself started work on the Yokohama docks. On high ground immediately above us stood an imposing house called "the mansion" by the neighbors; it belonged to a Mr. Naito, rumored to be related to the viscount of the same name. Mother did some sewing for the family, and it was through Mr. Naito's good offices—he was a senior official in the Dock Company—that I got the job.

Father was extremely pleased, and I too thought I was lucky to be taken on. Actually, being poor, we were inclined to exaggerate our good fortune in having someone like Mr. Naito intercede on my behalf. When I turned up at the Dock Company with his letter of introduction, I found to my surprise that I was given no examination; all they did was ask me how old I was. Mr. Naito had warned me not to give my real age, seventeen, the minimum age set by the company for dockhands being nineteen; so I said I was nineteen. I was immediately sent to join the sundry parts section. Of all the sections into which the workers were divided—the others included electrical, mechanical, and metal divisions—ours ranked the lowest, the miscellaneous tasks assigned to it requiring physical fitness primarily and no skill to speak of. The only work we did that involved any skill at all was painting the ship's hull, inside and outside.

Among the other things we had to do were helping to get ships in and out of the dry docks, hammering the rust off the hull, hauling up planks for the metalworkers, cleaning the docks, and helping out on ships in the open sea before they were brought in for repairs. Whatever odd jobs there were, we got them.

There were more than a hundred workers in our section, divided into six teams of seventeen or eighteen men each, the purpose presumably being to encourage competition. Each team had a leader and assistant leader. First thing in the morning, the leader would go to the foreman's office and come back with assignments for the day: to paint the ship in such and such a dock, for example, or to go out on a launch to a foreign vessel moored offshore and ready it for docking. Our regular working hours were from seven to half past five, and my daily wage was forty-five sen. If we put in an extra hour, twenty percent was added to our pay, and for late-night or overnight work we got much more. When I first arrived everybody asked me suspiciously, "How old are you?" Nobody believed that I was nineteen, partly I suppose because I was unusually small. Not one of my fellow workers in our section was quite as small as I was.

"*Don*" (the sound of a cannon being fired at noon) was one of the special words we used. "Hey, it's *don*!" meant it was midday, and we said "Let's have *don*" instead of "Let's have lunch." Another sound that shook the air over Yokohama regularly—in the morning, at noon, and in the evening—was that of the Dock Company's siren, or the "*bu*," as we called it. "There goes the dock *bu*" meant seven o'clock in the morning, or half past five in the evening. It acted as a clock for the entire city. To see thousands of workers, dressed variously in overalls, closed-collar jackets, or sailors' uniforms, pouring through the main gate of the company in the morning was an awesome sight. Since the seven o'clock siren signaled the start of work, it was at about half past six that the mass arrival reached its peak. If you showed up for work five minutes late the guard would note it down, and on payday you'd find that your unpunctuality had cost you half an hour's pay.

The fluctuating prosperity of the Dock Company was directly reflected in the economy of Yokohama as a whole. When you saw a great black mass of part-time workers gathered around the main gate, you knew that Nos. 1, 2, and 3 Docks had ships in them, with plenty of Japanese and foreign vessels anchored offshore awaiting their turn; it meant that good times had come to "Hama."

The people of Yokohama called these temporary workers *kan-kan mushi* [clang-clang insects], presumably because they crawled all over the ships setting up a great noise of metal being hammered. They ranged from old women with bent backs to thirteen-year-old boys and girls, but included, almost certainly, no strong men in their prime. Either way, the days when you could see them moving about like swarms of insects on the pier, or even on ships out at sea, marked the peak of Yokohama as a port city.

But for me the term *kan-kan mushi* has no humorous ring to it at all. Their work was not in fact limited to getting rust off ships, for they were made to do a great many other things, such as cleaning the hold, washing out the coal bunker and water tanks, and whatever else needed to be done in places where one would have thought only a rat could get in. Smeared all over with fresh paint, their nostrils and lungs filled with coal dust, they would crawl with cement brushes and cans into holes in the bottom that even the crew didn't know existed.

When they finally emerged into the gathering dusk, their appearance defied description. To say that they were coal-black, or that they were unidentifiable, would be an understatement. With only their eyes and noses showing, each of them presented an extraordinary sight. Yet as they took off their filthy headgear and washed themselves with the hot water from the drainage pipes behind some factory, there would occasionally emerge a girl with a touchingly pretty, fresh face, or a young woman, probably married but still innocent-looking, with stray hair falling over her face. Most of them, of course, were rather rough-looking men of the kind you wouldn't care to meet in large numbers at night, but none of them were like the really thuggish characters you saw hanging around the harbor. This was because the daily wage for people in the *kan-kan mushi* class was too low even for these types.

Nonetheless, despite their low wages, when work was over they gave the evening stalls and shops in the surrounding areas a great deal of business, buying cheap fish, pickled greens, and bags of rice to take home to their families. Watching them hurrying away from the stalls with their purchases, I could see no difference between their way of life and mine; they, too, were clawing their way up the same steep mountainside.

Nor were conditions in the sundry parts section of the Dock Company much different from those affecting the *kan-kan mushi*, except that we had to do risky work on hanging cradles and crushingly demanding manual work. In short, you might say that we were class-A *kan-kan mushi* who happened to be regularly employed by the company.

Facing No. 1 Dock, which handled ten-thousand tonners, was the office used by the foreman and pilots, and next to it stood our section's tin-roofed shed. Here the hundred-odd workers belonging to the section changed their clothes, left their lunch boxes, and in winter put firewood in a large, empty paint can, pouring on it whatever oil came to hand, then gossiped and grumbled around the roaring, smoky fire. You might well have encountered similar scenes in the miners' shed of a colliery.

In the way we dressed, though, and in temperament, we were probably different from those men of the mines. Practically all the painting of ships in dock was done by our section, so our clothes were covered with drops of paint of various colors which had hardened in layers like dry lacquer. Having only recently and by sheer chance joined the section, I was very self-conscious about my conspicuously clean overalls, and carefully daubed them with red, white, and black paint to disguise the fact of my being a beginner. Besides clothes stiff with paint, my fellow workers without exception wore wooden clogs—but more about these later.

I have said that there were six teams in the section. I myself was put in Team 6, whose leader was Inoko Saburo—a name I shall never forget, since I would probably never have been able to stay on the job if it hadn't been for that straightforward and understanding man.

But the other men I worked with were all cheerful and open too—purged, you might say, by the "Hama spirit" and by their exposure to foreign ships and ordinary sailors. They were kind, too. I was a seventeen-year-old who had lied about his age, trying to keep up with sturdy grown men; yet not one of them, knowing full well that I had lied, was ever mean to me or made me unhappy. The men in Team 6 in particular, though they had a hard time of it themselves, seemed to go out of their way to protect me.

A launch with a pilot on board would lead a ship into the inner harbor for docking. Waiting there, we got hold of the ropes and guided the vessel in. Then the water inside the closed dock was pumped out by electricity until the huge bottom of the ship was resting on the keel. The whole process took three to four hours.

The pilot, careful to an almost neurotic degree, constantly blew his whistle and shouted instructions at us, the entire sundry parts section, who were responsible for everything until the ship finally settled. The mood was that of a battlefield; any sign of confusion and you were mercilessly shouted at or got knocked down.

As the ship slowly subsided, it was kept steady with logs which were lowered at precise moments with ropes and pulleys, being allowed to rest between the hull and the stone wall of the dock on either side, forming what looked like a log bridge. The moment the vessel settled on its keel two men got onto each log on the side of the dock wall and facing each other hammered it down tight. With every blast of the whistle given by the pilot standing on the gunwale, the sledgehammers came down all together, filling the dock with a terrifying combination of sound. When this was done, a man holding a heavy mallet in one hand and a wedge in the other scuttled ape-like to the other end of the log and knocked the wedge in between the side of the ship and the timber. The logs were huge—a size larger in circumference than telegraph poles—some of them cut more or less square, others almost round with only narrow strips shaved off. The men, in wooden clogs, negotiated these things as though they were on level ground. It wasn't so bad while water still remained in the dock, but when all of it had been pumped out, there was only the stone-paved floor, a dizzying distance below. When I first watched the men working on the logs with such apparent unconcern, they seemed hardly human to me. Terrified, I stood there with my knees shaking; but terrified or not, I eventually had to do the same thing myself.

Securing the timber in the dock was not the only frightening and dangerous job we had to do. Working in a pitch-dark hold, climbing up a mast or a funnel, being lowered on a rope to the screw, daubing the sides—and yourself in the process—with red paint from a swaying cradle—all these tasks were not merely physically demanding to the limit of my capacity, but put me, every time, in fear of my life.

Often enough, as I left the house in the morning, I would find myself wondering, "Will I come home again this evening?" I was particularly susceptible to such sentimental thoughts on winter mornings, when it was still dark and there was frost on the streets.

Inoko, the team leader, must have lived somewhere near us, as I met him quite often on my way to the docks. My spirits always rose when I heard him hail me. There was a touch of bravado in his speech and manner, and though he was always dressed rather soberly in a jacket with a closed collar, he was a cheerful, dashing sort of man. He was fond of saké and gambling, and for two or three days after payday would abandon both work and home and go on a spree. A fellow worker told me that on one occasion his wife had to go in search of him, and finding him lying by the roadside, dead drunk, put him on a coal cart and hauled him back to their house all by herself. Other similar stories about him were told during lunch breaks in the shed.

"How are you doing?" he would say to me. "Do you think you'll manage? No moping, d'you hear? You'll be all right, don't worry, so long as you stay in Team 6!"

Though he was the kind of person who would always take the trouble to talk to me like that, with the foreman and the engineers he could be quite blunt, and it was said that, of the six team leaders, the company liked him least.

The teams were in competition with each other, and it was important for ours to perform well, so I could hardly take advantage of Inoko's kindness and let myself slack off. I wasn't strong, even so, and I was small—handicaps that became evident when one of those logs had to be shifted. It was carried by four men using chain slings, one man on each side at the front and rear. I had to stretch myself to my full height to be more or less on a level with my partner, which made it very difficult for me to keep my balance and bear my share of the weight. I would sometimes totter; I'd grit my teeth in the effort not to give up, but it was no good. To make up for my inadequacy I used to fetch things and run errands, even personal ones, whenever I could.

On rainy days we were given relatively easy tasks, mostly inside the ship or, if outside, knocking rust off the bottom.

One of the less strenuous jobs was sitting in a cradle in the hold with a lighted candle, loosening the rust on the sheet metal with a hammer. We all took it easy at such times, only resuming our work when the foreman appeared. I would bring out the pocket-size edition of Basho's haiku that I always carried with me and read it stealthily, or compose haiku in my mind, or just daydream.

If we were in the coal bunker, the darkness would seem to get deeper as the coal dust, to the sound of many hammers beating the metal, rose up into the air. But then, as particles of coal caught the light, the air would glow, and around the candle there would be constant displays of miniature fireworks. These tiny flickering lights, and the sound of the hammering, created a kind of strange, illusory world. My nose and throat would feel dry and obstructed, and when I tried to clear them what came out was like coal paste. Careless enough once to try to light a cigarette with the candle (I had begun smoking at the age of fourteen or fifteen), I came close to igniting the coal dust that was stuck to my whole face.

Even so, I enjoyed working in the hold, for there I could let my mind wander as much as I liked. I suspect it was this habit of day-dreaming in dark places that enabled me to keep on working on the docks for a year and some months. The darker the place was, the sweeter were my fantasies. And at times like these, the sound of the siren signaling the end of the day always came earlier than expected.

Overtime work at night could be pretty much of your own choosing, or it could be compulsory and hard.

It was very cold doing overtime at the bottom of a dock on winter nights. It was never dry there, and the cold—how many degrees below zero, I can't say—was a kind you never experienced on land. When it got late and the supervisor and engineers stopped coming around, the workers would either go up for a rest or start rolling dice by candlelight. There was always someone who had a pair of dice on him. So, provided there was no superior present, the men would start playing—anywhere, in the bottom of a ship, even on a launch on the way out to a boat lying offshore.

I was often made to stand guard while they played. At the end of the session, someone would give me five sen for my trouble. In time, I began edging up to the group to see how they played, and got to understand the rules of the game and their enthusiasm for it. Next, I began timidly putting a few copper coins down to bet on a throw, and finally started playing myself whenever I could. Then, one night as we were having a game, an old hairy-faced worker whom we all called "Padre" or "Father" looked up and glared at me from where he was crouching. "You stop that!" he said. Later, close to dawn, as I was trudging back to the shed, he approached me and patting me on the shoulder said, "What good will it do you to pick up a habit like that? Do you want to become like me?"

Back in the shed, he presented me with a pair of wooden clogs. I'd been envious of my fellow workers, all of whom owned a pair, but no shop seemed to sell them, and I didn't know how else to get hold of any; so I'd gone on wearing torn leather shoes or straw sandals, getting my feet soaking wet all the time.

On rainy days or during the night shift, the men would sneak over to the shed to make their own clogs. Using blocks of cedar wood they'd picked up somewhere, they would fashion them with a hatchet, saw, or knife into the right size and shape for the sole and heel. They then helped themselves to some canvas from the rope shed and cut out the two sections that joined over the front part of the foot. A strip of tin was put around the ends of the canvas reaching over the top of the wooden sole, and secured with metal studs. Finally, the metal eyelets for the laces to go through, which they'd bought at a shoe shop, were put in. The clogs were now ready to be worn, but for good measure the canvas was waterproofed with any kind of oil that was handy. These clogs were surprisingly sturdy; what was more important, they were very warm. There was no one in our section who didn't wear them. To look at a man's feet was one sure way of telling whether he belonged to our group or not. In those days at least, I imagine, it was only around the docks that you could see laborers oddly dressed like this—in clothes stiff with many shades of color, and wooden clogs.

Everybody wore a hat so covered with wart-like blobs of paint that it looked like a toad's skin. When you spent the whole day in a cradle painting the side of a ship, you ended up with your face also spotted in this way, for there was always a strong wind that blew drops off the tip of the brush and all over your head, giving you colorfully encrusted eyebrows. Back in the shed in the evening, we would look at one another and joke about our appearance. "I'd hate to have the old lady and the kids see me like this," someone would declare, and another, rubbing his face with a rag soaked in turpentine, would say, "And what's she going to think if I turn up like this? I've told her I'm in charge of the customs warehouse." The "she" probably referred to a woman in one of the pleasure quarters.

There was a small man in our section called Mori who was forever talking fondly about a woman he went to see regularly, and who seemed delighted to be teased about it by the others. After every payday—we were paid twice a month—he was sure to take a few days off. When he had used up the money at her place, he would come back and work again without missing a day until the next payday. He was very fit, had never been ill—I was told—and throughout the years had not once strayed from his routine.

He was supposed, accordingly, to be a bit of a fool. But he had worked in the section longer than anyone else. He always came to work with his pomaded hair neatly parted and wearing a suit, albeit of shoddy quality. You sometimes saw him leaving the docks with a slender cane tucked rakishly under his arm, his chest stuck out and a grin on his face. "Going again, eh?" someone would say. "You bet!" he would answer, puffing out his chest even more and stretching himself to his full height—he was shorter than I was. "He's at least forty-five, you know," somebody once commented. "For the rest of his life he's going to be the old hand here, and for the rest of his life he's going to keep strutting over to Magane-cho."

Most of the workers were married, Mori being one of the few confirmed bachelors. Few of the others had been there for ten or twenty years. I used to wonder how he had managed to avoid being badly hurt or killed for so long in a job so consistently dangerous.

I used to wonder, too, just how the wives and children of men who died there managed afterward. The condolence money that the company handed out was a pittance—a "sparrow's teardrop," as the saying went. To claim that they accepted their predicament only because they could do nothing about it wouldn't be quite right; rather, it was simply that the working class in general at that time had neither the awareness nor the organization that it has now. The number of men killed or seriously injured while working for the company, not only in our section but in all the others, was considerable.

Sometimes we would see two or three stretchers being carried out, with white-coated men in attendance, in the course of one day. When this happened, even the dock area would suddenly go quiet, and you would hear men saying to each other, "This is an unlucky day, so watch out!" But all would be forgotten again within an hour. If you let yourself be at all conscious of the dangers confronting you all the time, you couldn't have gone on working for even half a day.

It may be that anyone who, for twenty years, morning and evening as the siren sounded, had continued to pass through that gate separating the ordinary world from this first stop to hell, would have come to view life as Mori did. People laughed at him, yet—who knows—in his own fatalistic way he may have pitied all those fellow workers who had wives and children.

Much of the conversation among us took place during the half-hour lunch break in the shed. Here too, as in other places I had worked, food was followed by talk about sex. The stories the others told were quite unlike Mori's grateful, idealized reminiscences about women. I myself, fortunately or unfortunately, had gained through books a knowledge of the secret world of adults that (I thought) allowed me to imagine it accurately and exhaustively; but in the shed I discovered that I had much to learn. Their dirty stories were of the no-nonsense type, completely free of subtle nuance and leaving nothing to the listener's imagination. Facts were facts, and they were reported without adornment, obscene detail upon obscene detail, much to the gratification of the listeners, who clearly approved of such candor in the telling of personal experiences.

I listened intently, swallowing hard at each new detail and solemnly telling myself that, after all, there was still a whole new world I didn't know. And yet the impression the stories made on me was surprisingly short-lived—disappeared immediately, in fact, as soon as the siren sounded and I went back to work. I had acquired the habit of masturbating by now, and had spent whole days dwelling moodily on the evil of repeated "self-abuse." But as soon as I started working on the docks, the habit ceased without my giving it another thought; I was so exhausted when I got home that once I had filled my empty stomach all I wanted to do was jump into bed and go to sleep. Bedtime fantasizing was a luxury I had neither time nor energy for. It makes me wonder in fact—though my own experience may not apply here—if those men were as lecherous in real life as they appeared from their anecdotes. After all, in their kind of work any carelessness might have cost them their lives; they had to be on the alert all the time, they couldn't afford to be unsure of their footing because of any excesses the night before. And they were, indeed, very careful to keep themselves fit. If there was an accident, and the man involved happened to be known for his loose habits, they would say without much sympathy, "He must have been out last night." They were the kind of men who, seemingly nonchalant about the risks they faced every day, wore good-luck charms next to their skin.

Hama-chan

Working on the docks was hard. Every morning I felt tired, and left home with a heavy heart. But when I saw Mother's lined face and watched her packing my lunch box with such care, fussing over me as I prepared to leave, I couldn't bring myself to tell her how much I wanted to give up the job.

It was in May of my eighteenth year, when I'd been a dockhand for over six months, that my little sister Hamako, the fourth of the daughters, died. Nothing caused our family so much grief as her death.

Hamako was only eight, but some months before had been sent away to work in a restaurant in Boshu. It was the custom in those days for poor families to put children into service somewhere so that there would be fewer bellies to fill at home. All the same, how could my parents have sent someone so young to a place so far away? In later days Mother, desperately sorry that she had allowed such a thing to happen, explained to me in tears that they'd had to find fifteen yen in a hurry and, having been persuaded by the employment agency that the prospective employer was a decent person, had let Hamako go in return for fifteen yen paid to them as an advance on her wages.

Hamako was a lovely child, with a complexion so fair that she looked like a doll. Perhaps because she had grown up in the midst of grinding poverty, she was never one to make a fuss, and was quick to lend a helping hand. At an age when children want above all to play, she stayed with Mother, sharing the hardships with her. I feel sure she must have hated leaving her, but when told to go, she simply said yes.

According to her employer, from the day she arrived she would hardly eat anything, and cried all the time. The doctor who examined her said there was nothing seriously wrong, but she got thinner and thinner, so they had no choice but to send her back to us.

Arriving home, she was immediately put to bed; but by then she was already in a coma. We called a doctor, and he told us she had meningitis. With an ice bag on her head, she remained comatose for about two weeks, and all that time Mother sat beside her, begging to be forgiven, until I began to think she might lose her mind. I, too, would sit at her bedside when I came home from the docks. It may sound like an elder brother merely being sentimental, but I have never seen a living person's face that was so innocent and beautiful. She seemed peaceful: though unconscious, she may have felt the comfort of being home again. In the small hours, Mother would gaze at her sweet face and almost instinctively put her hands together as though in prayer; and I would do the same. From time to time in her delirium Hamako would say something hard to catch— probably just "Mother." And every time this happened Mother burst into tears and held her in her arms. That was how Hamako died, never waking from her sleep.

Even now I am filled with pity and remorse when I think of her death. I have never forgotten the date—May 13. Whatever allowances one makes for the contradictory ways in which people behave or the utter helplessness of the very poor, there are things about the incident that I still can't understand. I remember that in my anger I even bitterly attacked Mother. However urgent their need for money, there was surely some other way of finding it? If there had to be one mouth less to feed in the family, was sending Hamako to Boshu the only answer? I pushed her to the point where she looked as though she might try killing herself, which frightened me—another thing I can't forget.

They say that fate plays tricks on people; if so, then it played one on us, helpless as we were. Not long after Hamako died, our situation improved a little. Where the money came from, I don't know, but we moved to a house in Yoshida-cho 2-chome, beside Kane-no-hashi. I myself at the time was so worn out from forcing myself to go to work on the docks every day that the circumstances of the change in our fortunes quite escaped me.

The house in Yoshida-cho was a fairly substantial one, and stood just around the corner from the busiest street in the neighborhood. Now that we seemed better off, I thought it a good time to approach Father with the suggestion that I give up my job. What I most wanted to do was to go to Tokyo and study part-time while earning my living there.

But before I could summon enough courage to put my plans forcefully to my parents, I had an accident at work, thanks to another man's mistake: while I was painting the side of a ship, the cradle gave way and I fell with it to the bottom of the dock. I was taken to the Juzen Hospital on a stretcher.

One Morning
When I Was Eighteen

At some point while I was being lifted out of the dock on a stretcher, or being taken to the hospital, I lost consciousness. For some minutes, or tens of minutes, I was dead to the world.

Even when I came to in the white-sheeted bed in the hospital, I didn't know what I was being treated for or what the people around me were saying to one another. My only memory is that my whole body hurt, and that I lay there trembling with stiff, cold limbs stretched out and teeth and fists clenched.

Like a dropped watch, my brain seemed to have stopped functioning the moment my body hit the bottom of the dock, and for days all it could communicate was the sound and feel of that tremendous impact, so that from the rare experience of returning from apparent death, I gained nothing. I have even forgotten the day when the accident happened, though I'm sure that it was sometime in late November.

Had I been in the habit of keeping a diary, I would no doubt have recorded the incident later in detail; but I had never had the record-keeping instinct. Obviously, there was a careless side to my character. Or, more to the point, I still wasn't thoughtful enough to see such a serious accident as something that might change my youthful view of the world, as a landmark in my life. I was eighteen by then, but on the day that I found myself lying prone on the white sheets, my whole body reeking of some ointment, I hadn't yet completely grown out of the old, childish dreaminess that Mother had referred to as *annya-monnya*.

Needless to say, I was in a third-class room, but my bed, in one corner of the roughly six-mat space, was the only one. Whenever I woke up there was a nurse in a white uniform close by, and I could hear the kettle boiling on the porcelain brazier. The sight and sound of them helped to allay my fears, to calm the distress I felt at having been so badly injured.

When the doctor came on his morning round two nurses, one on either side of me, would open up my hospital kimono with their cool white hands and undo the bandage wrapped tightly around my body from chest to hips. The part of me that had been hit hardest when I fell was the area around the coccyx; the injuries to my right shoulder and arm were apparently not very serious. Peering down at me through his spectacles, the deputy head doctor said to me, "You got off lightly, I must say. It's a miracle you weren't hurt more badly—you could have been killed, you know."

I was pink from embarrassment as he spoke, not because of him but because of the two nurses who were gently winding a new bandage around me. Even in my grim condition, I was acutely aware of their white hands touching me. I wondered if my skin looked unwashed, if there were spots of red paint on it, if my scalp was caked with bits of rust. But despite such petty preoccupations, I was still able to respond with something like pleasure to their soothing touch and gaze, and to take some comfort in my surroundings. As I got better, I became more aware of the voices of people walking along the corridor and of the faint scents wafting though the door as the nurses approached with the doctor.

In time I was able to recall everything about the accident—what caused it, how I fell, and how I was so miraculously saved.

That day, every man in our section had been assigned the task of painting the outer hull of *Shinano-maru*, an oceangoing vessel of about ten thousand tons, in No. 1 Dock.

First we painted the upper part of the hull black, then the cradles were lowered to below the waterline, from bow to stern on either side, and we proceeded with practiced speed to brush on red paint, each team in competition with the rest.

It must have been half past three or four in the afternoon. The fresh red paint on the huge hull was brilliant in the western sunlight, but the bottom of the dock was already beginning to get dark, with patches of thin ice shining here and there. Evidently we would be working late that day.

The cradles were made of two foot-wide planks with their ends nailed to strips of wood. A pulley was attached to either end. On the upper deck of the ship was another pulley. The rope went around this and over the empty space between the ship and the side of the dock, where it was secured to a reassuringly solid, three-foot-high iron post with a rounded top.

Protruding horizontally near the top of the post was an iron bar to prevent the rope from slipping over it as it was being let out. We must have been shorthanded that day, since men from outside our section were in charge of some of these posts.

In charge of mine was an old man by the name of Hirai who normally worked in the warehouse. He had been watching me from the side of the dock, and I had barely finished painting the last bare patch within reach when I heard him shouting from behind me, "Hold tight, I'm lowering you!"

Taken by surprise, I started moving, cautiously but as quickly as I could, toward the end of the cradle. Anyone who worked on these contraptions had to learn to balance himself like a tightrope walker, for they swayed and rocked very easily. Before I had reached the end and got hold of the rope—he must have thought he had seen me do so—he started lowering the cradle. The next moment, it turned on its end and fell to the bottom—about forty feet below—with me on it. Had I been separated from it, I would probably have fallen head-first and crushed my skull. Luckily, though, the edge of the cradle and the lower part of my body hit the bottom together; and when I was flung off by the impact I fell on my right shoulder and arm. Even so, I lost consciousness.

When I came to I heard voices around me, near but distant-sounding. It seemed that I was being carried up the steep steps to the top of the dock. I looked at my body, and saw that it was almost entirely covered with blood.

At the sight of so much blood I fainted again. It was only much later that I realized it wasn't blood I had seen but red paint from the can I'd been holding when I fell. The sun was setting at the time, too, and its light shining into my eyes as I opened them must have added to the luridness of the red paint, giving me the illusion that blood was pouring down from my head.

I was told later how the accident had happened. It was cold, and Hirai was wearing gloves. He was old, and unused moreover to heavy dock work, so that when he loosened the rope around the post and it began to unwind too quickly, smoking from the friction, he instinctively let go. He could have tried to get hold of the rope again but, afraid of being dragged off the side of the dock by the weight of the falling cradle, he stood by helplessly and did nothing.

I had an odd feeling when I was told that the accident had been due to his mistake. Our first encounter had taken place outside the rope shed not long after I started working for the company. "Well—I could have sworn you were Arthur!" he said, popping his eyes in feigned amazement. Every time he saw me after that he'd say, "You really do look like Arthur!" It bothered me, so I finally asked a fellow worker who "Arthur" was. He was a Eurasian who'd once been in Team 3, I was told; he'd been lent out to the plating section one day, and while working on the stern of a ship in dock had fallen from his cradle and been killed.

After that I couldn't help having an ominous feeling whenever I saw old Mr. Hirai with his buck teeth and sallow, greenish face. He probably disliked me, too. Anyway, we weren't much drawn to each other. While I was in the hospital he came once to see me, on his way home, but I've no idea what he said.

The pain apart, lying in bed all day long was no ordeal for me.

Through the window I could hear the Dock Company's morning and evening sirens. What a rare, unexpected blessing it was, not to have to hurry toward the company's iron gate at the sound of the morning siren, to put on wooden clogs and engage in strenuous, acrobatic work for the rest of the day. I had not, in fact, known such comfort and peace of mind for many a year. I was served warm food regularly by the nurses, I could read books, I could daydream at leisure. So different were my days in hospital from those before that I could hardly believe they were real. People who came visiting all said what a dreadful experience it must have been, and how sorry they were; little did they know what a good time I was having on the quiet.

The first person to rush to the hospital must have been Mother, but for the first two or three days I wasn't fully aware even of her presence. All I did, apparently, was cry out, "It hurts! It hurts!" When at last I began to show signs of recovery she came and sat by my pillow and told me that even Father, stern though he was, had been shocked to the core by the news.

"The company sent a messenger over that afternoon to tell us you'd had a fall in the dock," she said. "I was standing in the kitchen at the time, and my legs almost gave under me. Your father, too, had a look on his face I can't describe. And he said something straight from the heart. . . ."

"What was it?" I asked.

"He said, 'Oh, he's gone, that son of mine' "

"He must have thought I'd been killed."

"Indeed he did. And *I* wasn't sure either until I got to the hospital. You didn't know that I sat here beside you all night long, did you?"

"No, I didn't," I said, shaking my head. Then I corrected myself: "Well, I did—sort of."

Very little else that occurred around then has stayed in my memory, but I do remember with uncanny clarity Mother's face and gestures and the things we said to each other when we were by ourselves in that hospital room. I remember in particular how on one occasion she showed her love for me in a way she'd never done in Father's presence. She drew my face to her breast and held me tight, as though her eighteen-year-old son were once again a suckling child, and whispered gently in my ear. The sweet smell of her breath and the feel of her warm, soft skin have stayed with me ever since. "I want to ask something, Hide-chan," she whispered. "What do you think of doing after you've recovered and left the hospital? I mean, you're already eighteen."

I had my eyes closed, and wanted to go on being held like a child. The area around my coccyx still throbbed with pain. I'd tried to avoid thinking about life after my convalescence was over, for I was frightened by the prospect of having to leave my comfortable bed in the hospital and return to a routine of poverty and hard work on the cold and windy docks.

"I'm sure you don't want to go back to the docks. The work's too tough for you, and you must hate it. Even before this accident I used to think, every time I packed your lunch, that it was high time you started thinking about your future and gave up that dangerous job."

"But if I quit now, how are you going to manage, Mother?"

"It'll be hard, of course. But never mind that. When you get out of hospital you've got to go to your father and tell him."

"What do I tell him?"

"What you've been wanting to do."

"That I want to go to Tokyo and study?"

"Yes. And in the meantime I'll say something about it to him. He was very shocked when you got hurt, and I'm sure he'll agree this time."

"But are you sure you'll be all right without me to help you?

Won't you be lonely?"

"You've got to stop worrying about the family—and about me. Do what you think is best for you. Go to Tokyo, find a job, work your way through school or whatever—please."

Then, suddenly switching to a more formal tone of voice, she said: "Thank you, Hide-chan, for working so hard for so long. You can start leading your own life now."

For ten or fifteen minutes after that, until the nurse appeared with my lunch, I stayed with my face against her breast.

Mother always brought a little gift for Yamada-san, the nurse, which she gave to her before leaving, asking her to take good care of her son.

When Mother came with Father she was never allowed to linger, as he was eager to leave the moment he saw I was all right. Since the move to Yoshida-cho their problems had continued, and no doubt he felt harried; nor could he have been expected to become a different man all of a sudden. Mother and I had no further opportunity to talk about my future, but there was no need, for our minds were made up.

I left the hospital in late December. Seeing me safe and sound at home again, Father for once showed genuine pleasure, and kept saying how glad he was. Thinking to tackle him while he was in a good mood, on my first or second day back I told him what I wanted to do. He might quite easily have lost me in the accident, I said, and it shouldn't be too much trouble to let me leave home. I wanted to work my way through school, and once I had found a decent position, I would bring the family to Tokyo and set up house there. So desperate was I to persuade him that I overdid it rather. When I had finished, Father answered simply, "You might as well give it a try." He was by no means pleased, and it came like a groan. He then added, more impatiently, "Working through school, eh? Well, why not, it's worth a try."

It was a time when phrases like "learning the hard way" and

"bettering yourself" were in fashion among ambitious youths who saw infinite possibilities of advancement and reward in a world committed to progress. Father no doubt dismissed me as yet another case of the fashionable disease. In this respect he was different from Mother who, growing up in Kondo Makoto's academy, had known the sort of things the students there were hoping to achieve. For her, I feel, the aspirations of her eighteen-year-old son were a more serious concern than they were for Father.

It was on December 30—this is one date I haven't forgotten—that for the first time in my life I bade a formal farewell to my parents and left the nest that was home. That morning, Mother cooked some red rice to mark the occasion and served it with a whole dried fish, and all of us, including my little brothers and sisters, had breakfast together. Then Mother with the young ones in tow accompanied me to Sakuragi-cho Station.

In retrospect, there is something a little comical about that leave-taking at the station. As the train began to move I stuck my head out of the window and with tears in my eyes waved my handkerchief to Mother and the children standing on the platform, going on waving until I could see them no more. But the scene would not have struck an onlooker at the time as at all funny, for Tokyo in those days seemed very far indeed from Yokohama.

As the train approached Takashima-cho, the Yokohama Dock Company came into full view on my right. I could see the masts of the ships in No. 1 and No. 2 Docks, and pictured my former companions in their wooden clogs, perched on their cradles, facing yet another day of hard, dangerous work. It was then that I remembered I hadn't said goodbye to my team leader, Inoko, who had been so good to me.

There was something else I felt bad about, too. For some time I'd been, from necessity, neglecting my repayments to our section's mutual loan fund—I can't remember whether it was ten or fifteen yen that I took out originally—and I was going away with some of the debt outstanding, leaving Inoko with the responsibility for paying it in my stead. I'm afraid I never repaid him, for which I've been inwardly apologizing to him ever since.

I got off the train at Shinagawa, mistaking it for Shinbashi Station, the terminus in those days. I must have imagined, in my nervousness, that the busy scene outside meant I was in Tokyo proper.

I was wearing a dark blue kimono with white splash patterns on it and a black cotton sash, both old. Only my wooden clogs were new; Mother had bought them for me. She also gave me a purse containing one yen seventy sen in silver and copper coins. That I still remember the exact amount would suggest that I valued it almost as much as my life.

In Tokyo

I n those days, to go up to Tokyo and "learn the hard way" was a cherished dream of young men without means. There, they believed, lay limitless opportunities to rise above their humble circumstances, if only they persevered.

In ancient China, young men used to shoulder their books and writing things, leave their hometowns, and set off for the capital, hoping to take their first leap toward advancement by passing the official examinations there. We of the late Meiji era had something in common with them.

It's not true that we were success-minded in the ordinary sense of the term, that the ambitious students of my generation all longed to be either rich businessmen or high-ranking bureaucrats. The emergence of capitalism and the general course of the nation's development tended, of course, to foster such ambitions, but there were those among us who sought learning purely for its own sake, or dreamed of devoting their lives to one of the arts, and who were willing to face all kinds of misery in order to make their dreams come true in Tokyo. Hongo and Kanda were full of idealistic young people seemingly undeterred by the prospect of lifelong indigence even after attaining professional standing, or by all the eminent artists and men of letters who still had barely enough to eat.

They were all poor. But they were proud to be students, and they had their own integrity and rules of conduct. They despised shallow-mindedness, and flaunted their rough country manners and shabby clothes on the big-city streets. These young men of late Meiji were very different from today's part-time students, in that they exuded optimism. Moreover, those in authority looked on their gaucheness and high spirits with a tolerant eye; the attitude of the average citizen too was was generous, and there was something akin to affection for them among the common people of the city, with none of the mutual antagonism and contempt seen in today's adults and students. Nor did the students themselves seek to make their way to the top by devious means. Thanks to the age's faith in the efficacy of sheer hard work, it never occurred to them to take advantage of the general sympathy shown toward youth. The *senryu*[17] poet Sakai Kuraki expressed their attitude well when he wrote: "There they go, strolling in Nagata-cho / Saying wait and see, wait and see."

In going to Tokyo I was undoubtedly driven by the same spirit that moved all those other youngsters. At Shinbashi Station I caught a streetcar and sitting by the window stared at the busy scenes that passed before my eyes. The ride was a long one, but I was too anxious and too overwhelmed by all I saw to be bored. I was of course completely ignorant of the geography of Tokyo; what's more, I had got on the streetcar with no particular destination in mind.

When it finally reached its terminus, which happened to be Midori-cho in Honjo, I got off.

I had intended to find a cheap lodging house for the night, but as I wandered about I saw a poster on a street corner inviting jobseekers to come to a certain address. It turned out to be that of an ordinary house on a back street in Aioi-cho. Hanging beside the sliding glass doors was a sign saying "Japanese Young Men's Christian Association: Employment Assistance Office." Telling myself

17. A seventeen-syllable verse form like haiku, but freer and more informal; a popular vehicle for social satire, trenchant observations on current fashions, affectations, and even politics. Associated in World War II with subversive tendencies.

that this looked promising, I went in hesitantly and found a young couple, Christian intellectuals, who ran the office as a home-based mission. I was given a room upstairs—not just for the night but, because it was December 30, for the several days of the New Year holiday.

I was lucky to have met these people. Thanks to them, I didn't have to roam the streets in search of lodgings, and was able to get through the New Year without spending too much of my one yen and seventy sen. I ate out, at a cheap place where I could get a meal for five or six sen. Having occasionally been to church when I was small, I was able to keep up some kind of conversation on religious matters with the Christian couple. And having been a dockhand until only recently, I gladly swept the front of the house and did other chores, without being asked and with no sense of injured pride.

The husband was a kindly man with the face of an intellectual; even his moustache had a gentle, thoughtful look about it. At our first encounter, he told me, "You must understand that a job leaving you time to study will be very difficult to find. But I can recommend you with confidence, so I'll make sure you get one." And while I was with them he went out every day for the sole purpose, it seemed, of finding the right job for me. One day—I think it was January 5—he took me to a baker's shop in Marunouchi. Unfortunately the master wasn't in, and after a long wait we left without having seen him. Then, the next day, my host said there was another job open—this time at a small screwnail factory—and asked if I was interested. I promptly decided not to wait to see about the job at the bakery, and went to the factory by myself with a letter of introduction from my host.

The place was in Kikukawa-cho in Honjo. The owner turned out to be a pleasant, simple-mannered man of about fifty who spoke slowly with a slight stammer. Dressed like his employees in oil-stained clothes, he worked all day beside them. My daily wage would be twenty-eight sen, with meals. I would have to pay for my bed. Work stopped at five-thirty, and I would have Sundays off. The job seemed all right, so I accepted it on the spot. That night, I slept in a room above the factory with eight or nine other workers.

The owner was himself a Christian—as were, presumably, all the prospective employers to whom my host introduced job-hunters like me. The work was extremely simple. All you had to do was sit in front of a threading machine, cranking and pedaling all day long and watching the brass shavings pile up on the floor. But I soon discovered that it was as exhausting in the end as any heavy manual labor. At the end of the day, back upstairs in our quarters, none of us had the energy to pick up a book and read. And as I looked about me, I felt we were stuck in a round of hopeless drudgery.

Mother wrote often, and I had written to her almost daily since coming to Tokyo. I was careful not to say anything to worry her, which may have persuaded her that I'd found employment allowing me time to study, for the parcels she sent me invariably contained a book or two, wrapped in a shirt or a pair of long drawers that she'd made herself. I remember my pleasure at receiving a book I had wanted for some time, Takekoshi Sansa's *2500-Year History*. On another occasion she sent me some Ayame-brand tobacco—she had always known that I smoked in secret, especially when Father wasn't there. It was wrapped in a piece of paper tied with an old red waist cord of the kind worn by women. I remembered Mother wearing it, and I couldn't bring myself to throw it away. So I used it as a belt for my cotton night kimono, and even wore it around my waist during the day, under my oil-stained trousers. This caused some amusement among my fellow workers. "Hey, look at lover-boy with the red thing next to his skin! I bet she'll be pleased!" I never minded their ragging, for when we were apart, Mother was indeed like a lover to me.

After two or three months I had to face up to the fact that I would never be able to study in my present situation. Desperate to get out of the trap I found myself in, I wandered out of the factory one evening in search of my uncle-in-law's house somewhere in Aoyama. I didn't expect anything specific from him; I was just groping in the dark.

I had met Saito Tsunetaro as a child when Mother took me to his previous house in the grounds of Prince Kitashirakawa's palace. I knew that he had moved to Minami-cho in Aoyama, but precisely where I had no idea.

I didn't have the five sen it cost to go by streetcar from Kikukawa-cho to Minami-cho, so I walked all the way, stopping at a number of police boxes to ask for directions. Having heard that my uncle had become a professor of English at the Peers' School, I used that information in the hope that it might help identify him. I found the house at last, but by then it was nearly midnight.

When I was announced I heard my uncle's voice from a room near the front hall saying incredulously, "Oiku-san's son, did you say? The boy called Hide-san?"

No one invited me in, however, and I remained seated in a corner of the old-fashioned wooden platform in the hall, feeling very small. A rather refined young woman came out with tea and cakes for me and, putting the tray down, went back inside. I knew that she was my cousin Sonoko, but not a word passed between us.

After a long time my uncle finally appeared in the hall. He was scowling. Of samurai stock, by now he was a noted English scholar, holding the junior fifth rank at the Imperial Court. He wore gold-rimmed spectacles, and his face was thin and nervous-looking. As soon as I saw him peering at me over his spectacles, I was sorry I had come. What understanding of my hopes and plans could I expect of people living in a world so removed from mine? Why had I come knocking at the door of these relations before whom I now felt such embarrassment? Becoming acutely aware of not belonging there, I knew I couldn't stay a minute longer.

But my uncle, taken aback by my sudden appearance so late at night, had to find out what had brought me there: "Did you run away from home?" he asked. "No, I didn't," I replied. "I came up to Tokyo to study, with my mother's permission." Then without much hope I added: "Do you think I might get a job as a student-servant or caretaker in some academy? It would be even better if I could be placed with a family as a student-houseboy."

My uncle absolutely refused to listen to me. Convinced that I was one of those aimless youngsters who came up to Tokyo on an idle whim, he lectured me angrily: "Tell me, what's your family going to do without you there? I'm told your father's no longer capable of working. And hasn't your mother got a lot of young children to take care of?" He went on in this vein for quite a while, winding up with: "Go home. I'll give you the train fare if you do, and no more. Go home and help your family. Have you forgotten you're your mother's eldest son?" And he dismissed me, giving me no chance to say any of the things I'd prepared so carefully on my way to the house.

I emerged from their front gate at about one in the morning. The streetcars had stopped running, but that didn't matter since I had no money on me anyway. From the far end of Aoyama I walked at a leisurely pace to the far end of Honjo. Perhaps it was my habit of daydreaming that saved me, then, from minding the distance too much, and from brooding unduly over life's hardships. What thoughts did I have as I walked all those miles through the streets of Tokyo? Surely I was hungry? As it happens, the memory of the long walk back involves no painful associations, no sense of humiliation or resentment at the cold reception and misunderstanding I'd met with. My mind, in fact, was remarkably serene as I made my way through the pleasant night and breathed in the soft, moist air of early morning. It was close to dawn when I reached the factory in Kikukawa-cho. After a short sleep, I went back to my threading machine and started pedaling and cranking as usual.

Later that day I came to feel that I had done Mother a disservice by going to see my uncle. In all our years of abject poverty, the only person who had bothered to find out where we were each time we moved, and had inquired after us, was this uncle. Moreover, Mother's elder sister, his wife, had been dead for some time, and he had remarried. To go to his house seeking help without Mother's knowledge, I now realized, was a thoughtless thing to do. I wrote to her immediately, saying that I would never do such a thing again and asking her to apologize to the Saito family for me.

Years afterward my Saito cousin Sonoko told me that the family had been mortified when they learned that I had indeed come to Tokyo with Mother's blessing. It was Sonoko who gave me many of the facts when I wrote about Mother's youth earlier in this memoir.

Among the many small factories in the Kikukawa-cho area was one owned by the S Portable Safe Company. It was in April, I think, that I moved there with the consent of the owner of the screwnail factory. My new job was better in several respects—working hours, pay, and opportunity for study. Portable safes were becoming very popular around then; the company seemed to be doing well, and there was an air of enthusiasm in the newly built factory.

The employees were divided into a number of small sections with special assignments such as metalworking, rinsing, lacquering, and packaging. I was hired nominally as a clerk, but half my time was spent on odd jobs. When, for example, a sufficient number of safes had accumulated in the factory and they were to be delivered to the warehouse in Yagenbori, I would accompany the carts with an itemized list of the different kinds of safes in the shipment. There was always a slim, middle-aged man dressed in a well-cut suit standing outside the warehouse or the company office, and one day he came up to me and asked, "Do you board in the factory?"

Having heard that he was the company president, I answered stiffly, "Yes sir, I do." He asked a few more questions, and that was the end of our conversation. But a couple of months later, on one of his visits to the factory, he gave me his card with his home address on it and said, "Come and see me sometime. The evening will do."

By appointment one evening, then, I went to the president's house in Hyapponkui by the bank of the river. Hyapponkui was a quiet neighborhood in those days, with trees still growing there. After dinner he said to me, "So you're trying to study part-time. But I don't see how you can, working as you do in the factory. And it won't do you any good to go to some night school in Honjo. If you want to work in industry, you should at least go to a technical school like Kuramae. Why don't you aim for Kuramae?"

I explained that because of family circumstances I hadn't even been to middle school. "But if you really want to study," he said, "I can give you a different kind of job. Besides, you don't have to go to Kuramae—there are other ways of getting training. I'll back you up, so think about it carefully." His business, he added, was expanding, and he intended to open up branches in China and the South Pacific.

I didn't know why he had gone out of his way to show such concern for my welfare, but I left his house that evening feeling so elated that back in the factory I had a hard time going to sleep.

The next morning, however, I abandoned any thought of taking advantage of his goodwill. Only six months had passed since my arrival in Tokyo, but from the dozens of letters I'd received from Mother in that time, I could tell—though she never said so—that she was having a hard time without the wages I'd been taking home. Sometimes I wouldn't hear from her for four or five days, and, afraid that she couldn't afford to buy stamps, I would enclose ten or twenty of them in my next letter. Whenever I had more cash to spare, I sent her a money order for two or three yen. But I couldn't rest easy with such gestures. My family had moved in the meantime from Yoshida-cho to somewhere in Takashima-cho, a place I didn't know.

There was a man in the lacquer section called Y-san. He was a fully qualified lacquer worker, a true artisan. He must have heard something about me, because during the lunch break one day he beckoned me to a quiet corner of the factory and keeping his voice down said, "There's a very good job open. It'll be hard going for the first year, but if you can put up with it, you'll make good money after that. You're from Yokohama, aren't you? Well, you'd be working on things that are sent to Yokohama for export." He sounded serious. He spoke with an Aizu accent, but had a no-nonsense, downtown Tokyo air about him, and was known for doing people favors. I trusted him, and was all ears.

I had by now lost faith in "part-time study." I was attending a technical school at night in Hayashi-cho in Honjo, where I had been admitted without difficulty. The school building looked like a renovated storage shed, and its one classroom had forty or fifty black desks arranged in rows. The students, apprentice boys and the like from the Honjo area, came to class in their heavy boots or clogs. It turned out that what the school meant by "technical" was mainly design drawing and elementary geometry. Deeply disillusioned by this and the quality of my fellow students, who seemed to me a bunch of idlers, I was thinking of finding another night school when Y-san told me about the opening.

The primary object of "working one's way through school" as I'd seen it so far was to become an educated man, however many years it took; earning money was merely a means to that end. But it had become clear that I owed it to my family to start making a decent income as soon as I could, and that I couldn't afford the luxury of further education. I felt sure that Mother, however prepared she may have been for adversity after I had gone, was by now in desperate straits. And so, through the kind offices of Y-san, I became a live-in apprentice to a Mr. T who made damascened wares for export at his house in Misuji-machi in Asakusa. My task would be to paint pieces of metal with the basic design in lacquer, and my apprenticeship was to last exactly a year.

Mr. T came from Wakamatsu in Aizu. Many gold lacquer workers hailed from Aizu, coming to Tokyo a few at a time, and had congregated in the back streets of Asakusa and Shitaya. Mr. T was a bachelor, living at the end of one of two rows of tenement houses standing in an alley near a theater. His house had only two rooms, one of six mats and the other of four and a half mats. The larger room was the workshop. The equipment needed in our work was minimal—a board the size of a small desk-top to keep the lacquer on; a lacquer brush; and little else. An outsider looking in would have had a hard time guessing what we were making. It was clearly not traditional lacquerware, since the material we worked on was brass.

After the design was painted on the piece of metal it was submerged in a corrosive liquid, which left little hollows on the surface that were carefully filled with ferruginous lacquer and polished; the rest of the piece was then plated with gold or silver, and delicate engraving completed the process. A tradition of making a unique damascened ware known as Komai had long existed in Kyoto, but ours was a modernized process aimed at mass production for export purposes.

We made bracelets, tiepins, cigarette cases, hairpins, earrings, napkin rings, vases, desk-top accessories, brooches, and even small household furnishings. They ranked high among the products handled by the Yokohama export companies—and middlemen were constantly badgering subcontractors like Mr. T to make more of them.

There must have been dozens of modest households in Asakusa and Shitaya engaged in this sort of damascene work, but I doubt if any of them was quite as humble as Mr. T's. He had the typical Aizu native's tenacity and attention to detail, and, for a man, was meticulous in his management of the household economy. As soon as I moved in he put me in charge of the kitchen and the shopping for food, but kept tight control of expenditures himself. "Get two sen's worth of miso," he would say, "and two slices of salted salmon at one sen five rin each," handing me the exact amount of money. In this way, instead of reading books under a lamp as a part-time student, I found myself, at the age of nineteen, learning for the first time in my life to wash and cook rice—and in a stranger's kitchen.

A Report Card

E ven now someone occasionally says to me—not very seriously, perhaps—"I hear you draw and paint well." This is nonsense. And it's particularly embarrassing to know how the rumor got started. In the course of learning a little about drawing with lacquer from Mr. T, I used to look at copies of paintings of the Rinpa or the Tosa School in order to get hints from their designs; and ever since in my doodlings I seem to have retained some basic awareness of such designs. But real painting is beyond me. And my training under Mr. T as a would-be craftsman has been more of a hindrance than a help in my efforts in that direction.

In the alleys and tenement houses of the Misuji-machi neighborhood the style of life was almost exactly as it had been in downtown Tokyo in the early years of Meiji. At the entrance to our alley a general store stood on one corner and a cooked beans shop on the other. Then came a row of four tenement houses on each side fronted by a covered gutter. The dark, ill-fitting front doors all bore the tracks of slugs. Mr. T's place was at the end of the alley.

The houses, sharing a common roof on either side, were all the same size, each with a six-mat room, a three-mat room, and a board-floor kitchen the size of two mats. Surprisingly, though, each had a tiny fenced-in garden at the back, with an evergreen bush or a small maple tree growing in it, and in the summer cucumbers and morning glories climbing up the fence. As gardens they were not much to speak of, but they gave some aesthetic satisfaction to those humble city-dwellers.

You could hear much of what went on in the four houses opposite and the other three on your own side—the laughing and the crying, the rattling of china, the coming and going—so that you came to know the circumstances and habits of your neighbors as though they were members of your own household. Sitting at work all day long on my designs, I was never bored.

In due course, I got to know the differences in style between the Yokohama working class and its equivalent in downtown Tokyo, and the manners and personalities described by Meiji-period Tokyo writers like Ichiyo and their Edo predecessors began to have rather more reality for me. Once again, I started reading Edo literature in earnest. Now, though, I found myself more drawn to people like Rijo than to the relatively highbrow Akinari and Saikaku.

Looking about me, I realized that there were still, in fact, many people in the streets of downtown Tokyo who could well have been models for characters in Rijo's or Ikku's[18] works. But being a freshly arrived and impressionable bumpkin, I was only too ready to marvel at what seemed to be thriving vestiges of old Edo, when in fact they were being steadily overwhelmed by the sprawl of a modern capital city.

I gave up haiku and began writing *senryu*. Then one day Inoue Kenkabo, the *senryu* poet and at the time a contributing editor with the *Nihon Newspaper*, paid me a surprise visit, and as a result I started attending his poetry meetings on my days off. I also became a member of the group associated with the magazine *New Senryu*.

In the meantime, Mr. T and I continued our bachelors' life to-

18. Ryutei Rijo (?–1841) and Jippensha Ikku (1765–1831) are two of the most famous comic writers of the Edo period. They can be very funny, but their humor is often scatological.

gether. When I wasn't preparing rice, grinding paste for pickling, or cooking miso soup, I would try to learn the techniques of gold lacquering and decorative design under his supervision. I was a quick learner, thanks to my fondness from an early age for drawing pictures. Mr. T's fellow lacquer workers from Aizu, who often dropped in, would watch me working with the thin brush and make gratifying comments in their dialect: "You must have done that before. No one can use the brush like that after only a few months of training," or "Hey, T-san, where did you find such a good pupil?" One frequent visitor was studying art in Terasaki Kogyo's studio. He also was from Aizu, and he liked making encouraging remarks: "Look, if you're really keen on painting, why don't you study Japanese art seriously? I'll have a word with Kogyo Sensei if you like." But I had given up all hope of becoming a painter—even, indeed, of being a student at night school. All I now had in mind was to complete my year's apprenticeship and bring my parents and siblings to Tokyo, so that we could somehow carry on as a family.

In the middle of April that year—just before I went to work for Mr. T—there was a big fire in the Yoshiwara pleasure quarter, and for several months, until reconstruction was completed, business was carried on in temporary buildings. Before the fire it had been Mr. T's rule to pay a visit to the quarter twice a month. He had never allowed himself even the occasional extra visit, presumably for reasons of money and time. But after the fire his visits suddenly increased in frequency. Perhaps he found the informality of temporary buildings attractive; and having me there to watch over the house in his absence was possibly another factor.

For a certain number of nights every week, then, I found myself alone in the house. These were enjoyable times for me, as I was free to write to Mother and read books. The next morning Mr. T would return, invariably accompanied by a few fellow revelers. Discussion of the night before would ensue—who had received favored treatment and who not, whether the cost of the whole night's entertainment had been shared fairly among them, and so on. Mr. T's friends obviously found his house a comfortable place to gather in, but being busy artisans, they none of them stayed very long. Mr. T, for his part, would work doubly hard after a night out; and if he still thought he hadn't caught up he would work all through the following night. His friends teased him about his obsessive habits. "A whore-mongering penny-pincher" was what one called him to his face. "Look at you," another said, "you can hardly keep your eyes open. What are you going to do with all the money you're saving anyway?"

And it was true that, his visits to Yoshiwara aside, there was something fanatical about his parsimony. For example, he once came back from a wedding party with a whole sea bream , the hosts' present to their guests. He put it away in the larder, then for several days afterward would bring it out at dinner time, heat it over the grill, and eat a little of it by himself, before returning the remainder to the cupboard. When the fish had finally been picked clean he told me to use the bones as stock in the miso soup. Having grown up among spendthrift Yokohamans, I found his behavior extraordinary at first; but in time I came to respect him for the thoroughness with which he did everything. His miserliness was notorious among the wholesalers he dealt with; but they, too, respected him as a man of integrity who could always be trusted to deliver his products on the day promised.

Living as I did with such a diligent person, I had no choice but to be diligent myself. At first, I was a little embarrassed to be seen in my dark blue cotton kimono coming back to the house carrying a large pickled radish or a dried fish, or going to the communal tap to collect water, but my neighbors were from the start kind to "T-san's pupil," as they called me. Before long, I even looked forward to going to the tap, for there I would sometimes see a girl from one of the houses who had caught my attention. She looked as fragile as a paper doll, and very innocent. Whenever we encountered one another, by the tap or in the alley, we would both lower our eyes and say nothing. As I worked, I faced the back of her house, and could hear her voice from morning to night and observe how her family lived.

They earned a living making the floral hairpins and combs then popular among girls in downtown Tokyo. Her parents and brothers all spoke with a Kyoto accent, so presumably she too was not Tokyo-born. Perhaps I imagined it, but she was apt to come out of her house to do her shopping just as I myself was stepping out into the alley. And I have always retained the memory, vivid still, of seeing her one evening at a local fair as she strolled among the stalls in the flickering, pale light of acetylene lamps. Someone was playing the melody of Azen's song "This World of Dreams." I remember, too, catching sight of her profile not far from me in the standing section of the local theater. But not once could we bring ourselves to speak to each other. When we met face to face, I saw a responsive look in her eyes that overwhelmed me; but it was only a brief moment of recognition, as though we were two swallows flitting past each other.

All my experiences of what might be called falling in love ended in this inconclusive way. What held me back was not timidity but my situation at the time. Toward the end of the year she suddenly disappeared. Later, her elder brother told me rather brusquely that she had become an apprentice geisha in Kyoto and had died shortly afterward. But then he added: "There's something else I should tell you: she said your name several times before she died." I have wished ever since that I'd had the courage at that point to ask him why she had been sent away and why she had died. He, on his side, said nothing more; I had the feeling as we parted that he disliked me for my reticence.

Mother came up to Tokyo a couple of times while I was with Mr. T. She became friendly with him and asked him if he would take my younger brother Sosuke under his wing too. He agreed, and soon afterward—how she managed it I don't know—she moved to Tokyo with almost the entire family.

I found them living under the railway overpass in Midori-cho in the Honjo district. It was a dreadful house, not only cold but dark as well. It was clearly an unhealthy place for Father, and I urged Mother to move elsewhere as soon as possible.

My younger sister Kae wasn't with them. I asked Mother why, and was told that she had gone to a city in Nagano Prefecture. She had been adopted, Mother said, by a family who owned a first-class inn-restaurant there; they promised they would take care of her, and it was for her own good that she'd been given away.

I was alarmed, for I had never been able to forget what had happened to poor Hamako. "Are you sure she'll be all right?" I asked. Mother seemed to have full trust in the adoptive family, who were good people, she assured me, and prominent locally too. But she omitted to tell me who had arranged the adoption or what its precise conditions were. Having by then acquired a certain measure of common sense, I couldn't share Mother's ready trust in the goodwill of these strangers who had adopted Kae. What did it mean to allow a fourteen-year-old girl to be entered in another family's register? What control over her, and prospect of material gain, did that give them? And what exactly was the business of an "inn-restaurant"? Mother couldn't be expected to know the answer to any of these questions.

In such matters, Father was equally out of touch. But of him it's truer to say that he had lost the will to resist whatever happened to our family. He had lost his bravado, too, and hadn't said "I'll show them!" for some time. Physically, he was a virtual compendium of illnesses, his main complaints being stomach ulcers, a bad heart, and bronchitis. Mother had by now been struggling for ten years under the burden of looking after a sick man and several young children. That she didn't choose to let herself and the rest of the family die is still a wonder to me. In this respect, she was a very strong person;

but her strength was like that of a willow tree in winter—she endured, but she accepted her fate without active resistance, just as she did her husband and children. If she was ignorant, she was ignorant in a way that invites only pity. If she was the embodiment of love, she was also the embodiment of sacrifice to the family, with only her children's tears to console her.

The family soon moved to rented rooms in Banba-cho in Honjo. Mother found piecework to do at home, such as making paper bags and sewing, sent the children to school, and one way or another began to settle down in her new surroundings.

Busy though she was, she found time to visit us often in Misuji-machi. While there she would clean the bachelor kitchen, tidy up the closets, do the laundry, mend our clothes, and even get the rice ready for cooking that evening. Mr. T was naturally grateful for Mother's fussing, and we two brothers—Sosuke had joined us by then—were pleased to have her bustling about, albeit in someone else's house.

But Father in his failing health wasn't happy about her going out so often. Sometimes when she was late getting back from Misuji-machi, Father—she told us—would rage at her in his usual fashion. She didn't mind that in itself, as she was used to it; what worried her greatly was that after such outbursts his condition invariably got worse.

Early that winter the family moved to two six-mat rooms on the second floor of a house beside the Ohaguro Ditch, just outside the Yoshiwara pleasure quarter. The landlord ran an employment agency downstairs, but from the outside the place looked like an ordinary private house.

On my first visit, I looked out of the window and saw, right in front of me, red undergarments hung out to dry at the back of a brothel; below me was the muddy ditch. I simply couldn't understand what had possessed Mother to move to such a place. Wasn't she concerned at all about my sister Chiyo and my brother Susumu, who were now going to school? At sunset the male customers went past in droves, and at night the air vibrated with the rowdy music issuing from the teahouses. I didn't question Mother at the time, but later I learned the reason for this move. She had made an arrangement with a certain brothel in the quarter to go there during the day to do whatever sewing was needed. It paid better than doing piecework at home; besides, she earned extra money by writing letters and doing other odd jobs for the prostitutes. Thanks to her increased income Father now dressed more neatly, and they were able to acquire a few additional pieces of furniture—a cabinet, a brazier, a tea table—to make their rented rooms a little more livable. But it was by dint of sheer hard work that Mother earned this money. And I can't help thinking that it was working in the brothel that ultimately caused her death ten years later; for handling clothes in a place like that had to be an insanitary and risky thing to do. No doubt, though, Mother couldn't afford to worry about the possible consequences of her newfound job.

At last, after being with Mr. T for about two years, I was able to set myself up as an independent worker.

When I was first employed there, I was given to understand by the lacquer worker Y-san that my apprenticeship would last a year. But when the year was up he told me that I owed it to Mr. T to work for him a while longer. Six months passed, and Y-san again objected when I expressed a wish to leave. Mr. T, for his part, showed no willingness to let me go. Another six months passed, not without some complications in our relationships. But thanks to the intervention of the senior clerk at O Company, for which Mr. T did the bulk of his work, and of other people in the trade, I was finally given permission to leave. My brother Sosuke remained with Mr. T, since it would have been awkward for him if both of us had left. I moved to a rented room in Shitaya Nishi-machi, and on the same day started looking for commissions. O company was the first to give me a subcontract, followed by another local firm.

The first room I had in Tokyo that I could call my own—my first base of operations, as it were—was above a hairdresser's shop. There were two rooms upstairs—a three-mat room at the top of the stairs and an eight-mat one beyond it. I had the smaller room, and a professional raconteur and his wife the other. We were separated by sliding doors.

I have tried hard to recall the name of the raconteur, but without success. Either way, I have the impression that he was a man of some standing in his profession. He and his wife did a great deal of entertaining, and since my room was at the top of the stairs, delivery men carrying food and saké constantly walked past me as I sat working at my desk and lacquer board. Trainees and younger fellow professionals would often gather in his room, and inevitably a party would ensue, even if it was still morning. His wife was a chic, lively woman, and she sometimes tried to get me to join them: "Hey, Mr. Student, come in and have a drink with us!" But I stayed where I was, listening to their banter and their ditties.

I started having a lot of visitors myself, too—not just men in my trade, but members of my literary group and the like. Our discussions were no less animated than those of the people next door. The husband of my landlady, who was a not very successful hairdresser, happened fortunately to make and sell honey dumplings to supplement their income, so I served these to my visitors; the tea he provided free of charge.

I learned much about Edo literature and poetry composition from Mr. Inoue, but he and his wife were personally very kind to me, too. I had had some contact with him before I came to Tokyo. Under the name of Inoue Shuken he used to judge poetry and prose submitted to such magazines as the *Middle School World*, and to write reviews of fiction for them, as well as doing social commentaries for the *Nihon Newspaper*. I met him only after I came to Tokyo, but he had once written to me in Yokohama in connection with a Chinese poem I'd sent in to some magazine. He remembered this when I met him, perhaps because Chinese poetry was quite out of fashion then, the Japanese "modern verse" being all the rage at the time.

I was taken aback when he suddenly appeared at Mr. T's door and asked for me. But, as I learned later, he was never one to stand on his dignity. He was a forthright, simple-mannered man who always wore a student's hakama and carried a pouch with the cord wound around his wrist. He did everything with gusto; when he laughed, he laughed with his whole body. Nor did he ever run out of steam: he could talk and laugh all day long without tiring. He and Father must have had something in common, for, oddly enough, they seemed to enjoy each other's company.

When I first met him he lived in Shiba, but later he moved to a house behind Tozenji temple in Takanawa. I would visit him at both places, and he often took me out to Rogetsutei, the Western-style restaurant. I found him a very interesting talker. He was particularly knowledgeable about history. Being one of the serious journalists of his day, he was familiar not only with the contemporary literary scene but with the political world as well, though the tendency to form cliques, noticeable in every field of endeavor in Japan at the time, was something he strongly disapproved of. Perhaps one of the reasons he was attracted to *senryu* was the opportunity it provided for sharp social satire.

I remember the first time I went to his house. For dinner, his wife cooked rice flavored with dried bonito. It was so good I can still taste it. I had come in muddy clogs with straps that were on the verge of breaking, and as I was putting them back on in the hall on my way out, I found that the clogs had been wiped clean and the straps replaced.

We transferred our family register to Tokyo, and I went to the Asakusa ward office for my army physical examination. When it was over, I presented myself to the grim-looking officer in charge. He stared at the doctor's report and then at my naked body. The room was full of other young men waiting for their turn, and he decided to make an example of me: "There's no excuse for anyone being so feeble in this day and age. Look at your weight, look at your height—what a puny specimen! Go home and build yourself up!" I weighed ninety-nine pounds, and was classified C.

I was extremely put out at being treated like this, but I knew in myself that I was no weakling; after all, I functioned perfectly well both at work and at play.

Speaking of which, I had gradually begun to explore the possibilities offered in the pleasure quarter, partly thanks to my new affluence since becoming independent: I was rather like a seed sprouting in the light of the sun after the snow and ice had melted. And, having a few like-minded friends of my own age by now, I got into the habit of going out as soon as the sun was down.

My initiation occurred one evening when I and a bunch of verse-spouting friends went to Yoshiwara after a visit to a temple somewhere. I lost my virginity willingly, to a cheap whore, for fifty sen, in a part of the area commonly called Fushimi Riverside.

Even in those days you couldn't do it for less. If you were short of funds, you only had to sell three or four books and the world of the night lay open to you. I remember a sukiyaki restaurant, in the same row as a number of large brothels, where hoarse-voiced waitresses in dark blue stockings rushed about all night serving the feasting throng—the educated and ignorant, the young and old, the tradesmen and students, mingling together, all distinctions cast aside, all linked in a sense of shared indulgence.

The rake's progress, in a way, is as easy as climbing a flight of stairs: you get to the top even without any money. I soon learned to make my own assignations at some teahouse or other. But, no matter how late it was, I never stayed all night at any of these places, preferring to get up and slip quietly away.

The elderly mother of the woman running one teahouse was so impressed by what she took to be a habit born of self-discipline that she said to me admiringly, almost as though she wanted to make me her son-in-law, "My, what an unusual young man you are!" But my late-night departures had nothing to do with self-discipline. My family was still living in the two rented rooms just outside the quarter. And every time I had to choose between remaining in bed next to a sleeping prostitute and going to see Mother, just a few steps away, I would decide on the latter.

Mother would get out of bed, give me a cup of tea, sometimes even go out and buy some cakes—shops around there stayed open all night—and we sat and talked until nearly daybreak. Then, lying down between my brothers and sisters, I would go to sleep. As for Father, I'm sure he knew perfectly well where I had been; given his own past, he must have had a nose for such things.

I was obliged to recognize that the way I was living was making a mockery of my hard-won independence. Inevitably, though, when evening approached, I hankered after the company of my night-prowling friends. As a way of restraining myself, then, I decided to give up my place in Nishi-machi and move in with my family. I could use one of their two rooms as a workroom; and after a while, if we went about it carefully, we could all move into a decent house.

I began to earn a steady income, and life became a little easier for us. Mother gave up her sewing work at the brothel, and Father on his good days took to visiting the local *go* club, looking like all the other retired old men you see hanging about in downtown neighborhoods.

It was there that I spent my fourth New Year since coming to Tokyo. I was twenty-two, and the incident I am about to describe took place on January 15. I can identify the date with some confidence, for once, because on that day I did something to Father that I have regretted ever since. On the same day every year without fail, I feel again a sense of shame.

I was working, lacquer brush in hand, in one of the two six-mat rooms. The sliding doors were shut, as it was winter. I could hear

Father getting angry with Mother in the next room. This wasn't an unusual event, and for a while I tried to ignore it, but that day he was being exceptionally persistent and mean. The tirade continued for an hour, then two hours, with no sign of abating. I could hear Mother apologizing and trying not to break down; I could only think that it was concern for his health that held her back. And as I listened I began to wonder if he was capable of feeling any gentleness or love toward her at all. I burned with resentment at all his endless bullying of her and his irresponsibility as a parent ever since I was a little child. I gritted my teeth and tried to go on working, but it was impossible, for the kind of hatred I felt then was overpowering, like some primitive physical force bursting out from deep inside me.

Father's voice had risen a notch, so that he sounded like the raging drunkard he had once been, the man he himself had probably long forgotten. I stood up uncertainly, not quite knowing what I was doing. I ran down the stairs into the kitchen, picked up a bucket filled with ice-cold water, and went back upstairs. Father, seated in front of Mother, was still shouting at her. I walked up to him from behind and emptied the bucket over his head. Both my parents must have cried out in shock, but I don't remember hearing or seeing anything at the time. Dropping the empty bucket I fled downstairs, slipped my feet into my clogs, and dashed out into the street like a thief on the run.

I spent the rest of the day in another part of Asakusa, mingling with sightseers in the amusement parks or on top of the twelve-story tower. Finally, just after midnight, I made my way home. Father had gone to sleep, but Mother was still up, sewing. She wouldn't speak to me. She had laid my bed out for me nevertheless, not doubting that sooner or later I would come back.

The next morning neither she nor Father made any reference to what I'd done. I went up to him and offered a brief apology. I expected cross words, but instead he gave me a strange, pained look, a look that I, his son, had never seen before. Then he turned to

Mother and said, "Oiku, let's all have some tea." Munching one of the crackers she had put out with the tea, I began to cry.

That year we rented a house in Eikyu-cho in Asakusa. It only had four rooms, but there was a small garden, and nearby was Shinbori Moat—not yet filled in—with willow trees growing along it. I think that at long last my parents felt they had a home where they could enjoy some peace of mind.

Father had by now finally come to terms with his past failures, and seemed to have surrendered his place as head of the household. He once said to my little brothers and sisters, "You can see for yourselves the condition I'm in. From now on you're to think of your elder brother as your father. And you, Hide, please bear in mind what I've just said."

The one missing member of the family was Kae, who had been sent away to a city in Nagano. I had learned in the meantime that the person who had acted as intermediary in her adoption was one of Mother's several sisters. And when I discovered what kind of woman she was, it became clear why Mother had not at first revealed the identity of the go-between. This woman—I don't even know whether she was an elder or younger sister—had owned a small restaurant in Rokku in Asakusa, then opened up a low drinking place somewhere in Hakku. She had a pretty daughter called Owaka, whom she installed in the bar to draw in customers.

With a person like her involved in the "adoption," it had to be supposed that Kae in fact had been sold. Mother now realized this, and when we talked about the girl she wept bitterly, her remorse made all the greater by the memory of Hamako. "What a fool I am!" she said repeatedly.

I took out my savings and caught the train to Nagano, a fair distance away from Tokyo. There I met Kae's adoptive father, the owner of the "inn-restaurant," and begged him to return her to us. Fortunately, he and his wife turned out to be good-hearted people, the sort you often find in the provinces. "We'll let Kae go," he said, "but please regard us as your relatives, and keep in touch with us." And for years afterward we did keep in touch, though their business eventually failed, and they are both gone now.

I don't suppose Mother's sister, the one who owned the drinking place, is still alive either. I wonder what became of the daughter Owaka, who was said to be so pretty. I remember hearing that Saito Tsunetaro's eldest son developed a passion for her, even though she was his cousin, and used to visit her at the bar. He was a university graduate, the author of a thesis entitled "A Study of Yin-Yang and Divination in the Middle Ages"; but not long after graduating he died.

In March of Taisho 7 [1918], Father died in another house we had moved into in Hama-cho 3-chome. The building, so narrow and deep that it looked like an eel's lair, faced the rear gate of Kibun, the restaurant.

Mother told me that about a week before he died he said to her worriedly, "Do you think Hide will be all right the way he is? Will he be able to manage?"

Because his ulcers and bronchitis were chronic, his doctor had not thought it necessary to give us any special warning. But two or three days before the end he began to have difficulty breathing, and Mother seemed to think that perhaps he would be more comfortable if we moved to a quiet house by the seashore in a place like Omori. The doctor saw no reason to object, so with a friend in tow I went to Omori to look for a likely place. When I returned I found him in a coma. The doctor who was there doubted that he would last the night.

That morning, Mother told me, something rather special had occurred.

It had been Father's habit for many years to wake up before sunrise and have Mother bring him immediately his morning cup of strong green tea, at just the right temperature. If he didn't get it, he was likely to be in a foul mood. That morning, then, Mother had got up as usual while it was still dark and gone into the kitchen to make his tea. She was waiting for the kettle to boil on the gas ring when she heard him call out in a voice full of longing, "Oiku, Oiku." "I'll be there in a minute," she answered, and waited until she had the tea ready before going back to him. When she knelt down beside him he sat up and said, "You know, Oiku, when I saw you in the kitchen just now I thought you were the goddess Kannon." And he brought his hands together before his face as though about to pray. "Don't be silly," Mother said and tried to make a joke of it, but she couldn't help shedding tears of happiness, for in all the years of their marriage he had never spoken to her like that.

A little while later he said, "I think I'd like some rice balls for breakfast today." When she brought them on a tray, he groped his way to the top of the bed—he couldn't see properly any more—and sat upright to eat them. Not once after he became ill did he allow himself to eat in any other position; he was that sort of man. At 11:35 that night he died. I was sitting beside his bed, and when I saw his face losing its color I went upstairs and sat curled up in the dark alone. A few moments later I felt someone's hand on my shoulder. Startled, I looked up, and the woman—a friend's wife who had been sent to fetch me—let out a shriek and ran out of the room. I was told later that from my expression she thought I'd gone mad. Even I hadn't realized the extent of my own anguish.

About Mother's death I can hardly bring myself to write even now. She died three years later, in June 1921, when I was twenty-nine. We were living then in a place called Uekiba in Mukojima, very near Rohan's[19] house. It was some consolation to us that we were able in the years following Father's death to give her a reasonably comfortable old age, with occasional spells at peaceful places like Atami and the Chiba coast, and with her children safely grown up. But she herself never stopped missing Father. "If only he were

19. Koda Rohan (1867–1947), a revered man of letters.

with us," she'd say, or "Did you know this about him. . . ?"

When the doctor told us she was dying of intestinal tuberculosis I immediately thought of the time she used to go to the brothel to do their sewing for them. Even now I'm haunted by the suspicion that she caught the germ then.

We were all, every one of us, with her as she lay dying. Intestinal tuberculosis is a painful disease. Wanting very much to comfort her in her last moments I foolishly whispered in her ear: "Mother, I know you're going to heaven. Look, can you see those pretty flowers? Can you hear the birds singing?"

Mother looked at me with dull eyes. Then in a barely audible voice she said: "Don't. That's enough." She was holding my sisters' hands under the futon cover. "Be good to one another," she said, and that was all. I can't remember her being cross with me more than two or three times in all the years I knew her. Yet her last words to me were, "Don't. That's enough."

Thirty or forty seconds later she left us, quietly.

Masahiro had often been on Mother's mind. From time to time she would say to me sadly, "I wonder what's happened to your elder brother. . . ." He and I did meet some years later, but it was an awkward occasion both for him—he is dead now—and for myself too, so I won't dwell on it here. Let me say simply that he suddenly visited me at my house in Shiba Park thirty-odd years after he disappeared from Yokohama, just when I had begun my career as a writer.

By then, though, both Father and Mother were dead. Life in the main is like that, I suppose.

I shall end my account here. There is little substance to what I have remembered and what I have had to tell, but there is one thing I would say in conclusion. I may have given the impression that I experienced a series of dreadful hardships in my childhood and youth, but for me those years in retrospect were in no way just a bleak ordeal. I suppose this is because I lived in an age when no one thought of questioning the realities of family and society. In other words, I, too, was a child of the feudal past, and many of today's lively young generation will dismiss me with a sneer. But until we ourselves have reached the end of the road, we can't know which way yields most of the fullness and joy of living. For me, the years of childhood and youth that I have written about were a source of ample pleasure. Comparing my life then with that of young people today, I am not in the least envious. In saying this, of course, I have no intention of judging my children's and their contemporaries' outlook by some arbitrary standard of my own; I am not *that* anachronistic.

Nevertheless, in looking back over the muddy road their parents trudged along, children may learn something of value that will help prepare them for the long road stretching ahead of them. My own father, perhaps, without intending to, made my road muddier than it need have been; but even so, at the time of his death, I had barely graduated from the middle school of life, and the foregoing account is my report card from that school. I was afraid of Father; yet, strangely enough, frightening fathers and teachers are sometimes remembered fondly and even gratefully by their offspring and former pupils.

Japan's Modern Writers

TUN-HUANG A Novel
Yasushi Inoue
Translated by Jean Oda Moy

An intriguing explanation of one of the great mysteries of western China—how the sacred scrolls of the Sung dynasty were saved from the barbarian tribes of the Hsi-hsia.

PB, ISBN 0-87011-576-6, 216 pages

INTO A BLACK SUN

Takeshi Kaiko
Translated by Cecilia Segawa Seigle

"No other account of Vietnam has been so vivid, so intimate or so moral." —Edmund White, *The New York Times*

PB: ISBN 0-87011-609-6 224 pages, 110 x 182 mm

HOUSE OF SLEEPING BEAUTIES
And Other Stories

Yasunari Kawabata
Translated by Edward Seidensticker
Introduction by Yukio Mishima

Three short stories which center on a lonely protagonist and his peculiar eroticism. Kawabata explores the interplay of fantasy and reality at work on a mind in solitude.

PB, ISBN 0-87011-426-3, 152 pages

THE LAKE

Yasunari Kawabata
Translated by Reiko Tsukimura

By Japan's first nobel laureate for literature. "Seizes the reader's imagination from the first page." —*Village Voice*

PB, ISBN 0-87011-365-8, 168 pages

MONKEY BRAIN SUSHI   New Tastes in Japanese Fiction
Edited by Alfred Birnbaum

Fresh, irreverent, and post-Zen, an astounding collection of the brightest and boldest voices in contemporary Japanese fiction.

PB, ISBN 4-7700-1688-3, 312 pages

SUN AND STEEL

Yukio Mishima
Translated by John Bester

Part autobiography and part reflection. "His literary testament."
—*The Times Literary Supplement*

PB, ISBN 0-87011-425-5, 108 pages

A WILD SHEEP CHASE   A Novel

Haruki Murakami
Translated by Alfred Birnbaum

"Haruki Murakami is a mythmaker for the millennium, a wiseacre wise man." —*The New York Times Book Review*

PB, ISBN 4-7700-1706-5, 312 pages

ALMOST TRANSPARENT BLUE

Ryu Murakami
Translated by Nancy Andrew

"A Japanese mix of *A Clockwork Orange* and *L'Etranger*."
—*Newsweek*

PB, ISBN 0-87011-469-7, 128 pages

H   A Hiroshima Novel

Makoto Oda
Translated by D.H. Whittaker

A surreal universe of people of varying racial and ethnic backgrounds struggle against the desecration of society and the environment symbolized by the first atomic bomb.

PB, ISBN 4-7700-1947-5, 218 pages

THE SILENT CRY

Kenzaburo Oe
Translated by John Bester

Awarded the 1994 Nobel Prize
"A major feat of the imagination." —*The Times*

PB, ISBN 0-87011-466-2, 288 pages

Japan's Women Writers

THE DOCTOR'S WIFE

Sawako Ariyoshi
Translated by Wakako Hironaka and Ann Siller Kostant

Japan's leading woman writer focuses on the role of women in Japanese society. "An excellent story."—*Choice*

PB, ISBN 0-87011-465-4, 184 pages

THE RIVER KI

Sawako Ariyoshi
Translated by Mildred Tahara

"A powerful novel written with convincing realism."—*Japan Quarterly*

PB, ISBN 0-87011-514-6, 248 pages

THE TWILIGHT YEARS

Sawako Ariyoshi
Translated by Mildred Tahara

"Linger[s] in the mind long after the story has ended." —*The New York Times*

PB, ISBN 0-87011-852-8, 216 pages

THE WAITING YEARS

Fumiko Enchi
Translated by John Bester

"Absorbing, sensitive, and utterly heartrending." —Charles Beardsley

PB, ISBN 0-87011-424-7, 208 pages

REQUIEM A Novel

Shizuko Go
Translated by Geraldine Harcourt

A bestseller in Japanese, this moving requiem for the war victims voiced the feelings of a generation of women. "Unforgettable and devastating." —Susan Griffin

PB, ISBN 4-7700-1618-2, 132 pages

THE PHOENIX TREE AND OTHER STORIES

Satoko Kizaki
Translated by Carol A. Flath

Women in search of home and a sense of self — caught between tradition and a need to define themselves in the modern world.

PB, ISBN 4-7700-1790-1, 242 pages

DISCOVER JAPAN Words, Customs, and Concepts
Volumes 1 & 2
The Japanese Culture Institute

Essays and photographs illuminate 200 ideas and customs of contemporary Japan. "The one book you must have if you're heading for Japan ..." — *Essex Journal*

PB, Vol. 1: ISBN 0-87011-835-8, 216 pages
PB, Vol. 2: ISBN 0-87011-836-6, 224 pages

GEISHA, GANGSTER, NEIGHBOR, NUN
Scenes from Japanese Lives

Donald Richie

A collection of 48 highly personal portraits of Japanese—both famous and obscure. "His portraits are unforgettable." — Tom Wolfe

PB, ISBN 4-7700-1526-7, 212 pages
Previously published in hardcover as Different People.

HAGAKURE
The Book of the Samurai

Tsunetomo Yamamoto
Translated by William Scott Wilson

"A guidebook and inspiration for ... anyone interested in achieving a courageous and transcendent understanding of life." — *East West Journal*

PB, ISBN 0-87011-606-1, 180 pages

THE HIDDEN ORDER
Tokyo Through the Twentieth Century

Yoshinobu Ashihara
Translated by Lynne E. Riggs

Looking at architecture as a metaphor for culture, a renowned Japanese architect considers the apparent chaos of Tokyo.

PB, ISBN 4-7700-1664-6, 160 pages

THE JAPANESE EDUCATIONAL CHALLENGE
A Commitment to Children

Merry White

Examines educational values in Japan, and differences between the Japanese and American school systems. "The best account I know of Japan as a learning society." — Ronald P. Dore

PB, ISBN 4-7700-1373-6, 224 pages
Available only in Japan.

THE JAPANESE NEGOTIATOR
Subtlety and Strategy Beyond Western Logic

Robert M. March

Shows how Japanese negotiate among themselves and examines case studies, providing practical advice for the Western executive.

PB, ISBN 0-87011-962-1, 200 pages

THE JAPANESE THROUGH AMERICAN EYES

Sheila K. Johnson

A revealing look at the images and stereotypes of Japanese produced by American popular culture and media.

PB, ISBN 4-7700-1450-3, 208 pages   Available only in Japan.

JAPAN'S LONGEST DAY

Pacific War Research Society

A detailed account of the day before Japan surrendered, based on eyewitness testimony of the men involved in the decision to surrender.

PB: ISBN 0-87011-422-0, 340 pages

MANGA! MANGA!
The World of Japanese Comics

Frederick L. Schodt
Introduction by Osamu Tezuka

A profusely illustrated and detailed exploration of the world of Japanese comics.

PB, ISBN 0-87011-752-1, 260 pages

NEIGHBORHOOD TOKYO

Theodore C. Bestor

A highly readable glimpse into the everyday lives, commerce, and relationships of some 2,000 neighborhood residents of Tokyo.

PB, ISBN 4-7700-1496-1, 368 pages   Available only in Japan.

THE INLAND SEA

Donald Richie

An award-winning documentary—part travelogue, part intimate diary and meditation—of a journey into the heart of traditional Japan.

PB, ISBN 4-7700-1751, 292 pages